BROWNING'S LYRICS:

D1521451

AN EXPLORATION

BROWNING'S LYRICS:

AN EXPLORATION

ELEANOR COOK

UNIVERSITY OF TORONTO PRESS

© University of Toronto Press 1974

Toronto and Buffalo

Printed in Canada

ISBN 0-8020-5291-6

LC 73-84432

To my parents

'I used to explain Mr. Browning – but the class won't stand that. They say that my reading imparts clear comprehension – and that is a good deal of a compliment, you know; but they say the poetry never gets obscure till I begin to explain it – which is only frank, and that it the softest you can say about it. So I've stopped being expounder, and thrown my heft on the reading. Yes, and with vast results – nearly unbelievable results. I don't wish to flatter anybody, yet I will say this much. Put me in the right condition and give me room according to my strength, and I can read Browning so Browning himself can understand it. It sounds like stretching, but it's the cold truth. Moral: don't explain your author; read him right and he explains himself.'

Mark Twain

(Hartford, Dec. 2, 1887,
from Benjamin Decasseres, *When Huck Finn Went Highbrow*)

CONTENTS

BIBLIOGRAPHICAL NOTE

Unless otherwise stated, quotations from *Pauline, Paracelsus, Sordello, Pippa Passes*, the *Essay on Chatterton, Dramatic Lyrics* (1842), and *The Return of the Druses* are from *The Complete Works*, I–III (ed. King *et al.*); quotations from *Aeschylus' Soliloquy* are from *New Poems*; and all other quotations are from the Centenary edition (ed. Kenyon). Full citations for primary sources may be found in the bibliography.

In quotations from the Barrett–Browning correspondence, two dots are as in the holograph and printed letters and indicate only a pause; omissions are marked by the conventional three dots.

Quotations from Browning material still in copyright are printed by permission of John Murray Ltd.

I have used the following abbreviations:

LEB: *Letters of Elizabeth Barrett Browning*
LRBEB: *Letters of Robert Browning and Elizabeth Barrett Barrett*
         (ed. Kintner)
PMLA: *Publications of the Modern Language Association*
RBAD: *Robert Browning and Alfred Domett*
RBJW: *Robert Browning and Julia Wedgwood*

PREFACE

Browning's lyrics readily find their way into anthologies, but not into critical literature. Many are powerful and at first seem simple, yet they prove difficult to get into. 'I found most of your pieces too hard of interpretation,' wrote Carlyle to Browning, speaking of *Men and Women*, 'and more than one (chiefly of the short kind) I had to read as a very enigma' (*Letters of Carlyle*, 298; Apr. 25, 1856). And Carlyle's perplexity, over even a collection like *Men and Women*, has been shared by many Browning readers. This essay is an attempt to read some of Browning's lyrics; it is only a beginning.

It has become, inevitably I think, three essays in one. First, it is something of a handbook on the lyrics, more so than I originally intended. But a glance at the critical literature on the lyrics shows that little can be taken for granted in dealing with them, and therefore I have included a number of detailed discussions. I have tried to avoid class-room obviousness, yet to demonstrate fully the basis for my reading. The selection of poems so treated is arbitrary; they are simply those about which I had something to say.

Second, this essay contains a study of Browning's imagery in the lyrics, which means in effect at least an outline of Browning's imagery as a whole. This proved necessary because Browning is nowhere more elusive than in his lyrics, and one of the ways he avoids simple predication is through the use of images. Imagery and theme are often so intimately associated that it is impossible to comprehend some lyrics without comprehending their imagery. I have tried to show how such imagery is related, first, to Browning's imagery in the longer poems, and second, when this is relevant, to certain important groups of images he used consistently. Most of these groups have not been worked on before, and some not remarked on before. C. Willard Smith has made an exhaustive study of one image in *Browning's Star-Imagery*, but a study could be made of all Browning's celestial imagery, of which this is only a part. Similarly, much has been written about the gold imagery in *The Ring and the Book* and *Andrea del Sarto*, but little about its extensive appearance elsewhere. The most interesting group, to me, is the group of what I have called enclosure images.

Third, this is partly an essay on Browning's poetics, chiefly as they bear on his lyrics. Like most Browning critics, I have weighted the discussion in favour of *Pauline, Paracelsus,* and *Sordello,* and this against Browning's express dictum: 'I myself have always liked to read a man's *collected* works, of any kind, *backwards*; and what I once thought a fancy I incline now to consider an eminently rational procedure' (*Letters*, ed. Hood, 165; Jan. 11, 1875). But other remarks on Browning's poetics may be found in 'Scenes and Song-Scraps,' and *passim*. The outline of Browning's imagery is, I think, inclusive if not always detailed; remarks on his poetics are rather more negative. I have included some on the ground that it is valuable to know how not to read Browning. For the rest, they make up thoughts towards, rather than an outline of, Browning's poetics.

Throughout, I have assumed more knowledge on the reader's part of Browning's common themes than of, for example, his imagery, because considerable work has been done on the former. This has the advantage of making Browning's kinds of reflection familiar, if it also sometimes makes them sound fatuous.

I have often had recourse to Browning's letters, especially his letters to Elizabeth Barrett, in order to shed light on the lyrics. I have tried to be careful not to imply that Browning simply transferred this or that discussion from his courtship to a later lyric. But it does no harm to repeat that the process is never direct.

> If you would – when you please to give them your attention – confine it to the poems and nothing else, no extraneous matter at all, – I cannot but think you would find little difficulty ... I say all this because you imagine that with more learning you would 'understand' more about my poetry – and as if you would somewhere find it already written – only waiting to be translated into English and my verses.
> (*Learned Lady*, 156–7; Mar. 17, 1883)

Browning's lyrics are, almost without exception, dramatic lyrics; his titles and *One Word More* make this clear. That is, they are not poems in which the poet is overheard by the reader, but poems in

which a speaker is overheard. It is always useful to begin by assuming
the existence and the coherence of the dramatic mask in reading the
lyrics. Character may be elusive. I call, for instance, the speakers of
Love Among the Ruins and *A Toccata of Galuppi's* the shepherd and
the scientist, chiefly for convenience, but we are hardly aware of
them in these roles. What we are aware of is a mood or a predicament
or a joy or a sorrow – the 'loves, hates, hopes, and fears' Browning
liked to probe. Many, perhaps most of these are not meant to be casual
or fleeting, though the songs may be short. Browning once wrote to
Milsand of *Men and Women*: 'My poems go under the distinctive
title of "Men and Women" – they being really dramatic attempts and
not a collection of miscellanies' (*Revue germanique* 14 [1923],
422–3; Aug. 10, 1855).

In the detailed discussions, I endeavour to establish the unity of
each lyric. It is important to try to work out what central effect
Browning intended in each poem. Otherwise the dramatic distance
may be ignored and the poem seem to go wrong. This is what
Browning himself says: 'He [a reviewer in the *National Review* 17
(1863), 417–46] says, I seek a central effect, and only wish the details
to be subordinate and seen by a reflected light from the whole:
exactly!' (*Browning to His American Friends*, 135; Nov. 26, 1863).

The lyrics include some of Browning's most concise effects, and
repay close reading. Browning can, of course, use chatter or verbosity
or tumbling nonsense-verse. 'So this time I whistle, not sing at all,'
he says in *Pacchiarotto* of the collection of that name. Or he notes his
variety of voice: 'Bless us! in the course of my musical exercises, and
according to the moods of many a year, I may have treated myself
to an occasional whistle, cherrup, and guffaw, besides the regular
symphonies' (*Francis Turner Palgrave*, 94–5; Oct. 19, 1864). He
ends *Pietro d'Abano* with: 'I have – oh, not sung! but lilted
(as – between us – / Grows my lazy custom) this its legend. What
the lilt?' A tune then follows, in musical notation, and the musical
tune is also (as Browning says) the metrical tune of the poem.
But there are few of these effects among the lyrics, and this may have
something to do with the fact that they are lyrics. Each speaker seems
to be provided with his appropriate song, which is another step
removed from his appropriate dramatic speech. Perhaps this is the
reason the lyrics have so few of the contracted prepositions and
articles (o' and i' and th') by which Browning liked to tighten the
language. These are close to speech and music leaves them behind.

Browning always declared that he favoured one effect in writing, that of concision.

> The vice I hate most in what little English literature I now see, is the inveterate avoidance of simplicity and straightforwardness. If a man has a specific thing to say, little or great, he will not say it, he says something else altogether in an alien tone to the real matter in hand, such as it is, and though, thanks to the triviality and obviousness of the matter, you understand it readily enough *by rebound*, as it were, yet you are expected to get along with and over and above the matter itself first ...
>
> Well, the absence of anything in your own articles but the precise thing you wish to say there, makes them hard to read, if you please, but not obscure in any way that I can account obscurity.
>
> (To Milsand, *Scribner's Magazine* 20 (1896), 115; n.d.)

The only fault Browning mentions in Elizabeth Barrett's poetry, when she asks him for criticism, is verboseness (though his tact is so exceeding, the fault is turned into a virtue) : 'An instructed eye loves to see where the brush has dipped twice in a lustrous colour, has lain insistingly along a favourite outline, dwelt lovingly in a grand shadow' (*LRBEB*, I, 7; Jan. 13, 1845). To Owen Meredith, concerning his poem *Lucile*, he once wrote: 'You detail effects too minutely, instead of leaving the causes (the actions, passions, words, and deeds of the "figures") to suggest the effects to the reader: that is the strong and succinct way, at least' (*Letters from Owen Meredith*, 158; Aug. 20, 1860). Ezra Pound notes how sound in Browning does not get in the way of sense, how it is organically part of the poem. (He is speaking of *Sordello*, where a peculiar overclarity is achieved by extreme concision.)

> There is here a certain lucidity of sound that I think you will find with difficulty elsewhere in English, and you may well have to retire as far as the Divine Commedia for continued narrative having such clarity of outline without clog and *verbal* impediment.
>
> It will be seen that the author is telling you something, not merely making a noise, he does not gum up the sound. The 'beauty' is not applied ornament, but makes the mental image more definite. The author is not hunting about for large high-sounding words, there is a great variety in the rhyme but the reader runs on unaware.

Again as in the case of Golding, the reader must read it as prose, pausing for the sense and not hammering the line-terminations. (*ABC of Reading* [Norfolk, Conn., n.d.], 191)

One final point should be made. If it is important to maintain the integrity of the dramatic viewpoint in Browning's poems, it is also important to remember that Browning repeatedly insisted poetry is meant to teach. In his letters to Elizabeth Barrett, in a letter to Ruskin ('it is all teaching ... and the people hate to be taught' [Collingwood, *Ruskin*, I, 200; Dec. 10, 1855]), in *The Ring and the Book*, in *Aristophanes' Apology*, the view is repeated. It also appears in a letter of October 1, 1855, to John Kenyon, concerning *Men and Women*:

> In your remarks on the little or no pleasure you derive from dramatic – in comparison with lyric – poetry (understanding the vulgar or more obvious form of drama, – scene & dialogue, for lyrics may be dramatic also in the highest sense) – I partake your feeling to a great degree: lyric is the oldest, most natural, most *poetical* of poetry, and I would always get it if I could: but I find in these latter days that one has a great deal to say, and try and get attended to, which is out of the lyrical element and capability – and I am forced to take the nearest way to it: and then it is undeniable that the common reader is susceptible to plot, story, and the simplest form of putting a matter 'Said I,' 'Said He' & so on. 'The whole is with the gods' as Cleon sums up in one of the things I send you.[1]

Yet again, while poetry teaches, it does not teach: 'obliquely' is Browning's word for the method in *The Ring and the Book*. He can inveigh against converting poetry into didactics. 'Do I take too moral a view of the poet's duty? I know you hate this, and I believe I do too' (*RBJW*, 163; Dec. 3, 1868). Victor Hugo 'won't let truth be truth, or a number of remarkable poetical pieces speak for themselves, without assuring you that he meant them to join Man to God, with the like pleasant practicabilities' (*Dearest Isa*, 48–9; Nov. 30, 1859). Whatever poetry may teach, it is not, any more than Browning's heart,

---

1 Holograph letter, to John Kenyon, London, Oct. 1, 1855; Houghton Library, Harvard University; by permission of the Harvard College Library

out for display on a ticket from the publisher. The 'spirit-sense'
must dive for it.

ACKNOWLEDGMENTS

My first thanks rightly go to F.E.L. Priestley, for this book really
began in his classes in Victorian poetry in the University of Toronto.
It is not the first book so to begin; I hope it may also pay some tribute
to the incisive and stimulating mind of so gifted a teacher.

I am grateful to the following libraries for placing material at my
disposal: the Armstrong Browning Library, Baylor University, Waco,
Texas; the British Museum, including its Bibliographical Information
Service; Columbia University Library; the Houghton Library and
the Widener Collection, Harvard University; the Library of Congress,
Washington, D.C.; the Pierpont Morgan Library, New York; and
the Humanities Research Center, University of Texas. Officers at
Baylor, Texas, and Harvard, and especially Mr Herbert Cahoon,
Curator of Autograph Manuscripts, the Pierpont Morgan Library,
have been very helpful; I appreciate their generosity in supplying
microfilm and xeroxes to scholars.

Because of my respect and affection for the memory of my former
teacher, A.S.P. Woodhouse, I am pleased to record, as requested, that
an earlier form of this study was awarded the first A.S.P. Woodhouse
Prize by the University of Toronto. A Canada Council research grant
helped me revise it, and it has been published with the help of a grant
from the Humanities Research Council, using funds provided by the
Canada Council, and of a grant from the Andrew W. Mellon
Foundation to the University of Toronto Press.

Among friends and colleagues, I should like to thank Jay
Macpherson for encouragement and assistance.

To the University of Toronto Press, to Gertrude Stevenson, and
especially to my friend and editor, Jean Jamieson, I owe more than
one debt. And to Ramsay, Maggie, and Markham.

ELEANOR COOK   *Victoria College, University of Toronto*

I PAULINE, PARACELSUS, SORDELLO: *THEORY*

1 THE LYRIC AS MUSIC:

PAULINE

Browning's finest lyrics belong to his middle period: they are those appearing in *Men and Women*, published in 1855 when Browning was forty-three, and in *Dramatis Personae*, published in 1864 when he was fifty-two. Hardly any lyrics, by any definition of the word, were published before Browning was thirty; indeed, by 1841, while he had written eight works of considerable length, he had published less than a dozen short poems of any kind besides the songs in *Paracelsus* and *Pippa Passes*.[1]

This is the more surprising because Browning seems to have associated the lyric in its most literal sense (sung or song-like poems) with youth. His boy-poet, revelling in the delights granted him by his natural endowment, bursts into song as unreflectingly as some bird. Akin to him is the child or young person who is no poet but who also, in the fresh exuberance of living, sings instinctively: Pauline, Michal,

---

[1] Park Honan points out this ratio in *Browning's Characters* (New Haven, 1961), 29. The eight long works are *Pauline, Paracelsus, Strafford, Sordello, Pippa Passes, King Victor and King Charles, The Return of the Druses,* and *A Blot in the 'Scutcheon*; not all, of course, were published by 1841 (see DeVane, *Handbook*, for the probable dates of composition). The few short poems are *Johannes Agricola, Porphyria's Lover, Eyes calm beside thee, Still ailing, Wind* (later used in *James Lee's Wife*), *A King lived long ago* (used, revised, in *Pippa Passes*), *Rudel, Soliloquy of the Spanish Cloister, Artemis Prologuizes,* and perhaps *Cristina*. Mr Honan also includes in this group *Lines to the Memory of His Parents* and *A Forest Thought*, though Browning never authorized these for publication and they appeared in print only after his death. He may have written and subsequently destroyed any number of poems, of course. Cf. 'Don't think I want to say I have not worked hard ... that there is no self-delusion here, I would prove to you, (and nobody else) even by opening this desk I write on, and showing what stuff, in the way of wood, I *could* make a great bonfire with, if I might only knock the whole clumsy top off my tower!' (*LRBEB*, I, 18; Feb. 11, 1845). Cf. also the reference to the MS of 'Only a Player-girl' (!) (ibid., I, 149; Aug. 10, 1845).

the boy who sings Sordello's surviving fragment, Pippa. These latter
are explicitly associated with the imagery of birds. Pauline is to
'sing / Thy native songs, gay as a desert bird / Which crieth as it
flies for perfect joy' (959–61). Paracelsus asks of Michal, 'Does she
still sing alone, bird-like ... ? Respect all such as sing when all alone!'
(III, 28–36). The child singing Sordello's poem goes 'Up and up, ...
singing all the while / Some unintelligible words to beat / The lark,
God's poet' (VI, 864–6) – that same lark which Paracelsus, dying, but
exultant as in his youth, had singled out for mention among birds
('the lark / Soars up and up, shivering for very joy' (v, 675–6]).
Pippa's songs all include references to singers ('the lark's on the wing';
'a page that carols unseen'; 'the maiden who singeth'; 'what are the
voices of birds / – Ay, and of beasts, – but words, our words, / Only so
much more sweet?'); and at the end of her day Pippa rather dis-
consolately assigns the world to the owl, the lark being 'day's apostle,'
like Pippa herself.

But if Browning did not publish songs in his youth, he did write
about the boy-poet, who appears oftener in his early work than
anywhere else. I am thinking of the *Pauline* poet, Aprile, the young
Sordello, David, and, in a review published in 1842, Chatterton; a
little later David reappears in the second version of *Saul*, and along
with him the boy-poet of '*Transcendentalism*.' Much later,
Aristophanes introduces the young Thamuris, and it is a mark,
I think, of how far Browning has come from the boy-poet's problems
(which are acute in *Pauline* and *Sordello*) that Thamuris is so contained, so set apart (a statue is made of him), so gently and freshly
evoked by even Aristophanes, and so finally set aside. The detachment
which we can see clearly in '*Transcendentalism*,' where the young
poet is contemplated as an object along with his poem, is here complete. In *Aristophanes' Apology*, when Browning wants to talk about
the poet's problems he uses Aristophanes and Euripides: Balaustion
is a singer, to be sure, but not a poet herself, and she belongs in the
happy company of Michal and Pippa. She is the medium, slightly
distorting,[2] through which we see the two great poets; as for herself,
she has no singing problems.

2 'I am confident that Euripides bore his fun and parodying good humoredly
enough ... but a friend of Euripides, – above all, a woman friend, –
feels no such need of magnanimity' (to Swinburne, in *Letters*, ed. Hood,
193; Feb. 5, 1881).

Browning's boy-poets do not fare so well, for their crucial difficulty is how to emerge and where to go from their early paradises – so much more paradisal for them than for even the happy band of instinctive unendowed singers. The *Pauline* poet moves into an emotional and religious crisis from which he is still convalescing at the time of writing. Aprile, dazzled by his enormous gifts, and unable to choose one fancy and thus reject others, does nothing. Sordello makes a brief essay at experiment, is rebuffed, and retires to his early shelter, thereby very nearly undoing himself. The '*Transcendentalism*' poet attempts the poem *Transcendentalism* in twelve dull books, with dismal result. Thamuris strains beyond his powers, the gods punish him for his hubris, and there his statue stands with broken lyre and blind eyes, a symbol and a warning. Only David moves forward smoothly from his instinctive singing to something else, and even he remained frozen in his song for ten years until Browning in the completed *Saul* gave him the flash of revelation that could release him.

The boy-poets are themselves beautiful; our eyes enjoy the sight of them while we listen to their song. Singer and song merge into one effect, the singer being object as well as creator. He does not disappear from the surface of his golden ring when the proper acid is applied, but makes up a sunny counterpart. (Indeed the ring-figure, in which the poem is a hammered and filed artefact, hardly applies to the songs of the boy-poets.) The *Pauline* poet has tear-dimmed eyes, and is altered and worn and weak, but he is young, he is going to recover, he can act as Pauline's lover; more than this, he exhibits a certain vitality in his feverish tossing and threshing about, and in his one prolonged imaginative exercise (the pre-dawn-to-noon excursion) he glides about like some Ariel. Aprile is not described in detail, but we know him to be fresh and young, and thus a contrast with the prematurely aged Paracelsus: 'Thine eyes are lustreless to mine; my hair / Is soft, nay silken soft: to talk with thee / Flushes my cheek, and thou art ashy-pale' (II, 354–6). With Sordello we come to more precise description, for his very features mark him out as a poet-soul:

> Yourselves shall trace
> (The delicate nostril swerving wide and fine,
> A sharp and restless lip, so well combine
> With that calm brow) a soul fit to receive
> Delight at every sense; you can believe

> Sordello foremost in the regal class
> Nature has broadly severed from her mass
> Of men, and framed for pleasure ...   (I, 462–9)

For David an observer is provided, Abner, who can do what David himself cannot very well – paint the contrast between the black, silent tent and the golden youth with his music: 'God's child with the dew / On thy gracious gold hair, and those lilies still living and blue / Just broken to twine round thy harp-strings ...' (11–13). As for the *'Transcendentalism'* poet, he is

> a poem, though your poem's naught.
> The best of all you showed before, believe,
> Was your own boy-face o'er the finer chords
> Bent, following the cherub at the top
> That points to God with his paired half-moon wings.   (47–51)

Thamuris is just such another: 'The voice of him was weak; face, limbs and lyre, / These were worth saving ...' (*Aristophanes' Apology*, 5171–2).

The boy-poets, being themselves objects for contemplation, belong before audiences who can see them; they are Davids who need their Sauls. Thamuris is immortalized in a statue which all may look upon (his earthly performance was all too well witnessed by the gods). The *'Transcendentalism'* poet is contemplated as he plays, and David sings a command performance before a royal audience of one. Sordello's moment of triumph, his win at Mantua, is before an audience (his time of trial is in solitude) ; indeed Browning says the young Sordello must ever live before a crowd. Aprile never does sing anything except a parody of his song, but the parody is fancied to be sung by a group of judging fellow-poets who haunt him; and before his death, peers circle to crown him as if he had won a singing-match. The *Pauline* poet, recalling his halcyon days, says that he never sang 'but as one entering bright halls where all / Will rise and shout for him' (78–9).

The touch of corruption comes upon the young singers when they try consciously to retain the applause originally won by their early unreflecting performances. The *Pauline* poet wishes to write the poems that 'encircle men with praise and love' (525; the 1833 version reads 'me' for 'men') ; he would at least bring back one golden branch, in fairy-tale fashion, from the magic kingdom to show he has been there. Aprile never faces the problem, for he never involves himself enough in the world to be tainted by corruption; it is Paracelsus, taking up Aprile's task without understanding Aprile's last words, who must grapple with the problem of an audience. Sordello, when his experiments fall on deaf ears, simply gives the Mantuans what they want to hear. This is what the '*Transcenden-talism*' poet also tries to do, in twelve dull earnest books ('grown men want thought, you think; ... Boys seek for images and melody, / Men must have reason – so, you aim at men. / Quite otherwise!'). And this is what David does in effect – not singing dishonestly like Sordello, or with blundering didactic earnestness, but singing what he supposes Saul really wants to hear, none of which does any good. David is singing the instinctive apprehension of joy and sorrow which belongs to youth; and he sings even of sorrow and death with a life that softens or diverts their force. The trouble, in this instance, is that it is David's life that is providing all this energy and not Saul's, and there is no way of transferring this life and energy to Saul. A different point of reference is needed, and a different poetry emerges ('No harp more – no song more!'). This day David comes happily into his poetic heritage as Aprile and Sordello never do. He leaves their company to come closer to a companion in the *Men and Women* volume, the poet of *How It Strikes a Contemporary*.

It may be seen from the above examples that Browning's boy-poets become increasingly distinct as they become detached, that is, looked at as objects along with their songs. The detaching and focusing progress steadily from the *Pauline* poet to David. But, with the impor-tant exception of David, while the boy-poets themselves become objects of contemplation, their songs are not very clearly heard. We hear none of the *Pauline* poet's songs, though the whole of *Pauline* is a lyrical enough effusion, and though the poet gives us a sample of his ability in a tour de force. Aprile creates no songs save for the mocking chant hummed by what I take to be part of his divided self. Of Sordello's work, in Browning's poem, only a snatch survives. The '*Transcendentalism*' poet is told to recreate the rose rather than elaborate its meaning, thus filling his audience with youth once more, but we hear nothing of how he does this. As for Thamuris of the weak voice and fine appearance, we hear only fragments of his attempt, though we are made to see vividly enough the ecstasy of his transport. David's is the one completed song of all the boy-poets'; he becomes the spokesman for the 'wild joy of living' shared by them all.

All these boy-poets are associated, as I have said, with lyric in its most literal sense of sung or song-like poems. Three are provided with musical instruments. I want to look a little more closely at their kind of music and their kind of poetry as they appear in *Pauline, Paracelsus*, and *Sordello*, to see what they can tell us about Browning's own 'music' when he comes to write lyrical poems. It is especially useful to keep in mind this background if we find ourselves praising *Pauline* as a type of lyrical poetry and regretting that Browning could not manage to keep up such productions. For Browning turned his back on this early work vigorously, deliberately, and finally. He attempted to suppress the poem,[3] and he set to work after its publication to develop quite another manner of expression.

In *Pauline*, poetry is so closely connected with music as to be one with it. The poem itself is called a song and a lay ('I will sing on fast as fancies come' [258]; 'this lay I dedicate to thee' [870]; 'this song shall remain to tell for ever ...' [1004], a wish devoutly abjured later). When the poet speaks of making poetry in the past, present, or future, he always uses the term 'singing' or 'weaving a lay,' and never 'speaking' or 'writing.' Other poets, as well as Pauline's ideal poet, are inevitably 'bards.' Shelley, of course, is something more, the unique 'Sun-treader' who provides illumination like some Apollo and whom the young poet desires to see clearly; he is connected with the complex of light and dark imagery, and hence with the fitful moments of insight in the

3 He dangled it before the eyes of Elizabeth Barrett very early in their correspondence, but did not reply to her response: 'Is there not somewhere the little book I first printed when a boy, with John Mill, the metaphysical head, *his* marginal note ...' (*LRBEB*, I, 28; Feb. 26, 1845). Elizabeth answered, taking the sense of Browning's cryptic remarks as best she could, 'And was the little book written with Mr. Mill, pure metaphysics, or what? (ibid., I, 32; Feb. 27, 1845) – to which there was no reply. When Browning wrote his defensive apology for the letter Elizabeth rejected, he returned to Mill's marginal remarks: 'Then, I had a certain faculty of self-consciousness, years and years ago, at which John Mill wondered, and which ought to be improved by this time, if constant use helps at all' (ibid., I, 75; May 24, 1845). *Pauline* reappears only with a discussion in January 1846.

poem. But his poems are seen as songs too: spring comes but 'thy
songs come not, other bards arise, / But none like thee' (154–5);
'I aim not even to catch a tone / Of harmonies he called profusely up'
(216–17); 'thy sweet imaginings are as an air, / A melody some
wondrous singer sings, / Which, though it haunt men oft in the still
eve, / They dream not to essay' (221–4).

Poetry is not only like music; it includes music, or at least musical
effect. This is why the young man decides to become a poet – because
poetry is more inclusive than the other arts. That is, painting and
music, or rather their effects, may be approximated in poetry. Other
arts are more particular and single in what they do.

> As peace returned, I sought out some pursuit;
> And song rose, no new impulse but the one
> With which all others best could be combined.
> My life has not been that of those whose heaven
> Was lampless save where poesy shone out;
>
> ...
> For music (which is earnest of a heaven,
> Seeing we know emotions strange by it,
> Not else to be revealed,) is like a voice,
> A low voice calling fancy ...   (357–61, 365–8)

Music thus not only provides effects that may be imitated in poetry;
it can also inspire the poet's fancy like some muse, or rather like some
elusive nymph who calls to fancy, charming it forth, as a piper charms
a child toward a magic kingdom. In fact, music as the inspirer and
releaser of fancy is like Pauline herself, that elusive phantom (the
word is Mill's) and convenient combination of beloved, mother,
singer, muse, and annotator. Music follows her ('that form which
music follows like a slave' [46]) though elsewhere it is independent
and mysterious enough. And it is thus through her that the *Pauline*
poet proposes in after-days to probe the riddle of music. 'Be still to me
/ A help to music's mystery which mind fails / To fathom, its
solution, no mere clue!' (929–31).

If music is like Pauline in its elusiveness and ability to inspire, and
also in its foretaste of heaven, it is like fancy in its ambiguity. For
music, like the fancy it can lead, seems capable of playing a sinister
role. When it leads fancy, it leads her on to some inhuman fairy

kingdom that sounds like a realm of unborn, ideal images, a world
which is also ambiguous, for it can madden those who enter it:

> For music ... is like a voice,
> A low voice calling fancy, as a friend,
> To the green woods in the gay summer time:
> And she fills all the way with dancing shapes
> Which have made painters pale, and they go on
> Till stars look at them and winds call to them
> As they leave life's path for the twilight world
> Where the dead gather.   (365-74)

Near the end of the poem, music becomes sinister again, or rather a
parody of sinister, in the role of a ludicrously villainous agent of
apostasy, as the young poet realizes he may backslide: 'As it may be; ...
music wait to wile, / And strange eyes and bright wine lure, laugh
like sin / Which steals back softly on a soul half saved ...' (988–90).
(In 1833 he was entirely resigned to future downfall: 'As it may be'
then read 'As it will be.'[4]) Music here appears to be earnest not of a
heaven but of a particularly conventional kind of hell. Of course, this
is a different sort of music, a cabaret tune say, perhaps like the
'unhonoured song' of the seductive soul's idol (541). But then there
must be music and music as there is fancy and fancy.

Fancy in this poem is not, it might be noted, synonymous with
imagination. The word imagination is used only in the poet's self-
analysis: it is the gift that allows him to alleviate his insatiable thirst
to 'be all, have, see, know, taste, feel all.' J.S. Mill in his notes on the
poem suggested the word should be printed with a capital, and
Browning at one time agreed but did not make the change in either
revision.[5] Imagination is not closely analysed, but it is said to be an
angel that always accompanies the young poet; it does not come and
go. Fancy, however, is often in the plural; a brood of fancies may be
sinister or benign; they do come and go; and they often seem to figure
as servants who hover about a master rather than august visitors from

---

4 For this reading, not given in the new *Complete Works ... with Variant
   Readings*, see N. Hardy Wallis, *Pauline by Robert Browning*.
5 Mill, note to line 284: 'not imagination but Imagination / the absence of
   that capital letter obscures the meaning'; Browning's note: 'make
   Imagination big I' (W.L. Phelps, 'Notes on Browning's *Pauline*,'
   Modern Language Notes, 47 [1932], 292–9).

another world. The important question seems to be who is master, or
rather who or what is the master's master. Imagination like fancy,
may have its mystery. In the description of Shelley's poems, his
'imaginings' (this form of the word is also used of the *Pauline* poet's
earliest efforts, but not of his later, sadder ones) partake of the
mystery of music: 'Thy sweet imaginings are as an air, / A melody
some wondrous singer sings, / Which, though it haunt men oft in the
still eve ...' (221–3). But imagination, whatever mystery may be
associated with it, does not wander into countries of madness; its
magic is white.

The *Pauline* poet sets himself as one future task the probing of
music's mystery, and it does occur to the reader to wonder whether the
real mystery of music may not be its dual role. In the same sentence
in which music lures fancy to a strange sinister world, it is also spoken
of as 'earnest of a heaven, / Seeing we know emotions strange by it, /
Not else to be revealed.' Since heaven in the rest of the poem is by no
means some sinister 'twilight world,' it seems a considerable mystery
how music manages to point both to heaven and to a certain kind of
hell. Of course, music is not of necessity a pointer at all. The young
poet retains his devotion to it even during his days of wickedness:
'music, my life, / Nourished me more than ever' (565–6). It is not
music but the arrival of Pauline that sets him on the path to virtue.
The dual role of music has rather more to do, I think, with the two
mental worlds which make up the two extreme poles of *Pauline*: one
is a world where the poet takes over the role of God, the other a world
in which God, a rather hazy God but a distinct other being, reigns.[6]

6 It is clear that I don't see such a polarization between God and Shelley in
   Pauline as do some recent commentators. Internally, at least, *Pauline* is
   quite consistent about Shelley. The speaker says he first embraced, then
   later repudiated his 'wild dreams of beauty and of good,' and that he
   afterwards lapsed into sin. The wild dreams, we surmise, were derived
   from Shelley. In the poem, the speaker is repenting, and he repudiates
   the sin, but not specifically the wild dreams. Here is what he says:

       I had been spared this shame if I had sat
       By thee [Pauline] forever from the first, in place
       Of my wild dreams of beauty and of good,
       Or with them, as an earnest of their truth. (28–31, italics mine)

   It is what the speaker does with Shelley's visions that is important. All this
   is argued, of course, from within the viewpoint of *Pauline*. Whether wild
   Shelleyan dreams could be reconciled with the speaker's enervated
   Christianity at the end is another matter.

I have noted that the *Pauline* poet sings rather than writes or speaks. He sings the present poem in unpremeditated strain, this being the way of the confessional genre.

> I must not think, lest this new impulse die
> In which I trust! I have no confidence:
> So, I will sing on fast as fancies come;
> Rudely, the verse being as the mood it paints. (256–9)

But this kind of singing seems to be the only kind he has ever done. The early songs are also 'rude,' and after the conscious decision to become a poet, the young man again makes 'rude verses.' At this time too, he is also moved by impulse – not impulsiveness ('song rose, no new impulse' [358]), but also not yearning: 'I had / An impulse but no yearning – only sang' (375–6); the word 'yearning' is a strong one for Browning even this early. The lines describing the young poet's first conscious efforts show us an even more unpremeditated art than *Pauline* is supposed to be: 'And first I sang as I in dream have seen / Music wait on a lyrist for some thought, / Yet singing to herself until it came' (377–9). The description is especially interesting because Browning later criticized this kind of poetry in phrasing that might have been aimed deliberately at these lines:

> I hardly know what to advise about the poems ... There is a distinct conception in each piece – something the writer had in mind to say before the beginning – and the working-out of the same has been a matter of less importance. There is not the usual *using up* of the effect produced by a sympathy with somebody else's poetry, which people suppose to be a spontaneous effect of their own minds, and treat accordingly. Above all, there is not the usual *singing away* till, peradventure, some thought or other turn up in the course of it; that is, the thought suggests the tune, not the tune the thought.[7]

It may be objected that in various of Browning's later poems on music, tune does lead thought (as in *A Toccata of Galuppi's*), but it is the musician's tune which the poet deliberately allows to provide a structure. It is the idea of a real tune, and not the poet's own strum-

---

7 The poet was Mrs Millais; from J.G. Millais, *Life and Letters of Millais*, 1, 439–40; Jan. 7, 1867.

ming. It may also be objected that no one supposes that in Browning's lyrics tune does lead thought (despite a contemporary reviewer's remarks that all his poetry is bang-whang-whang).[8] However, Browning himself remarked some ten years after *Pauline* that when young he wrote just such verses as the *Pauline* poet might have written, 'musical' ones, and that his reaction against such verses was so strong as to propel him into the opposite kind of writing: 'The fact is, in my youth (i.e. childhood) I wrote *only* musically – and after stopped all that so effectually that I even now catch myself grudging my men and women their half-lines, like a parish overseer the bread-dole of his charge' (*RBAD*, 96; Nov. 8, 1843).

Tune is not what leads thought in *Pauline* itself; mood does that ('the verse being as the mood it paints'). This is because it belongs to the confessional genre, as Pauline says ('... [le] seul mérite auquel une production si singulière peut prétendre, celui de donner une idée assez précise du genre qu'elle n'a fait qu'éboucher. Ce debut sans prétention, ce remuement des passions qui va d'abord en accroissant et puis s'apaise par dégrés, ces élans de l'âme, ce retour soudain sur soimême, et par-dessus tout, la tournure d'esprit tout particulière de mon ami ...' [*Complete Works*, 1, 42]). Or perhaps mood leads tune, which leads thought. Browning will certainly write again poems in which mood governs thought, but it will govern in a different way. The idea of a mood, or the type of a mood will govern, so that really the thought will come first after all, thought in the widest sense of the word. Mood to word will not be such a direct process; the verse will not be as the mood it paints in just this way ever again. In *Paracelsus*, for instance, Browning's next publication, he will 'display somewhat minutely the mood itself in its rise and progress' (Preface), but the result is far different from *Pauline*, and the difference is not just that of the two chief characters or the genre.

Something happened between *Pauline* and *Paracelsus* to determine the young Browning to begin the difficult task of working out a style of his own. He may have come to realize that the effects in *Pauline* were borrowed Shelleyan effects (despite denials of this in the poem[9]),

---

8 'Do you see the "Edinburg" that says all my poetry is summed up in "Bang whang, whang, goes the Drum"?' (*Dearest Isa*, 196; Oct. 19, 1864; the reference is to the *Edinburgh Review* for October 1864, 565).
9 'Yet I aim not even to catch a tone / Of harmonies he called profusely up'; '... dream not to essay' (216–17, 224).

that he was 'using up ... the effect produced by a sympathy with somebody else's poetry, which [he] suppose[d] to be a spontaneous effect
of [his] own.' He may have begun, as the *Pauline* poet intended, to
investigate the mystery of music, and discovered that his 'musical'
poems were not so musical after all. 'All this will show that I have
given much attention to music *proper* – I believe to the detriment of
what people take for 'music' in poetry, when I had to consider that
quality. For the first effect of apprehending real musicality was to
make me abjure the sing-song which, in early days, was taken for it.'
This was written in 1887,[10] but much earlier, in 1845, Elizabeth
Barrett reported: 'You said once that you had had a false notion of
music, or had practised it according to the false notions of other people' (*LRBEB*, I, 97; June 16, 1845). The false notion of music I take
to be sing-song, and sing-song I take to be poetry that is musical in the
sentimental sense of the word. Here I am following Northrop Frye's
remarks on music and poetry: 'This technical use of the word musical
is very different from the sentimental fashion of calling any poetry
musical if it sounds nice. In practise the technical and sentimental
uses are often directly opposed, as the sentimental term would be applied to, for example, Tennyson, and withdrawn from, for example,
Browning.'[11] Browning rejected very early sing-song and 'merely
making a noise.'

---

10 To H. Spaulding, June 30, 1887; *PMLA* 62 (1947), 1095–9.
11 See the entire discussion. *The Anatomy of Criticism* (Princeton, 1957),
255–8.

2   THE DRAMATIC LYRIC:

PARACELSUS

We do not hear a great deal about song in *Paracelsus*, but we do hear
four songs and see one singer, or rather one would-be singer. Each
of the four main characters of *Paracelsus* has a song or songs, has his
own music as well as his own dialogue, and both the song itself and
the circumstances of its singing are typical. Michal's songs are not
heard just as she herself is hardly seen, but they exert a strong and
unexpected influence, again like Michal herself, on Paracelsus.
She sings by herself, instinctively like some bird, bewitching the young
scholar and making him wonder why her simple song can distract
him from the studies he loves. Had he pursued this wonder, he might
have found another mode of knowledge long before he met Aprile.
Michal sings within her sheltered nest, a garden like the elusive,
magical, Keatsean garden in *Pauline* ('high-walled gardens thick
with trees, / Where song takes shelter and delicious mirth' [452–3]).
Paracelsus is far from such a peaceful refuge when he recalls
Michal's singing:

>   Does she still sing alone, bird-like,
>   Not dreaming you are near? Her carols dropt
>   In flakes through that old leafy bower built under
>   The sunny wall at Würzburg, from her lattice
>   Among the trees above, while I, unseen,
>   Sat conning some rare scroll from Tritheim's shelves,
>   Much wondering notes so simple could divert
>   My mind from study. Those were happy days.
>   Respect all such as sing when alone!   (III, 28–36)

To the last line Festus rejoins that she is scarcely alone now, with two
wild children scampering about her. Paracelsus' recoil from this
alteration of his perfect, static picture of the singing girl Michal is,

in little, his recoil against accommodating himself to this world. His consolation begins when he fashions an equally perfect and static picture of Michal as Madonna-like mother.

At the end of his life Paracelsus is soothed, then roused – as at the beginning he was diverted – by another simple song. He is again in a sheltered spot, not a friendly green garden however, but a bare austere cell that reminds both occupants of the narrower cell Paracelsus will soon occupy ('the tomb-like place') [v, 34]; 'an unexceptionable vault: / Good brick and stone: the bats kept out, the rats / Kept in: a snug nook,' [454–6]). The magic of song is what first breaks the spell of the sepulchral place; light will follow like the sun of the old days, literally as day dawns, and figuratively as Paracelsus begins his long last speech with ' I see' (and bids 'this wretched cell become / A shrine' [557–8]). Festus' song is simple like Michal's; it is a rocking lullaby and its chief effect is to soothe, for it is performed with Festus-like devotion as a service to a dying friend.

> Thus / the Mayne glideth
> Where / my Love abideth.
> Sleep's no softer: / it proceeds
> On through lawns, / on through meads,
> On and on, / whate'er befall,
> Meandering / and musical ...   (418–23)

(I have altered the placing of the lines to emphasize the swaying rhythm.) The song is like an imitative piece of music. It is not great poetry but it performs its office:

> My heart! they loose my heart, those simple words;
> Its darkness passes, which nought else could touch:
> Like some dark snake that force may not expel,
> Which glideth out to music sweet and low.
> What were you doing when your voice broke through
> A chaos of ugly images?   (447–52)

Music and musical verse still have something of the magic they had in *Pauline*, though here only white magic. And here tune does lead thought, which is right, for tune is thought, the poem being a lullaby.

Paracelsus' memory of song as a healer is strong, for in his most desperate moments after his expulsion from the university at Basel he composes verses as a diversion. Festus too recognizes the therapeutic effect ('this verse-making can purge you well enough' [IV, 546]). But the two songs Paracelsus sings take on the tinge of their creator's despair. The fact that Paracelsus' songs appear now shows how deeply embittered he is. Like Paracelsus himself, his songs have tangled motivation. Song has been associated with Michal and Aprile hitherto, and to both Paracelsus is devoted. But he is in the process of abandoning Aprile's ideals (or what he thinks are Aprile's ideals), and only now do we have a song that is relief and healing, but also flagellation and mockery. For both Paracelsus and Aprile, who fail (though not *sub specie aeternitatis*), actual songs are mockery and derision, no matter what they think of song or music in general. Paracelsus only turns the knife deeper in the wound by using song to mark his leave-taking of Aprile; Festus can accept the first song as a healer, but the second he sees as something different.

The first of Paracelsus' songs is a sweetly nostalgic elegy for his lost ideals ('Heap cassia, sandal-buds'), with drugs sensuously piled in the first stanza and the faint perfume of an ancient mummy strewn in the second. The exotic pile with its faint incense from a remote world is a funeral pyre ('on such a pile shall die / My lovely fancies'), perhaps an ironic variation on the fire in Book III if 'Heap cassia' is meant to echo the first line of that book, 'Heap logs ...' Paracelsus' interest in building such an impressive pyre is partly a tribute to Aprile, for Aprile was the poet who revered beauty as Paracelsus revered knowledge, and it is a beautiful farewell Paracelsus is giving to those ideas he had derived from Aprile. ('Still, dreams / They were, so let them vanish, yet in beauty ... I made this rhyme / That fitting dignity might be preserved' [IV, 187–8, 209–10].) The faint odour of death and the fact it is sweet, the weariness of a tired wind retiring from a howling sea to hoard its treasure, the inturning of the wind, and the stillness of the quiet closet where an Egyptian queen moulders – all breathe a lassitude so unlike Paracelsus' usual speech as to suggest how close he is to self-abandonment. Even so, it is the imagery and not the rhythm or syntax that suggests weariness and the attraction of easeful death. Paracelsus is still some distance from the languid incantation of Aprile's imagined voices before his death. When Paracelsus actually comes to his deathbed, he is plagued with a much more vigorous demon-troop, as his final words are more vigorous and more articulate than Aprile's. In that last dying speech Paracelsus has as quick an apprehension of the aliveness of all life as anywhere in the poem, even in his youthful days. The vision of life from stone up to man all pulsing together to the joy of the Creator contrasts sharply with the quiet defeatism here. There everything bursts its bounds, works and strains, thrusts upward: the lark soaring up and up is the bird mentioned there; like the ambitious eagle of Book I, she flies high; volcanoes break forth; fire is the fire of life at earth's core, not the fire of a funeral pyre.

Paracelsus' second song begins energetically enough but this is merely to accentuate the bitterness of what follows: knowledge that the energy has been misspent. Like the Lotos-Eaters, Paracelsus' sailors have been lured to their island by the promise of rest, and there, having unveiled and ensconced their gods, they feel compelled to stay even when they know of a real home for themselves and their deities. The whole adventure is given the bleakness of an Ozymandias setting, for the verse is engraved, Paracelsus fancies, on crumbling rock, and his voice singing it is the wind's voice: 'The sharp salt wind, impatient for the last / Of even this record, wistfully comes and goes, / Or sings what we recover, mocking it' (iv, 446–8). As so often in Browning, the wind is a wind of change, and its moaning the sad and sinister wail over the transience of this life. This poem, says Paracelsus, is inscribed as 'the sad rhyme of the men who proudly clung / To their first fault, and withered in their pride' (iv, 526–7). It is this poem which alarms Festus, not the del Sarto-like resignation of the first song, for in the fable the sailors see their own wretchedness but stubbornly remain in it like Satan proudly clinging to his own misery. There is no touch of enjoyment in the apparatus of despair, no rearing of a sensuous death-symbol, the sensuousness of which betrays some vitality. The sailors simply 'knew, too late, / How bare the rock, how desolate, / Which had received our precious freight' (iv, 516–18). And they will not move ('we have no heart / To mar our work'). The reiterated word in the inscription ('proudly ... pride') tells why, and prompts Festus to cry out, 'Come back then, Aureole; as you fear God, come! / This is foul sin; come back! (iv, 528–9). By the end of his life Paracelsus has come back, for in his delirium before his death he uses that same figure of men clinging to a worthless altar while a fair temple awaits them, but now he pleads with them to leave: 'Why should you linger here when I have built / A far resplendent temple, all your own?' (v, 303–4). Aprile too, before his death, had imagined how he might testify of a far-off glorious land to men living on barren isles: 'I would adventure nobly for their sakes: / When nights were still, and still the moaning sea ... I would ... load my bark, and hasten back, / And fling my gains to them' (ii, 534–40).[1]

The song Aprile hears before his death is the real Lotos-Eater chorus of the poem; Paracelsus' sailors awake before the end. Aprile has, his whole life through, heard the voices of fellow-poets chorusing to him that he is lost and has failed, that he must join their ranks and mourn with them, cut off from God. The scene of his song is reminiscent of the end of *Childe Roland* with 'we thy peers' leaning 'in an airy ring' and grieving:

'Must one more recreant to his race
Die with unexerted powers,
And join us, leaving as he found
The world, he was to loosen, bound?'   (ii, 319–22)

The beginning of the poets' song is especially hypnotic with the sing-song repetition of words and phrases. Here the tune again leads the thought, for the thought is simply to subside, rest, give up.

'Lost, lost! yet come,
With our wan troop make thy home.
Come, come! for we
Will not breathe, so much as breathe
Reproach to thee,
Knowing what thou sink'st beneath.
So sank we in those old years,
We who bid thee, come!'   (ii, 297–304)

As the verse goes on, the singers recall past hopes for Aprile and past efforts over him by their ghostly selves. Their comfort becomes more vocal and chattery as if they had already begun their post mortem on him, and he were there to confirm his death and join in the

---

1 Sordello is given a variation on the figure. He is not tied to one place, but accumulates treasure like an itinerant mariner, displaying it on request, and rushing off again at the call of the west wind.

diagnosis. There the lines fill out, and the slow short early lines, stretched out to their languid utmost, are no longer used. (The pause in the fifth line quoted above, for instance, is long enough to allow a full breath, but it must be a silent one after the injunction to silence in the hurried whisper of the fourth line. The effect of the pause is to leave the word reproach hanging like a weight in the silence, so that it is no surprise that Aprile sinks beneath some unnamed burden in line 6.)

The voices I conjecture are part of Aprile's own self. When he was young his own vitality drowned their chant, and he did not care whether they were real or unreal. Now they seem 'fatal-clear.' They may be seen to be part of his own self by their contradictory call. For they assert how they have yearned for Aprile's victory, how they have endowed him, how he is to be their champion. Yet their call is enervating, a siren song to abandon the struggle and join their melancholy ranks. It is Aprile's double consciousness of his poetic genius that produces the voices: his genius is a gift and a treasure, but it must be earned before it can be possessed and so is a burden. Thus the maddening ambiguity of the song, which reinforces his task at the same time it tempts him to abandon it. (The same form of torment – though over something different – afflicts the *Pauline* poet, who is haunted by 'dreams in which / I seemed the fate from which I fled' [96–7].) The result has been a paralysis of the will: Aprile has gazed so long on all he might do, on the full glory of possible achievement, that he has done nothing and now it is too late. This fate the *Pauline* poet avoided by forcing himself to produce *Pauline* ('I shall not know again that nameless care / Lest, leaving all undone in youth, some new / And undreamed end reveal itself too late' [1001–3]). But Aprile is perishing and has done nothing, like another poor singer who also did nothing and perished. Paracelsus hints at the connection: 'my Aprile ... the poor melodious wretch' (v, 852); his words echo the line on Ophelia, 'pulled the poor wretch from her melodious lay ...' (*Hamlet*, IV, vii, 182).

Yet Aprile has after all done something, if only to work out how much he might do. He also retains a loyalty to his first vision at a moment when Paracelsus is losing his. Thus he becomes a means of inspiration to Paracelsus, and closer to him in spirit than even the long-loved and long-suffering Festus. When Paracelsus dies, it is with one hand in Festus' live hand and the other in Aprile's ghostly one, for Aprile is with him all through his long death-struggle. But Aprile's vindication has come before, in the vision of his crowning just before his death and in his last, short moment of insight: 'I see now. God is the perfect poet, / Who in his person acts his own creations' (II, 648–9). The voices, then, for all their hypnotic power and paralysing effect, have not won out, though Aprile, always haunted by them, cannot believe his final victory. It is Paracelsus, wonderfully self-confident in his youth and always forceful even in despondency, who marches through the gates of death in conscious triumph.

We hear, then, four songs in Paracelsus, forerunners of Browning's later separate dramatic lyrics. And we see one singer, Aprile. Aprile is also, though this is often forgotten, a would-be painter, sculptor, and musician. But so well does he represent the conventional type of fervent, young, early-deceased Romantic poet that he is commonly thought of as the type of lyric poet. This despite his ambitions in the other arts and the fact that he sings nothing whatsoever except a semi-delirious incantation. Why this identification? Partly because Aprile himself associates poetry with song, ranks music as the highest of the arts, and at the same time uses the word 'poet' in the widest possible sense; we tend to choose the more precise and familiar meaning. Partly also because we so readily read 'Shelley' for 'Aprile,' and 'lyric' for 'Shelley.' Let us look a little more closely at these two reasons.

Aprile is closely connected with song in the poem. He is a 'melodious wretch'; Paracelsus thinks it fitting to bid farewell to his ideals in a song. Aprile himself, ironically, does not fashion any song at all; the would-be singer in the poem is the one person to whom this is not granted. What he does utter is a near-subconscious chant subversive of the very process of song-making. Aprile's scheme of embodying all beauty in sculpture, painting, poetry, and music indicates that he might better be thought of as an artist than a poet. Yet he himself with this scheme aims at being a 'poet'; he assumes Paracelsus has succeeded in a similar quest and hails him as 'poet'; in his moment of vision, God is the 'perfect poet.' And his urgent cry to Paracelsus is to sing: 'Sing them to me ... Sing thou ... thy songs ... Sing to me' (II, 373–8), although when he himself outlines his scheme for writing he says 'I would speak.' Music, of course, in Aprile's scheme is the highest of the arts and the last to be attained, and it may be he supposes that Paracelsus, having attained, will have produced 'solemn songs' (II, 360). It may also be that, since Aprile uses a concept of love and loveliness close to Shelley's, he also uses 'poet' in the wide sense in which it is used in the *Defence of Poetry*. Compare his 'all poets, God ever meant / Should save the world' (II, 289–90) and 'poets are the unacknowledged legislators of the world'; Shelley includes Plato and Bacon among the poets, and 'poetry' for him includes representations in the mediums of 'language, colour, form.'

This is another reason to connect the would-be singer Aprile with the singer Shelley besides the pertinent likeness of their concepts of love and loveliness. W.O. Raymond has developed the connection persuasively,[2] but his persuasiveness has, I think, tempted us to a too close identification of Aprile with Shelley. It is true that Aprile's infinite romantic thirst and peculiar sort of love are Shelleyan and that he sees them differently before his death: he does not abjure them, but sees their purpose in a new way, sees them as means rather than end. 'God is the perfect poet, / Who in his person acts his own creations. / Had you but told me this at first!' (II, 648–50). That is, if God can, the artist too can try to work out his full vision through a medium which will always be partly unsatisfactory.[3] And Paracelsus, when he takes over what he thinks Aprile has taught, begins the attempt to accommodate himself to the finite – an attempt which is not informed by his own wisdom and fails signally, but an attempt which is his most felicitous time on earth ('When but the time I vowed myself to man?' [V, 598]) – seen in retrospect, of course.

It may be that the young Browning is here giving Shelley a death-bed repentance and a new vision, that he is placing him, as the older Browning was to place him, with the Christians ('had Shelley lived he would have finally ranged himself with the Christians' ['Essay on Shelley']). But without denying the Shelleyan basis for Aprile's outlook, and the modification of it which Browning consistently made,

2 'Browning's Conception of Love as Represented in Paracelsus,' *The Infinite Moment and Other Essays in Robert Browning* (Toronto, 1965, second edition), 156–75

3 Aprile's cryptic remarks refer not to immanence but to the incarnation. Browning added, then deleted the lines that make this clear. 'God's strength his glory is, / For thence came with our weakness sympathy / Which brought God down to earth a man like us' (1849 edition of *Paracelsus* only).

Aprile as a character seems to me less a Shelley than a young
Browning inspired by a Shelley. (Raymond also notes that Aprile
'represents very definite impulses and sympathies in Browning's
nature' [*The Infinite Moment*, 164], but this is sometimes forgotten.)
What most suggests this is Aprile's fantastically ambitious scheme
for using all the arts to reveal all life. 'First: I would carve in stone,
or cast in brass, / The forms of earth ... I would contrive and paint /
Woods, valleys, rocks and plains, dells, sands and wastes, / Lakes ...
all filled with men ... I would speak; no thought which ever stirred /
A human breast should be untold ... This done, to perfect and consummate all, ... I would supply all chasms with music' (II, 421–77).
This scheme is close to the scheme proposed for himself by the talented
young Browning:

> The following Poem [*Pauline*] was written in pursuance of a foolish
> plan which occupied me mightily for a time, and which had for its object
> the enabling me to assume & realize I know not how many different
> characters; – meanwhile the world was never to guess that "Brown, Smith,
> Jones & Robinson' (as the spelling books have it) the respective authors
> of this poem, that novel, such an opera, such a speech, etc. etc. were no
> other than one and the same individual. The present abortion was the
> first work of the *Poet* of the batch ...
>
> Only this crab remains of the shapely Tree of Life in this Fool's
> paradise of mine.[4]

A note in Browning's own copy of *Pauline* reads:

> Kean was acting there; I saw him in *Richard* III that night and conceived
> the childish scheme ... I don't know whether I had not made up my
> mind to *act* as well as to make verses, music, and God knows what, –
> *que de châteaux en Espagne!*[5]

Aprile is represented as so dazzled by what he might do that he
achieves nothing, and certainly his or Browning's own scheme would
dazzle anyone. But to put Shelley in the position of achieving nothing

---

4 Note in the copy of *Pauline* used by John Stuart Mill; cited in DeVane,
  Handbook, 41
5 Note in Browning's copy of *Pauline*; cited in DeVane, *Handbook*, 40–1

('neglected all the means / Of realizing even the frailest joy' [II, 390–1], 'Thou didst not ... grow mad to grasp / At once the price long patient toil should claim, / Nor spurn all granted short of that' [II, 491–5]) is a curious way to treat the poet Browning most revered at this time. To be sure, in the 'Essay on Shelley' Browning does say that Shelley's work was incomplete and cut off by an early death. But he also says that Shelley may be misunderstood because of a failing quite opposite to Aprile's. He saw what wanted doing and seized too readily the first rough tools at hand: 'the early fervor and power to *see* was accompanied by as precocious a fertility to *contrive*: he endeavored to realize as he went on idealizing ...' ('Essay on Shelley'). This is just what Aprile is unable to do.

That Aprile should represent a certain part of Browning's own youthful self, a part strongly imbued with Shelleyan idealism, rather than Shelley himself also seems likely because of Browning's great admiration for Shelley both before and after *Paracelsus*. In the 'Essay on Shelley' he writes that it was 'the dream of my boyhood to render to his fame and memory' a 'signal service,' a service unlikely to be rendered by suggesting Shelley was a failure or at most a success in spite of himself. Nor does the opening *avanti* in *Sordello* sound very like a response to an Aprile figure:

> ... stay – thou, spirit, come not near
> Now – not this time desert thy cloudy place
> To scare me, thus employed, with that pure face!
> I need not fear this audience, I make free
> With them, but then this is no place for thee!
> The thunder-phrase of the Athenian ...
> Would echo like his own sword's griding screech
> ... wert thou to hear! What heart
> Have I to play my puppets, bear my part
> Before these worthies?   (I, 60–73)

No, Aprile, whose very name suggests dew-time freshness, seems closer to an earlier self of Browning's own remembrance: 'this ... is part & parcel of an older – indeed primitive folly of mine, which I shall never wholly get rid of, of desiring to do nothing when I cannot do all; seeing nothing, getting, enjoying nothing, where there is no seeing & getting & enjoying *wholly* ...' (*LRBEB*, I, 53–4; May 3, 1845).

There are Aprile-touches in *Pauline* (I have noted the split self and the doing something for fear of doing nothing) as there are also, of course, touches of Paracelsus. Between the two, in fact, the later heroes include the *Pauline* poet's 'principle of restlessness / Which would be all, have, see, know, taste, feel, all' (277–8).[6] The *Pauline* poet shares Aprile's ability to sympathize so closely with all life that he feels himself into every possible situation ('I can live all the life of plants ... I can mount with the bird' [716–20]). His journey through a varied landscape from night to noon has the voracious inclusiveness of Aprile's scheme, if the motive is a little different ('see how I could build / A home for us, out of the world, in thought!' [729–30]). The wealth of his imaginative endowment has also dazzled the *Pauline* poet:

> For fancies followed thought and bore me off,
> And left all indistinct; ere one was caught
> Another glanced; so, dazzled by my wealth,
> I knew not which to leave nor which to choose,
> For all so floated, nought was fixed and firm.   (878–82)

Aprile's memories of his crowds of unborn images reproaching him if one among them is chosen, and thus preventing him from developing any, is close to this. Aprile's feeling for the mystery of music is also close to the *Pauline* poet's, much closer than is Paracelsus', for he merely finds it puzzling that music can divert him. Aprile considers it the crown of the arts ('music, breathing / Mysterious motions of the soul, no way / To be defined save in strange melodies' [II, 477–9]). The *Pauline* poet uses some of the same words of it ('seeing we know emotions strange by it, / Not else to be revealed,' 'music's mystery').[7]

---

6 The *Pauline* poet, for that matter, includes the aspirations of Festus, who, if he were gifted like Paracelsus, 'would encircle me with love' (I, 633). The *Pauline* poet wished to write what would 'encircle me with praise and love' (525, 1833 version).

7 Aprile in the poem assigns to music a role like that Browning in his Preface to *Paracelsus* assigns to fancy: 'to perfect and consummate all, / Even as a luminous haze links star to star, / I would supply all chasms with music ...' (II, 475–7). Browning had written in the Preface: 'It is certain, however, that a work like mine depends on the intelligence and sympathy of the reader for its success, – indeed were my scenes stars, it must be his cooperating fancy which, supplying all chasms, shall collect the scattered

The *Pauline* poet also dreams of causing his own decay, but his sinister, highly coloured nightmares are more threatening than Aprile's quiet, persistent inner voices; of course, he is a more feverish fretful young poet, he is close to a crisis, and he has been falser to his ideal than has Aprile. In one sense, Aprile has never been false at all.

Browning has, then, in *Paracelsus* given us four dramatic lyrics, dramatic in the obvious sense of belonging in a drama and depending upon it. Later, in his dramatic monologues, Browning will condense one character's dialogue into a monologue and shear away the rest of the drama. The reader will reconstruct the whole drama – supply all chasms, as Browning has it – as best he can. The dialogue here is forerunner of such monologues, and it may be that the lyrics here are forerunners of dramatic lyrics in a similar way. For Browning will later condense one character's music into one song and shear away the rest of the drama, leaving the reader to reconstruct it too. The work toward this kind of lyric will come, however, chiefly with *Bells and Pomegranates*. Now Browning is still absorbed by the question of what the poet is, and what and how and for whom and why he writes.

lights into one constellation – a Lyre or a Crown.' I have already noted how, in *Pauline*, music and fancy are spoken of in a similar way.

Fancy presumably shows the *Pauline* poet how he might 'supply the chasm / 'Twixt what I am and all I fain would be' (676–7); this is wishful thinking. But Sordello's crowd of fancies enable him to 'supply each foolish gap and chasm / The minstrel left' (II, 73–4), and this is a real achievement. Browning will parallel the poet's and the reader's tasks later.

3 THE LYRIC AS SIGHT:

SORDELLO

In *Sordello*, the composing of poetry moves beyond the unreflecting, instinctive song with which it has been associated in *Pauline* and *Paracelsus*. Only in Book I is this concept a governing one, and in Book I Browning shows us a classic example of what I have called the boy-poet. The young Sordello is beautiful to look at and endowed with the singing gift. He is as he is by nature. *Nascitur poeta*, Browning insisted repeatedly. The 'mechanical part' of poetry may be, must be worked at by the conscientious poet; but the perceptions from which poetry is made cannot be commanded.[1] So with Sordello, who is born as he is. Browning uses two metaphors of him. First, his flesh-veil is thinner than that of ordinary mortals. He thus sees and hears more intensely, and his delight – a spontaneous, almost animal joy in his own exquisite perceptiveness – is ecstatic. What he sees and hears is the external world. For him its reds and blues are redder and bluer, its sounds intenser than for most men; everything is shot through with fire, as if, when his eye falls upon anything, it lights up. Phrases here recall Wordsworth's *Immortality Ode*, with the difference that Browning allows to the poetic soul alone what Wordsworth attributes to an ordinary child:

> ... round the rest is furled ...
> A veil that shows a sky not near so blue
>
> ... a coming glory. Up and down
> Runs arrowy fire, while earthly forms combine
> To throb the secret forth; a touch divine –
> And the scaled eyeball owns the mystic rod;
> Visibly through his garden walketh God.   (I, 479–504)

1 'One should study the mechanical part of the art, or [as?] nearly all that there is to be studied – for the more one sits and thinks over the creative process, the more it confirms itself as "inspiration," nothing more nor less' (*LRBEB*, I, 95; June 14, 1845)

Browning's second metaphor has a different emphasis. Here it is not so much what Sordello perceives as what he bestows on nature that is stressed. Sordello is like 'some happy lands, that have luxurious names' and are framed 'for loose fertility' (1, 470, 471). In such lands the lily and the rose flourish without a gardener's effort. But what seems to spring up of its own volition really owes its vitality and beauty to the soil in which it grows.[2]

Sordello is wonderfully happy in the sensations that his gift allows him. He is at first passive, receiving and learning, playing not working, but all this is his business for the time being. He is akin to Aprile, and Browning reflects briefly on the kind of love possessing such a young poet; it is as if he had heard the reader's bewilderment at Aprile's interpretation of love, and undertaken to explain it here in Book 1 and to show how it will be modified in the later books:

> How can such love? – like souls on each full-fraught
> Discovery brooding, blind at first to aught
> Beyond its beauty, till exceeding love
> Becomes an aching weight;
>   ... they are fain invest
> The lifeless thing with life from their own soul,
>   ... fresh births of beauty wake
> Fresh homage, every grade of love is past,
> With every mode of loveliness: then cast
> Inferior idols off their borrowed crown
> Before a coming glory ...
> Visibly through his garden walketh God.   (1, 483–504)

Thus we have the love of nature leading, in Platonic progression (like Aprile's progression of the arts from the material to the spiritual) and without any intervening love of man, directly to love of God. Or, say, the presence of God. Later Browning notes the capriciousness

---

2 Abrams notes that the metaphor is a familiar one. Addison used it in *Spectator* #160: '[Natural genius] is like a rich soil in a happy climate, that produces a whole wilderness of noble plants' (cited in M.H. Abrams, *The Mirror and the Lamp: Romantic Theory and the Critical Tradition* [New York, 1958, first published 1953], 187); so did Young, in his *Conjectures on Original Composition*: the mind of genius is 'a fertile and pleasant field' (ibid., 199)

of the boy-poet (Sordello is now a little older) who flits enamoured
from one entrancing object to the next. Enjoying the 'delights of
childish fancy,' Sordello is enthusiastic by fits and starts over each
new object: "Thus they wore / A fluctuating halo, yesterday / Set
flicker and to-morrow filched away' (1, 648–50). Browning also
writes at the end of Book 1, in a sharp clap of a couplet, that after
Sordello's prolonged and protected boyhood, there opened, 'like any
flash that cures the blind / The veritable business of mankind.' The
Platonic progression is thus set aside as Sordello comes to terms with
what is missing in it – mankind. The whole of *Sordello* is about
Sordello's coming to terms with mankind, or say with the finite. It is
another gloss on Aprile's final text: that God is the perfect poet, who
in his person acts his own creations.

But *Sordello* is not *the* gloss upon such a text, for Sordello belongs
in the company of failed poets. Browning, with his strong propensity
to work out a position by examining two opposite extremes, gives
Sordello the opposite weakness from Aprile's. Instead of despising
the finite, Browning says, Sordello tries to force all the infinite into it,
thus 'thrusting in time eternity's concern' (1, 566).[3] Such a weakness
according to Browning is worse than Aprile's.

Yet another image is used of the boy-poet's happy early fancies,
and this is an image that emphasizes how Sordello spins from his own
substance and resources the film he casts over the world. Like some
spider,

> so flung
> Fantasies forth and in their centre swung
> Our architect, – the breezy morning fresh
> Above, and merry, – all his waving mesh
> Laughing with lucid dew-drops rainbow-edged.   (1, 667–71)

Sordello is now a little removed from his first days of glory and arrowy
fire and God walking visibly about his garden. What now gives colour
to his 'spangled fabric' is sun and morning-fresh dew like the light of

---

3 'You are quite right about the classification of *Sordello's* ... it is the second
  [mood of mind] as "enervated" and modified by the impulse to "thrust
  in time eternity's concern" – *that*, or nothing' (letter to Dowden, in
  Letters, ed. Hood, 91–2; Mar. 5, 1866)

God and the morning-fresh boy himself. The effect is that of a prism, and this is the figure that Browning in the *Prologue* to his last volume, *Asolando*, uses to describe the phenomenon common to the youthful poet.

> 'The Poet's age is sad: for why?
>   In youth, the natural world could show
> No common object but his eye
>   At once involved with alien glow –
> His own soul's iris-bow.

> 'And now a flower is just a flower:
>   Man, bird, beast are but beast, bird, man –
> Simply themselves, uncinct by dower
>   Of dyes which, when life's day began,
> Round each in glory ran.'
> ...
> I found you [Asolo], loved yet feared you so –
>   For natural objects seemed to stand
> Palpably fire-clothed! No –

> No mastery of mine o'er these!
>   Terror with beauty, like the Bush
> Burning but unconsumed. Bend knees,
>   Drop eyes to earthward! Language? Tush!
> Silence 't is awe decrees.

> And now? The lambent flame is – where?[4]
>   Lost from the naked world ...

The burning bush figure had been suggested years before in *Sordello*, with the juxtaposition of the arrowy fire and the mystic rod and the presence of God. God of course walks in a garden, and thus Sordello is less a Moses perhaps than an Adam all blissful in his prelapsarian paradise. (It is Browning who takes up Moses' magic rod later in the poem.) Sordello has none of the awe of a Moses or of an older

---

4 Cf. the song of the boy-poet Thamuris: 'the morn-ray ... / If it gave
   lambent chill, took flame again ...' (*Aristophanes' Apology*, 5151–2)

Browning's remembering; his delight hints that he is a native in such a holy place. So does his attitude to language. 'Language? Tush! / Silence 't is awe decrees.' But Sordello carols in bliss, again like some young native (angels being given to song, we understand). Equally it is only when Sordello emerges from his paradise that he begins to work seriously at his use of language and to recognize the difficulties of manipulating it. In heaven, as the Pope in *The Ring and the Book* was to note, there is the Word and hence no need for mediate words or 'filthy rags of speech' – which must nonetheless be woven on this earth if we are not to be antinomians in our poetizing.

Sordello's emergence from Eden is delayed. Sheltered in the Goito castle, he can weave his colourful fancies long past the usual age for the reign of first fancy. No 'judgment, – care and pain' (I, 777) plague him,[5] and thus he might have gone on forever but for the 'flash that cures the blind.' The phrase suggests that the 'seeing' of the boy-poet is no longer true vision after a certain stage.

The acts of seeing and hearing both literally and figuratively are crucial images throughout the whole of Browning's poetry. He has already used them in *Pauline* and *Parcelsus* but considerably more simply than here. In *Pauline* the act of seeing is emphasized, and it is intimately connected with a whole scheme of light-dark images, most of which continue to be of major importance in Browning's subsequent poetry. Thus sun and star are images of illumination; Shelley is the Sun-treader and a star to men; the *Pauline* poet would give everything 'to see thee for a moment as thou art'; his yearning for God has been a lodestar; during his crisis, his soul, which he believed free, floated into the orbit of another star (the dim orb of self) and began 'reflecting all its shades and shapes' (94). His nightmares are wars between light and darkness, wars within himself ('I felt / A strange delight in causing my decay' [97–8]); he is a fiend in the darkness of an ocean-cave and he lures in a white swan, like a moonbeam, all silver-feathered; or he is a young witch seducing a god and watching 'his radiant form / Growing less radiant' (114–15). Recovery is

5 Cf. Browning to Alfred Domett: 'but, you see, when I was not even a boy, I had fancy in plenty and no kind of judgment – so I said, and wrote, and professed away, and was the poorest of creatures; that, I think, is out of me now, but the habit of watching and wording continues' (*RBAD*, 35; May 22, 1842)

associated with morning and with spring sunshine and with clear mountain-top vision. In *Paracelsus* the light-dark imagery is prominent in the death-scenes of both Aprile and Paracelsus. Aprile can see and hear only faintly, as a 'thick darkness' comes over him; but other lights begin to break on him from 'white brows, lit up with glory' and he exclaims, 'Yes, I see now.' Paracelsus' situation is more dramatic, for the setting is symbolic of his confined and darkened state; his final speech is prefaced by 'I see all' after Festus' song has charmed away his heart's 'darkness'; the light of day is dawning as he descends into the dark grave:

> If I stoop
> Into a dark tremendous sea of cloud,
> It is but for a time; I press God's lamp
> Close to my breast; its splendour, soon or late,
> Will pierce the gloom: I shall emerge one day.   (v, 899–903)

In *Pauline*, poetry, as has been noted, is associated closely with music. The art of singing is not drawn into the complex of light-dark imagery (except insofar as the poet cannot sing until he has returned to the world of light). In Shelley both the illumination of light and the mystery of music may be found, but the two are not connected; they simply exist together in the one Sun-treader. Apollo imagery – which Browning uses in later poetry – would make a connection but it is not put forward here. In *Pauline* the process of illumination seems almost exclusively spiritual; if there are implications for the shaping of poetry, we do not hear of them. In *Paracelsus* illumination does bear on the shaping of poetry, or rather would bear on it had Aprile lived. 'I see now. God is the perfect poet ... ' But the actual songs of *Paracelsus* do not elaborate this, nor is a poetics developed from it. It is in *Sordello* that process of 'seeing' is explicitly related to the art of poetry.

I have noted the interesting shift in Book I: first the young poet sees objects more clear-coloured than do other men because his flesh-film is thinner; then he sees what his own lively fancy throws in a rainbowed spiderweb over the world; then another world opens on him 'like any flash that cures the blind.' Through the rest of the poem, the metaphor of sight measures his growth. He wanders into a singing-match at Mantua, without premeditation leaps into the contest with a Goito song, and is crowned minstrel. Now the 'judgment, care and pain' kept from him at Goito begin; 'Sordello rose – to think, now; hitherto / He had perceived' (II, 123–4). He reflects on his poetry: can it be that other men have fancies which are 'not at their beck, which indistinctly glance / Until, by song ... all grow palpable, distinct?' (II, 166–8). Certainly Eglamor, the former minstrel, was an 'imbecile ... not to see' what to include in his songs (II, 135). The death of Eglamor occurs, Eglamor who had been granted now and then 'some sound or sight ... his own forever, to be fixed, / In rhyme, the beautiful, forever!' (II, 204–6). Sordello, meanwhile, ranges far and wide in imagination, casting his gaze everywhere and glorying in his powers of perception:

> 'So, range, free soul! – who, by self-consciousness,
> The last drop of all beauty dost express –
> The grace of seeing grace, a quintessence
> For thee.'   (II, 405–8)

Sordello will gain beauty through self-consciousness (the quality of which J.S. Mill said the author of *Pauline* had a morbid amount). He will live by seeing life and find grace by seeing grace. In the context 'express' has a double meaning, and so may 'grace'; the quintessence faintly suggests wine, perhaps the wine of a mass at which Sordello pledges himself to a Joycean aesthetics with the cry, 'Be mine mere consciousness!' (II, 429). Browning's comment is that Sordello only fancies himself free when he is actually floundering. Sordello 'loves not, nor possesses One / Idea that, star-like over, lures him on / To its exclusive purpose' (II, 395–7). The *Pauline* image of the free-floating soul which needs some lodestar to guide it, to give it a point of light, is again being used.

Sordello experiments with language, trying to get beyond this 'unreal pageantry / Of essences' (II, 564–5). He attempts to force into words a whole perception (cf. 'thrusting in time eternity's concern'), but language, being trapped in time, will hold only the sequence of thought not the unity of perception. Sordello is unable to 'diffuse / Destroy'[6] perception into thought as he must. (Similarly

---

6 Whether the verbs here (and perhaps the 'dispread, dispart, disperse' trio quoted on p. 45) are meant as a variation on Coleridge, I do not know. Coleridge's description of the secondary imagination is that it 'dissolves, diffuses, dissipates in order to recreate.' Browning's view seems to be that

the white light must be diffused by a cloud or broken [destroyed] into colour if it is to be of use to mortals and not to blind them.) Sordello has not considered seriously what he will ponder near the end of the poem: how much men can see. His experiments fail, he falters, man and poet war against each other. Naddo advises him to base his poetry on the average human heart, for the poet-soul is, 'after all, a freak / (The having eyes to see and tongue to speak)' (II, 505–6); admirers form a troubadour-style Browning society and plague him with questions; critics pester him like swarms of tiny noxious insects (Browning used this image for certain critics all his life). Sordello deteriorates, cannot sing, and wanders back to Goito one evening, pausing to brood 'on a blind hill-top' (II, 950). Reaching the castle, he explores its decrepitude: 'you hear / In the blind darkness water drop' (II, 986–7). He has retreated back to a dilapidated Eden; the second book closes like the first with images of blindness, and in the last line of bull-bait.

When Sordello begins to recover, he reflects on different degrees of being and perceiving. 'The common sort, the crowd, / Exist, perceive; with Being are endowed, / However slight, distinct from what they See, / However bounded' (III, 159–62). Their job is to 'become what they behold.' Sordello is just the opposite: he sees far, but before he can properly 'be' he must become one with all he sees. In Mantua, he says:

[I]

Preferred elaborating in the dark
My casual stuff, by any wretched spark
Born of my predecessors ...
My own concern was just to bring my mind
Behold, just extricate, for my acquist,
Each object suffered stifle in the mist
Which hazard, custom, blindness interpose
Betwixt things and myself.   (III, 195–204)

the imagination begins with an inspired and unified perception; the poet must then work to break up this perception into units of thought, so that it can be comprehended, even if by only a few. It is the reader's job to put the pieces together and 'recreate' what was originally whole. In the *Paracelsus* Preface, quoted in note 7, chapter 2 above, the reader does this by means of his 'cooperating fancy.'

There are now three kinds of obstacles to 'seeing': the common man's flesh-film, the colourful film spread by 'childish fancy,' and the film of 'hazard, custom, blindness.' (The last kind sounds close to *Fra Lippo Lippi*: 'we're made so that we love / First when we see them painted, things we have passed / Perhaps a hundred times nor cared to see' [300–2].)

Browning himself presently stops the time-processes of his poem and, holding it motionless, interjects remarks about his own poetry. One of the distinctions he makes is like Sordello's: it is between the see-ers and the doers. We are right, he says, to extol the men of action who turn the little that they do see into account. As for the seers, they are divided into classes:

> So occupied, then, are we: hitherto,
> At present, and a weary while to come,
> The office of ourselves, – nor blind nor dumb,
> And seeing somewhat of man's state, – has been,
> For the worst of us, to say they so have seen;
> For the better, what it was they saw; the best
> Impart the gift of seeing to the rest.   (III, 862–8)

These latter are the Makers-see. The present office of the seers will be over when the time comes that the powers of seeing and doing are equally strong. Seeing will then merge with doing as the end of the process by which Song slowly engendered Thought, which slowly engendered Act (a process outlined later in the poem). Then, presumably, a New Jerusalem will have been reached: 'then shake my hand / In heaven, my brother!' (III, 926–7). (One of the attributes of God in *The Ring and the Book* is 'the arch-prerogative / Which turns thought, act – conceives, expresses too!' Such ability in that poem also belongs solely to another world.)

This interesting interjection by Browning includes two slightly puzzling tales of 'seeing.' One concerns a reader who seizes upon some ready explanation of why the Maker-see describes a character as he does: the reader immediately supposing the character to have just the reasons for speaking which that reader himself would assign him (the reasons are biographical); he is corrected by the Maker-see and told to take the next sight offered on trust. For ''t is of the mood itself I speak.' The sentence recalls Browning's own aim as stated in the

Paracelsus Preface, and suggests that he is here trying to break the
reader's interest in action itself or in action as simple explanation for
character. Later lines (I shall come to them below) in which
Browning again speaks of moving away from characters in action to
the elements of character suggest that this is what he is getting at here.

The other 'seeing' tale is of Saint John.[7] John supposes that he
sees in his son's home the devil himself and he faints away; it proves to
be his own reflection in a mirror. Browning introduces the tale as
follows: 'Still, neither misconceive my portraiture / Nor undervalue
its adornments quaint: / What seems a fiend perchance may prove a
saint' (III, 986–8). The portraiture does not refer to the character
of Sordello, who neither descends to devilhood nor rises to sainthood.
It must refer, then, to the poem itself, and I take it that Browning
is bidding the reader to look at it closely before swooning away in
horror. It may be, indeed, that if the reader looks closer he will find
that it is he himself who makes the portraiture seem so fiendish; a
perceptive viewer will see that it belongs to the world of light. The
incident belongs in tone and in moral with the parting injunction to
the reader at the end of the poem; here it is sight that matters,
there smell.

All these 'seeing' remarks in Browning's interjection mean a lifting
of 'hazard, custom, blindness' – the efforts of the Makers-see, the
new kind of seeing suggested by a poem, and the right seeing of this
seemingly fiendish poem.

At the end of the next book, yet another kind of sight flashes on
Sordello – a vision. It is a vision of Rome, for Sordello sees in the
reintegration of Rome a symbol of the harmony of church and state,
an end to present strife, and the New Jerusalem come to pass. Rome
'looked an established point of light whose rays / Traversed the world'
(IV, 1003–4). Book V, however, opens on Sordello's disillusionment:
how can the present denizens of Ferrara be 'the shining ones / Meet
for the Shining City?' (V, 10–11). Progress from hut through town
to the Eternal City of Rome is dishearteningly slow. Sordello discards
his Rome-vision: 'Thou archetype, / Last of my dreams and loveliest,
depart!' (V, 78–9). It is at this point that 'a low voice' winds into his

7 The same Saint John who appears in *A Death in the Desert*. The supposed
   son of John, Xanthus, in whose home the *Sordello* incident occurs,
   also appears in the later poem. He is 'my wife's uncle now at peace' of the
   first writer on the script, was with John at the time of his death, and later
   burned to death at Rome.

heart, telling him that God concedes two sights to a man: one a completed plan for men, the other the minute's work for one man. Sordello has seen the first and must now look to the second.

From here on, the question is not of new sights, but of what to do with the two he already has (how to 'fit to the finite his infinity' [VI, 499]). One important related question is 'how much can men see?'

> I take the task
> And marshal you Life's elemental masque,
> Show Men, on evil or on good lay stress,
> This light, this shade make prominent, suppress
> All ordinary hues that softening blend
> Such natures with the level. Apprehend
> Which sinner is, which saint, if I allot
> Hell, Purgatory, Heaven, a blaze or blot,
> To those you doubt concerning!   (v, 583–91)

Two of the three examples which follow (Friedrich, Lombard Agiluph, and Matilda) are characters from Dante's *Divine Comedy*. Thus, what is appropriate for the age of Sordello is 'Life's elemental masque' in the form of a divine comedy. Such a masque shows the essential bent of each human being, like Don Juan's Venice-vision in *Fifine at the Fair* (Venice shows a literal masque, a carnival). When Don Juan surveys his crowds from the church steeple high in the heavens, what he sees are their 'masks' or their dominant traits. Such a sight, could Sordello have traced it as Dante did, would have altered history and prevented much misery; Sordello failed.

When Don Juan floats down from his Venetian steeple and finds himself on hard ground among his dream-figures, he discovers that their dominant traits are no longer so clear. Their types have melted into a common mortality, and 'the prominent, before, / Now dwindled into mere distinctness' (1747–8). No longer does one of 'a love, a hate, a hope, a fear' (1718) distinguish the Venetians, but a mixture. When Sordello peers into the future to see what kind of literature might succeed a divine comedy, he perceives a similar process. This age of poetry will show men and women in action in the world, 'how such ... love, hate, hope, fear' (v, 608–10).[8] At this stage it is not the

---

8 Cf. Aprile, who would sing of 'the hopes / And fears and hates and loves which moved the crowd' (*Paracelsus*, II, 462–3). Browning often uses the

lightness of light or the darkness of dark that is emphasized. For this kind of seeing, 'light, thwarted, breaks / A limpid purity to rainbow flakes, / Or shadow, massed, freezes to gloom' (v, 605–7). This kind of sight is closer to the uses of this world, and the process of breaking light recalls the process of breaking perception ('his office to diffuse / Destroy') into units of thought in Sordello's language experiments in Book II. It also, of course, recalls Browning's frequent use of the metaphor of breaking the white light of such perception into rainbow colours fit for earthbound seeing. (The boy-poet's dew-drop freshness breaking the sun's light for a 'rainbow-edged' effect is a variation on it. With age, the dew-drop dries – is dried, in fact, by the source of light, the sun. That Browning thinks such deprivation deliberate and necessary is suggested in 'This world of ours *by tacit pact* [italics mine] is pledged / To laying such a spangled fabric low' [1, 672–3].)

This stage I surmise is Renaissance literature, Shakespeare perhaps. (No characters are mentioned here.) The passage suggests a turning from types of men to the concerns of mankind, and a marshalling upon a platform. The suggestion is reinforced by Browning's later headings, where the epoist of the first stage evolves into the dramatist of the second ('or ... analyst') who becomes the synthetist of the third. The third stage is to

> 'unveil the last of mysteries –
> Man's inmost life shall have yet freer play:
> Once more I cast external things away,
> And natures composite, so decompose
> That' ... Why, he writes *Sordello!*   (v, 616–20)

The third stage, that is, goes behind action to what produces action (as the first comes after action, showing the results of it). Browning will not again 'decompose' as he does in *Sordello*, but the aim of decomposing will remain primary, and action remain subordinate in most of his poetry.[9]

Sordello realizes finally, in familiar Browning fashion, that man would be unable to bear full sight now. Full truth erupting like

four or six perturbations (cf. Burton, *Anatomy of Melancholy*, 1, 2, iii, 3; I am indebted to James Carscallen for this reference).

9 See the excellent recent studies, Donald S. Hair, *Browning's Experiments with Genre* (Toronto, 1972), 26–42; and W. David Shaw, *The Dialectical Temper* (Ithaca, 1968), 22–39

earth's inner fire would 'rip earth's breast, would stream / Sky-ward!'
(VI, 193–4). Or, in another metaphor, if man started at the top of
the mountain, without wings to fly, he would be left merely to gaze at
heaven and would become 'palled' like Sordello in the perfect Goito.
Man is to develop by climbing height after height and piercing veil
after veil. The metaphor is very like that of Dante's *Purgatory*.
Sordello finally dies with wide-open eyes, like a spent swimmer who
'spies / Help from above in his extreme despair' (VI, 616–17).

I have made the association of lyrics as sung or song-like poems
with the early instinctive singing of the boy-poets. Such instinctive
singing would be, I suppose, like the *'Transcendentalism'* poet's,
full of images and melody, recreating the rose, bringing back youth in
a flood, and pouring heaven into this shut house of life. The boy-poet
in his first singing seems able to make people see something of his
own paradisal world and feel something of his own wild joy in living.
There are, of course, other kinds of lyrics: the song, for instance, in
which one sight would be put and which would be connected, if its
roots were traced, to a whole body of poetry. (I make this a different
kind from first singing because it is the kind of song Sordello would
fashion, were he able, in Book II, when he has left Goito and begun his
apprenticeship in 'judgment, care and pain.') And the lyrics of the
sentence 'I am writing ... lyrics with more music and painting than
before, so as to get people to hear and see' (a sentence written by
Browning in 1853 of the *Men and Women* lyrics).[10] How far people
may see by means of lyrics or into lyrics will depend partly on them
and partly on the Maker-see. A 'Rome-vision' will hardly appear in
one song, for a song is short and circumscribed. (Perhaps a group of
songs might mark out a vision, as stars a constellation, if the reader's
'cooperating fancy' connects them.) But a Sordello-nature cannot
write even songs until its seeing has penetrated all the way to a
Rome-vision. If Browning resembled Sordello in this respect, the
seeing and hearing inspired by his lyrics may at least lead the reader
past the first sensuous apprehension of the boy-poet, and perhaps
eventually much farther.

But the boy-poet's clear and vivid seeing of the natural world
comes first, as *'Transcendentalism'* says. There is no use trying to leap
ahead and embrace a Rome-vision all at once, no use trying to

10 Letter to Milsand, cited DeVane, *Handbook*, 207; Feb. 24, 1853

scramble via a short-cut up the mountain and into the Shining City instead of following the laborious path – and this in poetry as well as in other things. The listeners in 'Transcendentalism' tried this: during their youth they pursued meanings of the rose in erudite books; they close the books, their youth has gone and so has the rose; now the boy-poet must start them at the beginning again. Browning repeated this moral more prosaically near the end of his life in the Parleying with Christopher Smart: first live, then learn; first earth, then heaven; first the rose, then the meteor. And Smart's marvellous chapel, like the boy-poet's creations, does succeed in 'pouring heaven into this shut house of life.'

Browning always valued the first and literal kind of seeing – that of the clear, observant eye. He found Mary Shelley, for instance, unbearably vague in her descriptions of Italy:

> Mrs. Shelley found Italy for the first time, real Italy, at Sorrento, she says. Oh that book – does one wake or sleep? The 'Mary dear' with the brown eyes, and Godwin's daughter and Shelley's wife, and who surely was something better once upon a time – and to go thro' Rome & Florence & the rest, after what I suppose to be Lady Londonderry's fashion: the intrepidity of the commonplace quite astounds me. And then that way, when she and the like of her are put in a new place, with new flowers, new stones, faces, walls, all new – of looking wisely up at the sun, clouds, evening star, or mountain top and wisely saying 'who shall describe that sight!' – Not you, we very well see ... but she is wrong every where, that is, not right, not seeing what is to see, speaking what one expects to hear – I quarrel with her, for ever, I think.
> (LRBEB, I, 189–90; Sept. 11, 1845)

Shelley himself, however, had had an eye as sharp as a botanist's:

> And which of you eternal triflers was it called yourself 'Shelley' and so told me years ago that in the mountains it was a feast 'When one should find those globes of deep red gold – Which in the woods the strawberry-tree doth bear, Suspended in their emerald atmosphere.' So that when my Mule walked into a sorb-tree, not to tumble sheer over Monte Calvano, and I felt the fruit against my face, the little ragged bare-legged guide fairly laughed at my knowing them so well – 'Niursi – sorbi!'
> (Ibid., I, 54–5; May 3, 1845)

From all these remarks about seeing, it may be surmised that the 'hearing' half of the 'hearing and seeing' pair is left behind in *Sordello*. It may also be surmised that the apprehension of poetry is moving from ear (the association of music with poetry in *Pauline*) to eye (seeing, life's elemental masque, and so on). Both these surmises are in part correct, I think, in *Sordello*. The ear accompanies the eye by courtesy, but its faculties are not developed as are those of seeing. Both Sordello's eye and ear are fine, but it is the colour and fire he sees and the rainbow he produces that are mentioned. Songs he produces literally, but no play is made with the image of hearing. Throughout his poetry Browning was to stress the act of seeing rather than hearing, though as modes of apprehension the two are commonly linked in phrasing. But hearing does not lend itself as a symbol to such interesting and consistent development as seeing. I can think of no word for hearing, for instance, which carries the double meaning of apprehension by sense and soul (to use Browning's pair) that 'perception' or 'vision' does for seeing. Similarly we speak of the mind's eye but not of the mind's ear. Seeing involves light, either white, or diffused by cloud, or broken into colour by a prism; light as produced by fire; sun, stars, moon – a whole complex of celestial imagery.

Of course hearing can follow part of the same pattern. There can be a perfect harmony of which on earth we hear only imperfect approximations. This parallel is developed in *Abt Vogler* – though it might be noted that when the musician concludes, he comes back to an image that is seen (or felt) : 'on the earth the broken arcs; in the heaven a perfect round.' The parallel may also be developed by the perfect-Word / imperfect-words figure used, for example, by the Pope in the *Ring and the Book*. And the Word is used by Browning himself in the *Asolando Prologue* partly quoted above. Here he does say that hearing gives superior apprehension to seeing, and places himself in the Hebrew tradition that hears the still, small voice but distrusts idols and images. But all this is many years hence. There is just enough of it in *Sordello* to allow the peroration on the two sights to be given by a 'small voice'; but the connotations are not Christian, for the voice is said to be like the low voice of some oracular pythoness.

I have stressed the magic and mystery associated with music, and it may be thought that so much illumination and so much seeing may make the world and poetry prosaically plain. But Browning preserves from *Pauline* through *Sordello* another figure which has to do with the making of poetry and which emphasizes the inexplicable and the miraculous. This figure also changes in these early years (like the sight imagery) and is also important in later poetry. It is the mage-figure.

The mage-figure and his world, as Robert Preyer has shown,[11] are important in *Pauline*, and they haunt the discussions of poetry in *Sordello*. What Preyer suggests is that we pay some attention to the lines in *Pauline* hinting that the *Pauline* poet had a previous interest in the occult, and to the warning from Cornelius Agrippa in the poem's epigraph. It does seem impossible to interpret such words except as indications of an earlier curiosity and investigation and involvement in some form of mysticism or occultism.[12] Preyer points out how such mysticism would engender a poetry rather like *Pauline*. It would be a poetry connecting the seen and unseen worlds by musical, alogical discourse, and not a poetry governed by syntax and sequence. The poet's function would approximate that of the mage.

Some of the 'strange fair worlds' in *Pauline* have been noted already. The maddening, unearthly realm to which music can lead is one; so is the dim star of self with its sinister pull of the soul into its orbit; so is the nightmare world where chained fiend and blue-eyed witch seduce and ruin their radiant companions; so is the temple where a dark spirit sits in the seat of God; and there are more. Most of the magic and charm and mystery of the poem is of this sinister variety, though the magic of music may be either black or white. When the *Pauline* poet turns away from such worlds, he turns back to some form of orthodoxy, as his avowal near the end makes clear ('A mortal, sin's familiar friend, doth here / Avow that he will give

---

11 In 'Robert Browning: A Reading of the Early Narratives,' *ELH* 26 (1959), 531–48

12 Preyer does not cite the case of Sludge, but this later and cheaper delver into things unseen echoes sentiments and phrases of the *Pauline* poet. Both come to believe in signs and omens: 'and thence I date my trust in signs / And omens, for I saw God everywhere' (*Pauline*, 301–2); 'I live by signs and omens' (*Sludge*, 971) and '... a course of signs and omens' (*Sludge*, 1072). Both occupy the centre of things and constitute their only reality; in *Pauline* the poet reigns in an enclosed universe, while in *Sludge* the outer world bends constantly around the medium to signify what might be the pleasure of the infinite.

all earth's reward, / But to believe and humbly teach the faith, / In
suffering and poverty and shame ...' [855–8]; this follows an evocation
of Christ). What comes out of this avowal is not made specific, nor is
the assertion at the end ('I believe in God and truth / And love'
[1020–1]). But there has been established a second point of reference
and the dim enclosed orb of self has been broken. The poet's job has
been revised: in Don Juan's image, it is no longer to connect frag-
mented points into a circle, but to connect one such point with the
infinite.

When the uncanny strange fair worlds of *Pauline* are left behind
for the more ordinary scenes of *Paracelsus*, mage and magic and
mystery are not altogether abandoned. They retire certainly, and one
kind of mage is disposed of: the mage created by popular credulity,
on closer inspection, turns into Paracelsus. But the black and white
magic of music still persists, whether in Michal's carols or Aprile's
insidious chant or Festus' lullaby or even Paracelsus' contrived songs.
Aprile speaks of his torment among his fancies as does the *Pauline*
poet, and as if his mind had been enchanted:

> Dazzled by shapes that filled its length with light,
> Shapes clustered there to rule thee, not obey,
> That will not wait they summons, will not rise
> Singly, nor when thy practised eye and hand
> Can well transfer their loveliness, but crowd
> By thee for ever, bright to thy despair?
> Didst thou ne'er ...
> ... laugh that man's applause or welfare ever
> Could tempt thee to forsake them? ...
> Didst thou ne'er strive even yet to break those spells
> ... that charmed so long ...   (II, 576–603)

One would not expect *Sordello* to be ghost-ridden; it has no
thematic reason for being so, as Preyer has suggested *Pauline* has.
Sordello is more resilient and interested in his future than the *Pauline*
poet. His experiments with language, as well as Browning's own remarks about poetry, are not centred on a mystical, alogical discourse.
But the mage and the world of enchantment reappear several times
in *Sordello* as though Browning could not be rid of them. Of course
their sinister power has been exorcised, and they are now beneficent

or at worst mischievous. Once again, they are connected with poets or the making of poetry. Browning himself steps into the role of mage at the beginning of the poem as he summons up a ghost, 'Sordello, compassed murkily about / With ravage of six long sad hundred years,' bidding 'the dim Abysmal past divide its hateful surge' (1, 8–9, 18–19). He also calls up a ghostly audience: 'Confess now, poets know the dragnet's trick, / Catching the dead, if fate denies the quick' (1, 35–6). In the middle of the poem when Browning wishes to interject a few remarks in his own person, he steps in again, freezes the time-sequence, and has his say. 'Entrance thy synod, as a god may glide / Out of the world he fills, and leave it mute / For myriad ages as we men compute, / Returning into it without a break' (III, 610–13). At the end, the whole poem is conceived as a spirit conjured up by Browning:

> but, friends,
> Wake up! The ghost's gone, and the story ends
> I'd fain hope, sweetly; seeing, peri or ghoul,
> That spirits are conjectured fair or foul,
> Evil or good, judicious authors think,
> According as they vanish in a stink
> Or in a perfume. Friends, be frank! ye snuff
> Civet, I warrant. Really? Like enough!
> Merely the savour's rareness; any nose
> May ravage with impunity a rose:
> Rifle a musk-pod and 't will ache like yours!
> I'd tell you that same pungency ensures
> An after-gust, but that were overbold.
> Who would has heard Sordello's story told.   (VI, 873–86)

(The rose is the flower of sweet, youthful song in 'Transcendentalism.' Browning did not have to be told that his poem was rare.[13])

But the mage-figure is more intimately connected with the making of poetry. Fancies, as in *Pauline* and *Paracelsus*, are portrayed as so many spirits ready to be mastered by the right magician. Ordinary

---

13 Could the comparison have been suggested by Browning's beloved Donne? Cf.: 'As the sweet sweat of Roses in a Still, / As that which from chaf'd muskrats pores doth trill ...' (Elegie VIII, The Comparison, 1–2)

people, Sordello conjectures, have fancies, but 'not at their beck'
(II, 166). Eglamor's fancies are far above him:

> He, no genius rare,
> Transfiguring in fire or wave or air
> At will, but a poor gnome that, cloistered up
> In some rock-chamber with his agate cup,
> His topaz rod, his seed-pearl, in these few
> And their arrangement finds enough to do
> For his best art.   (II, 213–19)

Sordello can transfigure at will, but when he comes to grips with
'the stuff / That held the imaged thing,' his language, then mastery
of another kind is required. Then the struggle is with some Protean
object – 'let it writhe / Never so fiercely' (II, 570–2) – and Sordello's
first welding of a new 'stuff' is unsuccessful, breaking to pieces.

Browning connects his own poetry and the work of Sordello in
several ways. I have noted how they are set on the same path, with
Sordello being assigned (had he been able) the writing of a divine
comedy and Browning the writing of a *Sordello*. The same phrase
too is used, first of Sordello's early Goito-songs, then of Browning's
own lines:

> songs go up exulting, then dispread,
> Dispart, disperse, lingering overhead
> Like an escape of angels ...   (I, 881–3)

> my rhymes – that spring, dispread,
> Dispart, disperse, lingering overhead
> Like an escape of angels! Rather say,
> My transcendental platan! mounting gay
> (An archimage so courts a novice-queen)
> With tremulous silvered trunk ...   (III, 593–8)

And Browning goes on to conjure up the tree, buds, blooms, fruit, and
all, and to sprinkle the reclining queen with its 'bloom-flinders and
fruit-sparkles and leaf-dust' – 'the weird work prosecuted just / For
her amusement.' A magical tree would spring, spread, and disperse
like the group of angels, but would also be rooted in the ground. It

would be less etherial than the angels and closer to Coleridge's plant metaphors for poetry, though preserving a sense of magic. (Browning's metaphor might be an attempt to have the advantages of the plant image – organic unity of the poem, for example – together with more sense of the creator's control than in Coleridge's usage. The tree must have tree characteristics or it would simply astonish and not delight the young queen. On the other hand, her delight is not because the tree is so tree-like, but because it departs from nature.) But the metaphor proves unsatisfactory: no sooner is the queen all delighted and the archimage dozing nearby, 'decrepit' and 'stark,' than Browning rejects the figure: 'Yet not so, surely never so.'

Another mage-like figure connects Sordello and Browning, and that is the figure of Moses. Sordello as a boy lives in native innocence in a burning bush setting. Later in the poem Browning pictures himself as a Moses using the 'mystic rod' of Sordello's boyhood to find the water of life for a parched people:

A hungry sun above us, sands that bung
Our throats, – each dromedary lolls a tongue,
Each camel churns a sick and frothy chap,
And you, 'twixt tales of Potiphar's mishap,
And sonnets on the earliest ass that spoke,
– Remark, you wonder any one needs choke
With founts about! Potsherd him, Gibeonites!
While awkwardly enough your Moses smites
The rock, though he forgo his Promised Land
Thereby, have Satan claim his carcass, and
Figure as Metaphysic Poet ... ah,
Mark ye the dim first cozings? Meribah!   (III, 819–30)

Browning thus insists on retaining the emphasis on the inexplicable in poetry – the endowment of a Sordello and the miracles of a Moses, to say nothing of the conjuring of a Browning. Naddo, the critic who relies on common sense, is held up to scorn. He counsels Sordello:

'[the poet] can't stoop
'To sing us out ... a mere romance;
'He'd fain do better than the best, enhance
'The subjects' rarity, work problems out

'Therewith.' Now, you're a bard, a bard past doubt,
And no philosopher; why introduce
Crotchets like these? fine, surely, but no use
In poetry – which still must be, to strike,
Based upon common sense[14]; there's nothing like
Appealing to our nature! what beside
Was your first poetry? No tricks were tried
In that, no hollow thrills, affected throes!
'The man,' said we, 'tells his own joys and woes:
'We'll trust him.' Would you have your songs endure?
Build on the human heart! – why, to be sure
Yours is one sort of heart – but I mean theirs,
Ours, every one's, the healthy heart one cares
To build on! Central peace, mother of strength,
That's father of ... nay ...
                              I restrict
The poet?
                        ... As well you hid
That sense of power, you have! True bards believe
All able to achieve what they achieve –   (ɪɪ, 784–816)

A mage or a Moses has no intention of hiding his power, or building
on the average human heart. He is quite unashamedly out to make
use of his gifts, even if this means producing a rarity ('the savour's
rareness' is Browning's phrase for the odour of his poem at the end
of it). He will not sing his own joys and woes in order to be trusted.
Indeed, perhaps he will not figure as a bard at all ('bard' was a
favourite *Pauline* term); he may even work out problems in poetry,
even (as Browning threatens in the Moses passage) turn Metaphysic
Poet. The mage, we see, has changed since *Pauline*. His power is still
stressed but not his autonomy; he has lost his eeriness and become
more human; the one full-dress mage, an archimage indeed, is
de-glamourized and left decrepit and stark. The mage pays some
attention to the recipients of his gifts. Browning addresses himself
to both ghostly and quick readers at the beginning of the poem and
the end; Moses foregoes a promised land to bring water to his people;

14 'Mr. Kenyon ... says my common sense strikes him, and its contrast with
    my muddy metaphysical poetry! (*LRBEB*, ɪ, 75; May 24, 1845)

even the archimage courts a queen. Poetry has not been confined
to Naddo's finite, but neither has it wandered into some infinite
non-human strange fair world.[15]

This change in the mage figure is part and parcel of the change
in the poet's task from *Pauline* to *Sordello*. Mage and poet have
turned from self-absorption to concern for mankind. W.O. Raymond
has noted how the change in the concept of love in *Paracelsus* is
marked by a changed attitude toward mankind. Both Aprile and
Paracelsus do an about-face at the end of their lives. Sordello also
tackles the problem of what to give mankind. When the low voice
winds into his heart, it tells him that he may continue mere dreaming,
may satisfy himself in fancy, if he wishes to remain at the Goito-stage
(or what I have called a boy-poet):

> you have but
> To please yourself for law, and once could please
> What once appeared yourself, by dreaming these
> Rather than doing these, in days gone by.
> But all is changed the moment you descry
> Mankind as half yourself, – then, fancy's trade
> Ends once and always: how may half evade
> The other half?   (v, 246–53)

Browning in his own person says in *Sordello* that he himself has
changed Muses. What was once 'her I looked should foot Life's
temple-floor' (III, 750) has now altered to the 'sad dishevelled ghost'
(III, 696) of all mankind rolled into one ('care-bit erased / Broken-up
beauties ever took my taste / Supremely' [III, 747–9]).

The mage may thus retain some power which sets him apart from
men, but at the same time work under laws not of his own making.
This is what Moses, whom I have classed as a mage-figure, does; so
does another Old Testament figure whom Browning later distinguishes as a type of mage – Elisha. The movement in Book I of *The
Ring and the Book* from the conventional mage to Elisha is a further

---

15 The mage, incidentally, is connected with all the senses, and not only
with seeing or hearing; he may stimulate smell like Browning, or satisfy
thirst, again like Browning, or raise a magic tree whose flowers and
fruit can be felt.

development of the change in the mage figure from *Pauline* to
Sordello: 'Oh, Faust, why Faust? Was not Elisha once? ... 'Tis a
credible feat / With the right man and way.' And the mage moves
into another tradition. What connects the Faustian mage and Elisha
is the process of resuscitation, a process just touched upon in the
calling up of the dead at the beginning of *Sordello*. It is not further
developed in *Sordello,* but I think Browning's playing with the mage-
figure is a groping toward it, for the germ may be seen as early at
Paracelsus ('God is the perfect poet, / Who in his person acts his
own creations').

But all this is still to come at the time of *Sordello*. If Humanity is
Browning's mistress, she is courted in a fiendish and stinking poem –
saintly and pungent if approached properly, to be sure. Browning
is still in the period of which he said later to Elizabeth Barrett: 'So
far differently was I circumstanced of old, that I used rather to go
about for a subject of offence to people; writing ugly things in order
to warn the ungenial & timorous off my grounds at once. I shall never
do so again at least' (*LRBEB*, 1, 95; June 14, 1845). When he does
turn to producing the shorter poems of 1842 and 1845, it is not 'so
as to get people to hear and see' but rather more condescendingly as
a favour to his publisher Moxon 'for popularity's sake' (*RBAD*, 36;
May 22, 1842). Moses is still closer to Faust than Elisha.

II BELLS AND POMEGRANATES:

PRACTICE

5 'SCENES AND SONG-SCRAPS'

Pauline ends with a vague desire, and *Paracelsus* and *Sordello* with a strong one, of turning toward the needs of mankind. The *Bells and Pomegranates* series is Browning's own effort to do so, and the title may be instructive of his purpose. In *Sordello* he had chosen for himself the role of a Moses, isolated, misunderstood, and reproached, but a prophet who could draw living water for a parched and exiled people in the wilderness. His pamphlet series, however, is a priestly garment, designated for Aaron 'that he may minister unto me in the priest's office'; it is rich in colour, the hem having alternate golden bells and blue, purple, and scarlet pomegranates. 'And it shall be upon Aaron to minister; and his sound shall be heard when he goeth in unto the holy place before the Lord.' When Browning came to explain his choice of title, he stressed the combination of effects at which he had aimed and which the bells and pomegranates symbolized.[1] But implicit in the choice is also, I think, his wish at this time to reach a wider audience. The prophet usually stands alone; he is not noted for his popularity; his inspiration, if from God, is vindicated in the end. The subjective poet in Browning's 'Essay on Shelley,' who writes with reference only to God, is closer to prophet than to priest. But the objective poet casts about to consider what men need, and he has their needs in mind as he writes. He is rather priest than prophet, being the people's representative before God, instead of His before them. He is part of the communal life rather than a challenger of it; he leads an

---

1 His explanatory note is in the last pamphlet between *Luria* and *A Soul's Tragedy*. DeVane says that 'by placing the explanation where he does, Browning in effect excludes *A Soul's Tragedy*, or half desires to exclude it, from the series' (*Handbook*, 189–90). But Browning denied any conscious exclusion: 'The explanatory note fills up an unseemly blank page – and does not come at the end of the "Soul's Tragedy" – prose after prose – still it does look awkwardly – but then I don't consider that it excludes this last from the "Bells"'' (*LRBEB*, II, 623; Apr. 14, 1846).

established ritual rather than performs miracles; he belongs to a
settled people rather than to wanderers. And there was more than one
reading, perhaps, for Browning of 'his sound shall be heard.' The
format of the *Bells and Pomegranates* series, pamphlets selling at 6d.
to 2/6 each, was chosen to attract a wide audience. Browning's letters
in the early 1840s show, too, that he was working at how to reach out
to an audience.

> The one point that wants correcting is where you surmise that I am
> 'difficult on system.' No, really – the fact is I live by myself, write with
> no better company, and forget that the 'lovers' you mention are part and
> parcel of that self ... I am busy on some plays ... that shall be plain
> enough if my pains are not thrown away – and, in lieu of Sir Philip and
> his like, Stokes may assure himself that I see him (first row of the pit,
> under the second oboe, hat between legs, play-bill on a spike, and a
> 'comforter' round his throat 'because of the draught from the stage'),
> and unless he leaves off sucking his orange at the pathetic morsels of my
> play, I hold them nought ... After all, writing unintelligible metaphor is
> not voted as bad as murder.   (*RBAB*, 28–30; [Mar., 1840])

Some six years later Browning wrote to Elizabeth Barrett, with the
same emphasis on his endeavour at clarity but a more explicit demand
that his audience make some endeavours of their own:

> A writer who fails to make himself understood, as presumably in my case,
> may either believe in his heart that it is *not* so .. that only as much atten-
> tion and previous instructedness as the case calls for, would quite avail
> to understand him, – or he may open his eyes to the fact and be trying
> hard to overcome it ... Of course an artist's whole problem must be, as
> Carlyle wrote to me, 'the expressing with articulate clearness the thought
> in him' – I am almost inclined to say that *clear expression* should be his
> only work and care – for he is born, ordained, such as he is – and not born
> learned in putting what was born in him into words – what ever *can*
> be clearly spoken, ought to be: but 'bricks and mortar'[2] is very easily said
> – and some of the thoughts in 'Sordello' not so readily even if Miss
> Mitford were to try her hand on them.   (*LRBEB*, I, 439; Feb. 6, 1846)

But a good deal had happened in the six years between these two

---

2 'Brick and mortar' thinking was Coleridge's description of the reasoning

letters. In *Paracelsus* and *Sordello* the responsibility of the gifted man toward the less gifted is emphasized not only for the sake of the recipients but also, the heroes gradually realize, for their own sakes. For both, the break from self-enclosure is a necessary humanizing process. Browning's stress on this no doubt stemmed partly from that Puritan conscience of which Elizabeth Barrett Browning later spoke.[3] The burdens of responsibility both toward one's fellow man and toward God would have been laid upon him, and there are numerous references in his letters to the duty of the poet before God.[4] The two duties would not be in conflict ultimately, but might for a young poet be so temporarily. At the least the two duties might demand different kinds of poetic productions. This is what Browning argues in his 'Essay on Shelley,' and what, I suspect, he practises in his later poetry. (*Fifine at the Fair* would represent the work of the subjective poet, writing for himself and God, and *The Inn Album* or the two *Dramatic Idyls* the work of the objective poet, writing with reference to his fellow-man.) Just before *Bells and Pomegranates* Browning had produced a poem assuredly written with reference to himself and God rather than an audience. His letters and prefaces indicate that he had practical reasons, besides his principles, for putting his name before the public again.[5] Principles and practical reasons alike, then, would dispose Browning to be amenable to a publisher's suggestion that, as well as his plays, he print a few short poems 'for popularity's sake.'

of the mechanical philosophy (*Biographia Literaria*, XII). A comparison of Coleridge's theory of the fancy and the imagination and Sordello's poetic experiments would probably shed much light on the latter (cf. note 6, chap. 3 above).

3 'Robert, though a poet and dramatist by profession, being descended from the blood of all the Puritans, and educated by the strictest of dissenters, has a sort of horror about the dreadful fact of owing five shillings five days' (*LEB*, I, 390; Dec. 3, 1848). The connection between Puritanism and paying debts would have pleased Tawney.

4 Cf., for example, *LRBEB*, I, 18, 39, 206, 336; Feb. 11, Mar. 11, Sept. 18, Dec. 21, 1845. Cf. also the following text, said to be written in Greek in Browning's hand some time between 1837 and 1840 (one of fourteen such jottings of his on a wrapper of some poems): 'For if the trumpet give an uncertain sound, who shall prepare himself to the battle? So likewise ye, except ye utter by the tongue words easy to be understood, how shall it be known what is spoken? for ye shall speak into the air' (I Cor. 14: 8–9; in M.D. Conway, *Autobiography* [London, 1904], 2 vols., II, 16–17).

5 'Ever since [*Strafford*], I have been desirous of doing something in the same way that should better award their [the audience's] attention ... help me

Another factor may have contributed to the making of the *Bells and Pomegranates* series, dramas and poems both. Browning attributes to Paracelsus, Aprile, and Sordello great anguish over the question of how and why to communicate with mankind. For Naddo (cf. p. 46 above) there is no problem, but for these geniuses the hiatus between the gifted and the ungifted man, or between the gifted man's capacities for desire and his performance, is painful. Browning himself did not by nature communicate readily with other people, that is, communicate things of importance. And it may be that he pushed himself into popular productions after *Sordello* with all the more determination because he knew his own temperament so well. He chose to attempt a form of literature where communication is most mandatory – the drama. He published dramas and poems in a format designed to attract a wide audience. The humility of the letters and prefaces referred to above (note 5) can be almost embarrassing. Browning the poet practising the active drama also writes about action in most of the plays and poems of the series. The emphasis is on heroic performance, on action versus words, on theories in action. It is as if Browning had chosen to go back from a *Sordello* to what he described as the stage before *Sordello*: 'behold / How such [men and women] ... love, hate, hope, fear, peace make, war rage, / In presence of you all!' (v, 607–11).

But his first enthusiasm ('the original hour [that is quarter of an hour] of confidence and creation') was not to last. He could write to Eliza Flower (probably in 1840 and no later than 1841): 'I have a head-full of projects – mean to song-write, play-write forthwith ... When these three plays are out I hope to "build" a huge Ode[6] ... ' (*Letters*, ed. Hood, 4; Mar. 9 [1840]). But by 1842 he was less sure of himself:

> to a sort of Pit-audience again. Of course such a work must go on no longer than it is liked' (advertisement to *Pippa Passes*, 1841; cf. the remarks on the pit-audience to Domett, cited p. 70 above, and written a year before!). 'I have written a spick and span new Tragedy (a sort of compromise between my own notion and yours – as I understand it, at least)' (to Macready, in *Letters*, ed. Hood, 5; autumn 1840). 'I ... work double-tides to bring out something as likely to be popular this present season – for something I *must* print, or risk the hold, such as it is, I have at present on *my* public' (to Dowson, in *Letters*, ed. Hood, 10; Mar. 10, 1844).
>
> 6 Could this be *Saul* so early? It was influenced by that ode-like poem, Smart's *Song to David*.

... to write a book now will take one at least the ten or dozen years you portion out for your stay abroad. I don't expect to do any real thing till then: the little I, or anybody, can do as it is, comes of them going to New Zealand [Domett had just gone] – partial retirement and stopping the ears against the noise outside; but all is next to useless – for there is a creeping, magnetic, assimilating influence nothing can block out. When I block it out, I shall do something ... At present, I don't know if I stand on head or heels: what men require, I don't know – and of what they are in possession know nearly as little. (*RBAD*, 35–6; May 22, 1842)

In July he wrote: 'Here everything goes flatly on, except the fierce political reality (as it begins to be). Our poems, &c., are poor child's play ... There is much, everything, to be done in England just now, and I have certain plans which shall either fail, or succeed, but not lie dormant. But all my heart's interest goes to your tree-planting life. Yet I don't know' (ibid., 42–3; July 13, 1842).

Throughout Browning's 1842–4 letters the same restless alteration of moods is evident: he chafes to begin something new; he is ebullient, then downcast; his heart turns to 'tree-planting,' then back to London; he has still to make his name, and his ambition is often high.[7] In the May 1842 letter he had seemed content to let the early *Bells and Pomegranates* efforts go: he would 'print a few songs and small poems which Moxon advised me to do for popularity's sake! These things done (and my play out), I shall have tried an experiment to the end, and be pretty well contented either way ... The true best of me is to come, and you shall have it' (ibid., 36–7; May 22, 1842). But he did not know 'what men require.' A year later, 'I seem only beginning to see what one (someone, you) might do, writing' (ibid., 55–6; May 15, 1843; cf. *Waring*: 'happy as Waring then, / Having first within his ken / What a man might do with men'). But in the same letter he advises: 'Don't leave off ploughing, for poetry will come of that.' And by autumn there is a note of depression – 'Saying, or writing – what is it, or what does it?' (ibid., 94; Oct. 9, 1843) –

7 'He sat and talked of his own early life and aspirations; how he marvelled, as he looked back, at the audacious obstinacy which had made him, when a youth, determine to be a poet and nothing but a poet' (Edmund Gosse, *Robert Browning: Personalia* [London, 1890], 84). Cf.: '... Meaning, on the whole, to be a Poet, if not *the* Poet .. for I am vain and ambitious some nights' (*LRBEB*, I, 75; May 24, 1845).

that echoes the former sentiment of poetry as child's play. With midsummer of the next year comes new vigour: 'I feel myself so much stronger, if flattery not deceive, that I shall stop some things that were meant to follow, and begin again. I really seem to have something fresh to say ... I never took so earnestly to the craft as I think I shall – or may, for these things are with God' (ibid., 106; July 31, 1844). Long afterwards, Browning remembered these years, and some to follow, as years of neglect and misery in his work: 'Then, with complete frankness, he described the long-drawn desolateness of his early and middle life as a literature man; how, after certain spirits had seemed to rejoice in his first sprightly runnings,[8] and especially in *Paracelsus*, a blight had fallen upon his very admirers. He touched, with a slight irony, on the "entirely unintelligible *Sordello*," and the forlorn hope of *Bells and Pomegranates*.'[9] And Browning admitted to Julia Wedgwood in 1864 how he envied those like Tennyson, who knew from the beginning what they wanted to do.[10]

Browning's letters to Elizabeth Barrett are full of remarks about a new beginning in his poetry, a beginning to be inspired by her presence, and to issue in some work worthy of such inspiration. The urge to begin again was not evoked solely by her. The 1844 letter to Domett quoted above shows this, for Browning had not met or written to Elizabeth Barrett at that time. And he mentions a new start very early in the correspondence with her: 'I will simply assure you, that meaning to begin work in deep earnest, BEGIN without affectation, God knows – I do not know what will help me more than hearing from you' (*LRBEB*, I, 12; Jan. 27, 1945). This is Browning's third letter to Elizabeth. If he had cast about for an auspicious inspiration for his new beginning, he could hardly have hit upon a better one.

8 Dryden's 'sprightly runnings' is a favourite Browning phrase. 'Speaking of a classification of Wordsworth's poems, in my heart I fear I should do it almost chronologically, so immeasurably superior seem to me the first sprightly runnings' (Browning to Professor Knight, in Anne I. Thackeray, Lady Ritchie, *Records of Tennyson, Ruskin, and Browning* [London, 1892], 220; Mar. 21, 1883). 'The book [W.W. Story's *Roba di Roma*] runs along more sprightly than ever' (to Mrs Story, in *Browning to His American Friends*, 132; Nov. 26, 1863).

9 Gosse, *Robert Browning: Personalia*, 84–5

10 'Nobody more than Tennyson has more fully found out *at the beginning* what he was born to do – nor done it more perfectly' (*RBJW*, 75; Sept. 2, 1864; italics mine).

'These scenes and song-scraps ... such mere and very escapes of my inner power' (*LRBEB*, I, 17; Feb. 11, 1845) : this is Browning's description of a collection that includes *My Last Duchess, Rudel,* and *Artemis Prologuizes,* and it may seem unduly depreciatory. But brilliant as his 1842 and 1845 collections are, their brilliance is not that of *Men and Women.* This early brilliance reminds me strongly of the letters to Domett, written over the same period. There is the same exuberance, the same thirst to try this and that, the same current of energy. It would be unfair to call this posturing, but there is an enjoyment in exhibiting strength. The technique displayed is considerable, but the subtlety of the speakers' attitudes, compared with those in *Men and Women* (and taking into account the sizes of the collections) is not remarkable. Nor is there much development from the speakers' situations (as in, for example, *Andrea del Sarto* and *Fra Lippo Lippi*). Rather, the novelties, colours, ironies, gestures – the aliveness of the various positions is what remains with the reader. This is true of even the renowned figures in the group, the Bishop of St Praxed's and the Duke of Ferrara. They are less interesting because less human than Andrea or Fra Lippo Lippi. The eye tends to stop with them, examine their curiosities, look at them as objects, but not to involve itself with them. Sometimes, indeed, Browning's search for the intensely vivid leads him to overreach himself, as in the lines on Metternich in *The Italian in England.* (Perhaps a similar impulse inspired the lines in *Count Gismond* – notably the dripping sword lines – which have helped engender a new reading of the poem.[11])

These poems are generally full of surface action, and the action tends to be colourful, as colourful as the situations imagined in *Pippa Passes*: the steely fastidiousness of the Duke of Ferrara and what it conceals, the blood in *Count Gismond,* the romantic heroism of the boy in the *Incident of the French Camp,* the sudden stabbing from the mysterious three in *In a Gondola,* the maniacal murder in *Porphyria's Lover,* the flight to the gypsies by the duchess. To many might be applied Bowning's wry remark about *A Blot in the 'Scutcheon*: 'There is *action* in it, drabbing, stabbing, et autres gentillesses.'[12] In *Men and Women* the romances on the whole do not

---

11 Cf. John W. Tilton and R. Dale Tutton, 'A New Reading of "Count Gismond," ' *Studies in Philosophy* 59 (1962), 83–95
12 To Macready, in *Letters,* ed. Hood, 5; autumn 1840

show such swashbuckling, flair, and dash, or such simple ironies as
do those of *Bells and Pomegranates.* When they move toward the
melodramatic, it is toward the macabre (*The Heretic's Tragedy,
Mesmerism, Holy-Cross Day*), but the romances also include *The
Last Ride Together, A Grammarian's Funeral, Protus, The Statue
and the Bust,* and *Childe Roland.* Of the *Men and Women*
poems later classified as lyrics, very few have lurid situations (like
those in the *Soliloquy of the Spanish Cloister, The Laboratory,*
and *The Confessional*). *A Serenade at the Villa* and *In a Year*
just verge on melodrama, and so perhaps do *Before* and *After.*
But these are four dubious possibilities out of thirty lyrics. The
1842 and 1845 pamphlets represent Browning's most extended poetic
excursions into action and narrative until much later in his life, from
Red Cotton Night-Cap Country (1873), through *The Inn Album*
(1875), *Dramatic Idyls* (1879, 1880), many *Jocoseria* poems (1883),
and a few *Asolando* poems (1889).

I have already suggested reasons for Browning's own literary
activity at this time, and hazarded the guess that the emphasis on
action, deed, commitment, and so in the poems and plays is connected
with this activity. In two plays, *The Return of the Druses* and *A Soul's
Tragedy,* the chief character talks and theorizes and postpones the
decisive deed; it is another and a better who puts the theories into
action and pays the price. In the personal sphere, too, action is to
fulfil and confirm the word, as works faith. (If the parallel seems
fanciful, it is worth remembering that the pomegranate of *Bells and
Pomegranates* is, as Browning says in his explanatory note, '*simbolo
delle buone opere.*') 'The words are words, and faulty, and inex-
pressive, or wrongly expressive –, but when I live under your eyes,
and die, you will never mistake' (*LRBEB,* II, 613; Apr. 10, 1846) ;
'and now, no more of words? & will there indeed be need of no more,
– as I dare hope and believe, – will the deeds suffice? – not in their
own value, no! – but in their plain, certain intention, – as a clear
advance beyond mere words?' (ibid., II, 950; Aug. 10, 1846). There
is something in Browning that wants the corroborative deed, and that
not so much mistrusts as views with detachment, waiting for the test
of action, the man of words. A touch of such sentiment, or perhaps of
the man waiting for a prophecy to be fulfilled (if there is an echo of
Simeon below), is seen after his marriage: 'How you have dared and
done all this ... I believed you would be capable of it – What then?

What is a belief? My own eyes have seen – my heart will remember'
(ibid., II, 1067; Sept. 13, 1846). Some of Browning's severest strictures
were to be on men whose word means nothing, like the lawyers in
The Ring and the Book: 'language – ah, the gift of eloquence! /
Language that goes, goes, easy as a glove / O'er good and evil,
smoothens both to one' (I, 1179–81).

But it does not do to read the *Bells and Pomegranates* poems too
sternly. Much of the action is connected with a great youthful vitality
that plays through the collections, and again such vitality is both
displayed by Browning and extolled in his poems. 'Life' here seems a
positive good (the criticisms of the Santayana school are more pertinent here than elsewhere) : life versus pretension or dead tradition
in *The Flight of the Duchess*; life versus pedantry in *Sibrandus*; life
versus the form of sloth which is timidity in *Pictor Ignotus*. Blacks
and whites, in youthful confidence, are sharply black and white.

Browning published two collections of short poems in the *Bells and
Pomegranates* series, *Dramatic Lyrics* in 1842 and *Dramatic Lyrics
and Romances* in 1845. These were the first short poems he had
published on their own and not as part of a longer work. In 1863 he
rearranged these short poems, along with the *Men and Women*
poems, into three groups: *Dramatic Lyrics*, *Dramatic Romances*,
and a new short group of *Men and Women*. In this rearrangement he
transferred many of the dramatic 'lyrics' of 1842 into the class of
romances, and from the 1842 and 1845 collections some twenty lyrics
remained. Of the fourteen poems in the 1842 *Dramatic Lyrics* he
retained only four as lyrics in 1863 (*Cavalier Tunes, Soliloquy of the
Spanish Cloister, Cristina, Through the Metidja*), possibly five if
Rudel (inserted in the new *Men and Women*) is considered a lyric.
Browning's 1863 classification provides a useful working list of lyrics
for the reader. His final division between romance and lyric is made,
I think, on the principle that romances centre on a plot, an action,
and lyrics do not. *How They Brought the Good News to Aix* (a lyric)
might seem to be an exception to this, but Browning always insisted
that he meant the chief emphasis of the poem to be on the rhythm and
excitement of the ride. The two poems whose classification as lyrics
greatly puzzles me are *The Laboratory* and *The Confessional*. If *My
Last Duchess* is a romance, why not *The Laboratory*? If *The Heretic's
Tragedy* or *The Patriot* is a romance, why not *The Confessional*?

A glance at the collected lyrics and romances shows that Browning began to work much more extensively at the lyric after 1845. In the two *Bells and Pomegranates* pamphlets, the number of romances and lyrics is approximately the same, but the romances include poems of considerable length or substance such as *In a Gondola, Waring, Italy in England, England in Italy, The Flight of the Duchess,* and *The Glove.* Only twelve of the romances of the 1863 collection come from the 1855 *Men and Women; The Statue and the Bust* is the longest and most are quite short. But *Men and Women* furnishes thirty of the collected dramatic lyrics from among its fifty poems.

6 LOVE LYRICS

In 1863, when Browning re-grouped his short poems, he opened the new *Dramatic Lyrics* with *Cavalier Tunes, The Lost Leader, How They Brought the Good News from Ghent to Aix, Through the Metidja,* and *Nationality in Drinks.* The first four poems centre on patriotism, or more precisely on patriotic enthusiasm on behalf of one cause in a divided country. The last is a piece of whimsy turning on the supposed approximation of a country's drink to its national characteristics. After these drinking fancies come two *Garden Fancies, The Flower's Name* and *Sibrandus Schafnaburgensis,*[1] and the *Soliloquy of the Spanish Cloister* (originally also a 'garden fancy') follows. The impotent scheming of the latter is followed by the macabre plotting of *The Laboratory,* then by the unrelieved horror of *The Confessional,* and the love interest in these last two poems may be meant to lead into what follows, a group of *Bells and Pomegranates* love poems – *Cristina, The Lost Mistress, Earth's Immortalities, Meeting at Night, Parting at Morning,* and the *Song* 'Nay but you, who do not love her.' This group leads, in turn, into love lyrics from the 1855 *Men and Women.* Thirty *Men and Women* lyrics in all follow the *Bells and Pomegranates* lyrics listed above. Only the two *Home-Thoughts* are separated from the other *Bells and Pomegranates* lyrics and inserted later.[2]

---

1 A garden fancy perhaps inspired by a passage in its own Rabelais concerning 'a great, greasy, grand, grey, pretty, little, mouldy book, which smelt more strongly but not more sweetly than roses ... At the end of the book was a little treatise entitled *Corrective Conundrums.* The rats and moths, or – to be more truthful – some other venomous vermin, had nibbled off the opening; but the rest I have put down, out of reverence for antiquity' (*Gargantua,* I, I).

2 Is this in order to dilute any inordinate emphasis on the patriotism of the second *Home-Thought*? This is the poem containing the lines 'Here and

The progression Browning follows, then, is from patriotism to
love, with whimsy, eccentricity or aberration between; from public to
private commitment; from social to individual sphere. The patriotism
all sounds laudable, the lovers all praiseworthy. The oddities inspire
amusement or abhorrence, or a mixture of both. Yet the groupings
give us pause, for it cannot be by accident that the first two poems
celebrate two opposed traditions, and the next pair two such different
rides. These are *dramatic* lyrics, as Browning tells us in his 1842,
1845, and 1863 titles, and in *One Word More*, the epilogue and
dedication to *Men and Women*. But he has chosen to arrange the
dramas in a certain way; to encourage the reader to look at different
patterns, different traditions, different commitments. The numerous
groupings of the 1842 and 1845 poems suggest the same purpose.[3]
There is patriotism and patriotism, as there is love and love.

Most of these *Bells and Pomegranates* love lyrics concern lost love,
as most of the *Bells and Pomegranates* plays concern lost power.
Lost love and power are easiest, and may have seemed purest. 'No
disheartening Before, / No affrighting Hereafter ...' Among the
love lyrics only *The Flower's Name* and the *Song*, 'Nay but you, who
do not love her,' celebrate a united pair. *Parting at Morning* is enigmatic, but the emphasis is on leave-taking. *Love* from *Earth's
Immortalities* is on the familiar theme of desertion. *The Lost Mistress*

there did England help me: how can I help England? – say, / Whoso
turns as I, this evening' – lines which have doubtless been quoted in
circumstances to make Browning wince. Perhaps he had had occasion to
wince before 1863, for in the 1863 collected *Dramatic Lyrics, Home-
Thoughts* are removed from the opening group of *Bells and Pomegranates*
lyrics and inserted among those from *Men and Women*, the only poems
so to be transferred. They are made to follow '*De Gustibus* –' in which
a friend chooses an English lane as habitat for his ghost; but as for the
speaker himself, 'Open my heart, and you will see ...'

3 The three *Cavalier Tunes, Italy and France* (later *My Last Duchess and
Count Gismond*), *Camp and Cloister* (later *Incident of the French
Camp* and *Soliloquy of the Spanish Cloister*), *Queen-Worship: Rudel*
and *Christina, Madhouse Cells* (later *Johannes Agricola* and *Porphyria's
Lover*), *Italy in England* followed by *England in Italy, The Lost Leader*
followed by *The Lost Mistress,* three *Home-Thoughts, Garden Fancies:
The Flower's Name* and *Sibrandus Schnafnaburgensis, France and Spain:
The Laboratory* and *The Confessional,* the two *Earth's Immortalities,
Night and Morning, Claret* and *Tokay.* Some of the pairings seem a little
forced, and Browning later abandoned many of them.

describes a loss that is mitigated because the speaker, like the speaker of *Cristina*, keeps intact the image of his mistress.

But the *Cristina* speaker is no grateful worshipper of his lady's virtues, though his poem appeared under the heading *Queen-Worship*. His curious attitude gives the poem a double effect. His retention of the one moment when 'mine and her souls rushed together' is familiar in a Browning lover. A man and woman previously unknown to each other may be seized decisively by mutual attraction: the power of the eyes in such first meetings is often prodigious ('she should never have looked at me ...'). The lazy lovers of *The Statue and the Bust* experience this unforeseen kindling. Pompilia and Caponsacchi find such an initial reaction vindicated. The former pair remind us that Browning liked to make unorthodox cases, and what is unorthodox about the case in *Cristina* is not the speaker's loyalty but his attitude to the lady. She 'fixes' him as the lady in *The Flower's Name* does the nameless flower, catches him in a spell; but then she abandons him. For 'next moment, / The world's honours, in derision, / Trampled out the light for ever.' These are the honours that perish in the sudden insight of a moment of vision, but for the lady they perish only temporarily. So, 'she has lost me, I have gained her; / Her soul's mine ...'

Yet there is an unshakable petulance in the opening lines ('She should never have looked at me / If she meant I should not love her!') and also later ('I'm not so, and she knew it / When she fixed me, glancing round them'). It seemed hard on the lady, whatever her character, that she cannot look at an observer without being accused of infidelity to ideal love. In *The Statue and the Bust* the case is clear; Browning tells us the attraction was mutual. But here, despite the thrice-repeated verb 'fix' we remain unsure. 'What? To fix me thus meant nothing? / But I can't tell (there's my weakness) / What her look said!' If the speaker cannot tell this, how does he know their two souls did rush together? And is not Browning deliberately introducing doubt into the reader's mind by the above quotations and by the belligerently reiterated question 'Doubt you ...?' later attached to the speaker's speculations? Doubt would be a listener's natural reaction; why should this bother the man blessed with revelation? It is clear, too, that the speaker's attitude becomes surer as he progresses, as if, the glance being gone, he can elaborate and reinforce his own interpretation of it. Browning wrote later of his own love

for Elizabeth that 'it was, in the nature of the proceeding, wholly
independent of any return on your part' (*LRBEB*, 1, 176; Aug. 30,
1845). The worshipper of Cristina has had his moment independently
of the lady, but he is not disposed to be so generous toward her if
she does not respond.

So many of the poem's phrases recall Browning's own sentiments
that it is tempting to posit a normal if unusual speaker, and let it
go at that. The purpose of this life, he says, is to achieve the 'love-bliss'
of mingling with another soul. Would Browning have thought this
in 1842 (if he ever thought it)? The danger of reading answers
from his dramatic works becomes clear when we look at his cast
of characters up to now. For Sordello, the answer is no; for Valence,
yes; and so on. Browning's personal testimony is that before 1845
he himself did not believe in deep 'love-bliss.'[4] The last lines of
Cristina echo another Browning view: life is for the proving of 'our
powers.' But the speaker can try his power now because he has 'grown
perfect'; and he has achieved this state because 'her soul's mine.'
It is a curious development. The woman is prey to the world's temp-
tations, which are said here to be a snare of the devil. Nevertheless,
the possession of this spotted soul brings perfection. Or does he
possess her essential soul while she, hollow within, pursues those
swollen ambitions? There is no such suggestion. If Cristina had
revealed to the speaker nothing but the possibility of the existence of
love, there would be no difficulty. It is her soul that causes the trouble.
In Browning's own life, as well as in the life of Caponsacchi, respond-
ing love is evoked by the kind of soul the beloved possesses. She is
(in both instances) said to be like a Beatrice, a symbol of both secular
and sacred love, shedding light on the connection between the two.
How such a soul lends itself to *Queen-Worship* is clear, but the
Cristina speaker chooses strange gods. There is enough of the self-
righteous, the belligerently assertive, the disdainful in this speaker to
to make him, for me, an appropriate neighbour to Johannes Agricola,
as he was in 1842.

Perhaps the clearest indication of what Browning meant to

4 'If you ask Mrs Jameson she will tell you ... that I once, two or three
years ago, *explained* to her that I could not believe in "love" nor understand it, – nor be subject to it consequently. I said – "all you describe
as characteristics of the passion – I should expect to find in *men* more easily
and completely –" now I know better' (*LRBEB*, II, 709–10; May
17, 1846).

imply in the poem is in its companion-piece under the heading *Queen-Worship: Rudel to the Lady of Tripoli*. Rudel is possessed of a devotion beyond parallel; not a breath of reproach passes his lips, though his suit is of longer duration than the *Cristina* speaker's. His whole petition, contained in the fervent central triplet, is to end just where the *Cristina* speaker began, with one look: 'Oh, Angel of the East, one, one gold look ...'[5] In the Rudel legend, in fact, Rudel dies under the lady's gaze, she having rewarded his devotion by coming to him in his fatal illness.

Browning of course may not have meant the *Cristina* speaker to be an oddity. Perhaps the doubt in our minds is a mark of his inexperience at this time – the same inexperience that did not make it clear how to read *Count Gismond*. Or is it a mark of his demands on the reader, that he expects these lyrics to be read as carefully as, say, *Bishop Blougram's Apology*?

Rudel is one of the most beautifully contrived of Browning's poems. It concentrates on three images and their various relations; its three parts focus in order on mountain, sun, and sunflower; its blank verse is sweeping and ardent, broken only by one beseeching couplet; verse, imagery, and thought show a persistent but controlled fervour.

DeVane asserts that the sun symbolizes love and the Mount symbolizes the lady; the sunflower is, of course, clearly Rudel (*Handbook*, 121). But try as I will, I cannot make the lady and the Mount correspond. The Mount is impervious to the gaze of love: fine. It is cold; it is prominent; it is honoured among men: all fine. But when that first 'large calm front of snow' reappears in this fashion, I have difficulty transforming it into a beloved lady.

> Men nobly call by many a name the Mount
> As over many a land of theirs its large
> Calm front of snow like a triumphal targe
> Is reared, and still with old names, fresh names vie,
> Each to its proper praise and own account.

If I were Rudel's lady, it might please me to hear that I was honoured among men. But I would not enjoy being told that I reared my

---

5 Cf. Rudel's own poem 'L'amour de lonh' (cited in Helen Waddell, *The Wandering Scholars* [London, 1927], 225–6)

large calm front of snow like a triumphal targe over many a land. And what is Rudel doing underneath the shade of the Mountain which hides from him the gracious gaze of his worshipped sun?

But the chief difficulty with the image comes in the second and third parts of the poem. In the second part Rudel pleads with the 'Angel of the East' for one gold look to his twilight nook. Surely the Angel of the East is the lady: the poem is titled *Rudel* TO *the Lady of Tripoli* and if this petition is addressed to the sun (and the lady is the Mount), Rudel nowhere speaks to the lady. Tripoli is in the east, where the sun rises; that golden look is surely solar, and the fervour granted to the twilight nook is what is sadly lacking in the first stanza. In DeVane's reading the petition may be addressed to the Mount (can it look? would its look be golden? why petition the Mount to look down at the sunflower when the sunflower wants a glance from the sun?). Or it may be addressed to the sun as the symbol of love. But then, what about the lady? Is she to stop being a Mount and start being a sun? This makes the reading of the first stanza difficult. Or is she to show a little more susceptibility to the sun as love? If so, why not petition the sun to melt her?

In the third part of the poem, the mountain is also ignored. The Pilgrim is bid to continue travelling east, saying as he goes that Rudel has chosen as his device the sunflower, that men feed on his song as bees on the flower, but that his sole concern is for the sun. He cares nothing for men's applause (such as that with which the Mount is honoured), but looks only to the east, hoping constantly that his look will be returned.

Unless the lady is the sun, the poem should be called *Rudel to the God of Love* because the relation of sun and sunflower is the central one of the poem. But it seems to me that lady and sun combine happily in one symbol. The sun, to be sure, is called 'he' in traditional manner in the first stanza, though not afterwards, for all pronouns are avoided later. But the point of this poem's symbolism is that tradition is turned upside down, the lady being assigned the ruling and masculine role of the sun, and Rudel the dependent role not even of earth, but of one of its products, and not even a remarkable product, but a sunflower, a 'foolish mimic sun.' His appropriation of feminine imagery may be seen in his baffled attempts at embroidery ('these inexpert / And hurried fingers ... 't is a woman's skill / Indeed'). Such inversion is appropriate to the courtly love tradition (which Rudel the Troubadour's poetry and devotion to his lady recall). The sunflower 'outspread like a sacrifice / Before its idol' seems a perfect courtly love stance. Such a stance stresses the inversion of conventional male-female positions. The lady is the leader, the arbiter, the worshipped one: the lady for what she pleases, and he for god who is her. The sun image is a happy one in this context, for the sun has associations with divinity and the lady in courtly love is worshipped. (This poem is one of Queen-Worship.) In the triplet the lady is not deified, but she is assigned to the heavenly order as the Angel of the East. And Rudel prides himself, like the true courtly lover, on his perfect prostration and his emulation of the lady. Like the sunflower, an emblem of constancy,[6] he follows the sun's course from afar; he has abjured his own proper qualities to become the adoring embodiment of her glory, with his yellow disk and rays mimicking her;[7] he feeds men as she nourishes the earth.

This is the only reading which, to me, makes sense of the rapture of the poem and renders its petition appropriately powerful. But, of course, I have the Mount left over. I should like to cast it (with a little hesitation) in the unappreciated third role of the courtly love situation, that of the husband. This may at first sight seem far-fetched. But suppose the 'gracious Sun' (the adjective suits the lady, and Rudel picks it up later when he says the sunflower has parted with a flower's graces for the grace of being but a foolish mimic sun) is the lady. Then she favours with her day-long presence some Mount, who repays the favour with 'no change of its large calm front of snow.' The sun, like the lady, does not even see the flower, shaded as it is by the Mount – the flower which has made not merely one change, but an alteration of its entire being. The sentiment is like that expressed in *Cristina*: 'there are plenty ... she may discover / All her soul to, if she pleases, / And yet leave much as she found them.' The Mount does not appear to be collective, that is, to be all those upon whom the lady's influence shines. It is a prominent, honoured person, known through several lands; for the lady's husband, the image of the triumphal targe would be appropriate; he would indeed

---

6 Cf. Rosemary Freeman, *English Emblem Books* (London, 1948), 12
7 In the first proofs of *Dramatic Lyrics* (in the Widener Collection at Harvard University), Browning has sketched a sunflower – circular centre, wide pointed petals – beside this description (ll. 10–12).

collect most of the sun's rays, he is firmly established, and beside the prominence of this person, a sunflower would indeed be in the shade. As the sunflower presses its modest claim, however, the mountain as husband is ignored, the sole interest here being the sun-flower relation.

The short lyric 'Nay but you, who do not love her' is the only poem of Browning's entitled simply *Song*. It resembles the Pippa songs in its clarity, quiet fervour, and touch of idyllic rapture, though it belongs to this world and not another. The tress of hair here is made to stand for the entire 'pure gold' of the mistress. It can be pointed to, but the lover cannot speak properly: 'This tress, and this, I touch / But cannot praise, I love so much!' His adoration places him beyond appraisal and close to worship. Like Rudel or the speaker of *The Flower's Name* his passion remains veiled;[8] dispassionate assessment is for outsiders. He has gone beyond names or words, like the devoted apostrophizer of Tasso, quoted by Browning in his second letter to Elizabeth, who could not get beyond 'O tu.'[9] The lover here is like Browning himself in *One Word More*, when he evokes a moon image to convey some of his feeling for Elizabeth, then finally steps away from the world, out of the poem, and leaves words behind: 'Where I hush and bless myself with silence.' In another later poem, associated with Elizabeth, the image of a lock of

8 And like Herrick:

> You say I love not, 'cause I doe not play
> Still with your curles, and kisse the time away,
> ...
> Now since my love is tongue-lesse, know me such,
> Who speak but little, 'cause I love so much.

(*To his Mistresse objecting to him neither Toying or Talking, Complete Poetry of Robert Herrick*, ed. J.M. Patrick [New York, 1963], 24). Browning's lyric ends with 'this tress, and this, I touch / But cannot praise, I love so much.'

9 'My poor praise, number one, was nearly as felicitously brought out, as a certain tribute to no less a personage than Tasso, which I was amused with at Rome some weeks ago, in a neat pencilling on the plaister-wall by his tomb at Sant' Onofrio – "Alla cara memoria – di – ... Torquato Tasso – il Dottore Bernardini – offriva – il seguente Carme – *O tu*" .. and no more, the good man, it should seem, breaking down with the overload of love here!' (*LRBEB*, i, 6; Jan. 13, 1845).

hair does duty for the whole woman: the poem is *In Three Days*, and the other image connected with the woman there is the familiar moon image.

'Is she not pure gold, my mistress?' As the tress must stand for the whole outer woman, so must the image of pure gold for the whole inner woman. The imagery of gold had already been used by Browning, and it would continue to be used and to be much elaborated. I shall reserve most remarks on it until later, and make only a few observations here. First, in another love poem we shall see gold associated with the aspiring, outside world. In the 1863 collected *Dramatic Lyrics*, the *Song* follows *Parting at Morning*, where gold is so used. Is it significant that here gold is associated instead with the woman? I believe so. In *Love Among the Ruins*, gold also belongs to the 'world of men': it is yellow, a thoroughly domestic variation of the gold colour, which is assigned to the lady ('a girl with ... yellow hair'). The same contrast is used in *Parting at Morning*, between the sun's path of gold and the low 'yellow' half-moon. On the other hand, in *Rudel* the lady is given a dazzle of golden sun imagery, while Rudel himself appropriates the mere yellow (he does not use the word) sunflower. (I always suspect, too, the colour in Porphyria's lover's repetition of 'her long yellow hair.' Perhaps if he had seen her hair as golden, he might not have used it as a noose.)

Browning and Elizabeth regularly assay each other as pure gold: 'And shall I allow myself to fancy how much alloy such pure gold as *your* love would have rendered endurable? – Yet it came, virgin ore, to complete my fortune!' (*LRBEB*, I, 335; Browning to Elizabeth, Dec. 21, 1845). 'So I accept the promise as a promise of pure gold, & thank *you*, as pure gold too, which you are, or rather far above' (ibid., II, 574; Elizabeth to Browning, Mar. 30, 1846). The letters abound with images of gold. Luria is early introduced to Elizabeth as 'golden-hearted' (ibid., I, 26; Feb. 26, 1845). When she sees *Luria* in print she remarks: 'You have made a golden work out of your "goldenhearted Luria" ... as once you called him to me ...' (ibid., I, 453; Feb. 12, 1846). But, of course, each could see only one heart of the auspicious colour: 'that golden heart of yours' (ibid., I, 532; Elizabeth to Browning, Mar. 12, 1846); 'and I have learnt since, that "*golden-hearted*" is not a word for him [Luria] only, or for him most' (ibid., I, 557; Elizabeth to Browning, Mar. 4, 1846); 'the golden heart of my own Ba!' (ibid., II, 761; June 5, 1846). And not only hearts were golden. Very early in their correspondence Browning applied the image to their friendship, later to the accumulated letters, looks, words, fancies given to him: '... the octaves on octaves of quite new golden strings you enlarged the compass of my life's harp with ...' (ibid., I, 32; Mar. I, 1845); 'you will never drop *me* off the golden hooks, I dare believe' (ibid., I, 129; n.d., written between July 18 and July 21, 1845, in response to Elizabeth's remarks about his 'gold-headed nails of chivalry,' quoted on p. 96 below); 'when I see a line blotted out; a *second-thoughted* finger-tip rapidly put forth upon one of my gold pieces ...' (ibid., I, 284; Nov. 21, 1845); 'you crust me round with gold and jewelry like the wood of a sceptre' (ibid., I, 302; Dec. 3, 1845); 'I feel every single sand of the gold showers' (ibid., I, 313; Dec. 9, 1845); 'if I had begged never so gently [for a letter], the gold would have fallen ... Let me count my gold now – and rub off any speck that stays the full shining' (ibid., I, 334–5; Dec. 21, 1845); 'and so the golden links extend' (ibid., I, 534; Mar. 12, 1846); 'all your corrections are golden' (ibid., II, 638; Apr. 19, 1846). The catalogue grows almost wearisome, and might be matched by as profuse a one of Elizabeth's. It demonstrates the frequency of the usage; the image is probably the most common one in the letters.

The occasional reverse usage should also be noted: '... when the foolish baton had been broken into ounces of gold, even if gold it *were*, and spent and vanished .. for ... such gold lies in the highway, men pick it up' (ibid., I, 485–6; Browning to Elizabeth, Feb. 21, 1846). Or the reviewers give 'gold currency' for the 'cabbages' of verse-merchants in their Rialto (ibid., I, 18; Browning to Elizabeth, Feb. 11, 1845; did Elizabeth recall the remarks when she bartered curl for curl in 'the soul's Rialto'?). Or 'you cannot despise the gold & gauds of the world more than I do' (ibid., I, 196; Elizabeth to Browning, Sept. 16, 1845).

In traditional fashion, Browning commonly associates flowers with women and by extension with love, but his links are by no means necessarily traditional, for he displays great variety in his flower symbolism. He had a personal passion for flowers, part of a larger loving fascination with most plant and animal life.[10] In later

10 'I have, you are to know, such a love for flowers and leaves – some leaves – that I every now and then, – in an impatience at being quite unable to

poems, the flower of flowers, the rose, was to figure prominently (*Women and Roses, One Way of Love, Another Way of Love*, for example), but up to 1845 it did not. In *Sordello*'s closing lines the rose symbolizes poetry of immediate sensuous appeal and popularity; Browning's own, of rarer but more lasting odour, is the musk-pod. Pippa and Phene are connected with flowers, as was Ottima in the days of her glory; the rose is not among them. *Colombe's Birthday* abounds in not very striking flowers imagery. But the rose's time has not yet come. It comes with Elizabeth Barrett ('Ba who first taught me what a rose really *was*' [*LRBEB*, 1, 566; Mar. 27, 1846]), roses being Browning's most frequent gift to her and the language of flowers playing some part in their letters. *The Flower's Name* is a pre-Barrett poem and like *Sordello* relegates the rose to second place.

The lover of *The Flower's Name* addresses most of his remarks to the roses, which stand prominently in valiant rows, but by the end of the poem, 'Roses, you are not so fair after all!' The reason is that the lady has paused to favour another flower by touching it and pronouncing its name. The secret of its name preserves the flower's privacy and this indirection is of a piece with the whole poem. For, just as in the song 'Nay but you ...' the lover cannot praise, he loves so much (we see only one tress to stand for the mistress's perfections), so here. This lover expresses his devotion by his attitude to the garden: his lady has passed through the gate and is at a distance. We do not see her except by means of the garden, and we read her in her action there. Mistress, flower, lover – none is seen wholly and distinctly, and each chiefly by what the other two show us. The lover notes what his lady notes; he bids the recipients of her favours to value them as they ought; he would preserve the chosen bud as it is forever, catching and holding as in a spell the good minute. There is no overt connection here with Browning's later development of the good minute or the infinite moment. This is simply the lover's natural reaction; as the flower opens, blooms,

> possess myself of them thoroughly, to see them quite, satiate myself with their scent, – bite them to bits ... so there will be some sense in that. How I remember the flowers – even grapes – of places I have seen! – some one flower or weed, I should say, that gets some strangehow connected with them' (to Miss Haworth, in *Letters*, ed. Hood, 1; July 24, 1838).

blows, falls, it moves farther and farther away from the magic instant. There is no hint of pain in the lover's knowledge of coming change, no tragic motif even lightly touched on.

This is the garden of the seasons of love: it shows June passion, for 'June's twice June since she breathed it with me.' June is the month of roses (cf. the play on this in *One Way of Love* and *Another Way of Love*; or the *Parleying with Furini*: 'show beauty's May, ere June / Undo the bud's blush, leave a rose to cull' [559–60]). It is marked here by a flourishing row of roses (Browning uses these words in one line, but without this jangle, for they are separated: 'Roses, ranged in valiant row'). It is marked, too, by awareness of the roses, referral of actions to their observance, remarks addressed to them. The rose may be the flower of love and of June, as June is the early summer of love, but for the moment its claims are set aside. The roses at first appear masculine, even military ('Roses, ranged in valiant row ... She loves you noble roses, I know'). By the end of the poem, they are some flirtatious beauty who has been spurned ('Ah, you may flout and turn up your faces – / Roses, you are not so fair after all!'). They represent another kind of emotion than the present. Now all is tenderness, newness, pink and white, in bud. Love has other colours too, but it is not yet time for them. Their season may come later: the lady may 'fix you fast with a fine a spell.'

To the roses belongs the hard *r* sound: they are ranged in valiant row. But most of the poem is given over to the *s*s and *f*s which seem to grow from the words Spanish and flower. The third stanza makes special use of the *s* sound, this being the verse in which the name is given: 'This flower she stopped at ... Stooped ... settling its ... she ... slip ... soft meandering Spanish name ... Was it love, or praise? / Speech half-asleep or song half-awake? / I must learn Spanish, one of these days, / Only for that slow sweet name's sake.' In the next verse the *f*s join in: 'fix you fast with as fine a spell, / Fit you each with his Spanish phrase'; in the next 'Flower, you Spaniard' again brings the two sounds together and both are used to the end of the poem. When the roses mix with this sound pattern at the end, entering as it were into the present competition, they are defeated: 'Ah, you may flout and turn up your faces – / Roses, you are not so fair after all!' Elizabeth Barrett notes the use of sound in the central stanzas on the flower's name. The whole poem pulls in to the centre with its description of the name, or rather of the lady's pronouncing and the lover's hearing it. It is as if the flower's name, as the title indicates, spreads

its influence out over the entire poem, which is, like the name, soft,
meandering (literally, for lover and mistress are strolling), slow and
sweet. The 'speech half-sleep or song half-awake' recalls the gypsy's
spell in *The Flight of the Duchess*: 'was it singing, or was it saying ...?'
In both poems the lady knows how 'to fix you fast with as fine a spell.'

There is a later poem in which women and flowers figure, and in
which a spell is contemplated, but unsuccessfully. The development is
interesting and complex; I do not wish to pursue it here but simply
to note points of similarity. The connection of women and flowers is
clear in *Women and Roses* as in *The Flower's Name*. In the former,
however, it is the man and the artist, not the lover of one woman who
reaches out toward beauty, and he reaches toward all the beauty of
women, past, present, and future. He is the one who begs the magnificent women of antique time to 'stoop, since I cannot climb' and asks
'How shall I fix you ...?' In the earlier poem the lady herself chose a
flower ('This flower she stopped at, finger on lip, / Stooped over ... ')
and later she may 'fix you fast.' The lady has consented to work her
magic in the early poem as the dazzling crowds of women refuse to do
in *Women and Roses*. The lover playfully desires a literal fixing of the
enchanted moment, a fixing of one favoured flower to correspond
to the fixing of that Spanish name in his own memory: 'Stay as you
are and be loved for ever! / Bud, if I kiss you 't is that you blow not: /
Mind, the shut pink mouth opens never!' The lover would try his
own magic on the flower and the delicate sensuousness is finely
handled. The bud seems called upon to bear the exquisite pleasure of
this moment and preserve it: June will pass, perhaps into something
better, but into something different. As for *Women and Roses* the
man and the artist cannot reach across to those women and those
flowers, and they will not stoop.

The Lost Mistress is a *Cristina* without recrimination. Its force,
like that of 'Nay but you, who do not love her,' lies in its control and
understatement, by which the quality of the lover's devotion may be
gauged. This is especially notable (again like 'Nay but you') at the
end of the poem; both lyrics begin quietly and end quietly too, but the
quietness of the endings is charged and full. In the last two quatrains
here, the effect is achieved by making them one sentence; by reiterat-
ing 'though ... though ... Yet I will ... I will'; by inserting a sudden
fervent line ('though it stay in my soul for ever'), which has to do
with only a voice and one remark, one memory; and by allowing such

fervour only a shade more strength of expression than the calmest friendship would use. The lover is already practising his self-abnegation. (The 'for ever' contrasts with the ironic refrain remembered by one *Earth's Immortalities* speaker, 'Love me for ever!')

Browning once again, as in *The Flower's Name* and *Love* of *Earth's Immortalities*, uses the symbolism of the time of year to signify a type and a stage of love. Here it is springtime: the leafbuds are about to open, and the lover can recollect his mistress longing for snowdrops. Perhaps her choice of flowers was ominous: the first flower of the season, which is gone even by the time of full spring, and a small white flower of such a cool name.[11] When the snowdrops are over, so is her passion; like the leafbuds, the 'red turns grey.' This, then, is spring passion that is suddenly halted; the leaves are not allowed to open. The lover may, incidentally, recall 'your voice, when you wish the snowdrops back' from the winter, or from the present; if the mistress yearns for snowdrops after they have gone, the lover's suit is chilled indeed.

The imagery is prettily domestic, deliberately scaled down to sparrows twittering in the eaves of a vine-covered cottage. Why, precisely, I do not know, although a glance at other Browning love poems will show how important dwellings may be for the fortunes of love – the farm in *Meeting at Night*, the home in *By the Fireside*, the mountain nook in *A Lovers' Quarrel*, the deliberate homelessness in *Two in the Campagna*, the ruined tower in *Love Among the Ruins*, the house of love in *Love in a Life*, the house into which Elvire nearly draws Don Juan. Browning wrote one love lyric that talks only of rooms, *Appearances*.

The relation of the poem to Browning's experience is probably fairly direct. DeVane proposes a composition date in May 1845, mentioning that Elizabeth threatened to break with Browning then because of his precipitate and misinterpreted declaration of his feelings after their first meeting in May. I suspect that the poem's May imagery induces DeVane to such a dating (cf. his reasons for dating *The Flower's Name*). One slight difference from the poem would have obtained had Elizabeth in May 1845 become the lost

---

11 When Elizabeth was sparring with Browning about the date of their spring meeting, she wrote; 'To me unhappily, the snowdrop is much the same as snow – it feels as cold underfoot' (*LRBEB*, 1, 29; Feb. 27, 1845).

mistress, for she declared that with any repetition of the offence she would not see Browning again (*LRBEB*, I, 72–3). The poem, I think, belongs to any time in the summer of 1845 when Browning – and Elizabeth – repeatedly confirmed their friendship; Browning declared himself blessed in it, whatever more might happen, when he proposed to Elizabeth in the autumn of 1845. Each is in early correspondence 'my friend' or 'my dearest friend' to the other.[12] But Browning did not need his own experience to tell him the pain of pushing love back into friendship.

The two short poems published under the heading *Earth's Immortalities* are a complementary pair, the poet having selected two of the supposed immortal things of earth, fame and love. The earth and the immortality of the title are incompatible, earth being (Browning stresses this thoughout his work) a place of mutability, where things alter and often corrupt with time. The two immortal goals, fame and love, are those commonly associated with masculine and feminine spheres respectively, and a man and a woman are shown as failing to achieve the goals. Browning seems to have wished to present in as simple a manner and as few lines as possible a quiet but bitingly ironic treatment of the supposed immortality of these human aspirations. Each of the short stanzas represents a type of death.

The first is literal death, followed all too rapidly by the death of fame, and of even a place in the memory of followers and friends. The 'by-and-by' echoes sadly, for the promised brickwork will not come to this unkempt grave; instead of brickwork, lichens are building 'plate o'er plate.' Minute and grey, they resemble the sands of time

12 Elizabeth: 'writing as from friend to friend – as you say rightly that we are (*LRBEB*, I, 35; Mar. 5, 1845); Browning: 'I will joyfully wait for the delight of your friendship, and the spring' (ibid., I, 7; Jan. 13, 1845); Elizabeth signs herself 'Always your friend' on May 15 and intermittently thereafter during the summer. After their first meeting, Browning writes: I am proud & happy in your friendship – now and ever' (ibid., I, 70; May 20, 1845). Browning will call Elizabeth 'my dear friend,' later 'dearest friend,' but will not sign himself 'your friend'; presently Elizabeth leaves off too. He says, as they arrange to meet regularly: 'I do believe we are friends now & for ever' (ibid., I, 90; June 9, 1845). 'And you are NOT, NOT my "other friend," any more than this head of mine is my *other* head, seeing that I have got a violin which has a head too!' (ibid., I, 164; Aug. 20, 1845).

piling in slow inevitable layers over one man's achievement like the sand in Paracelsus' 'Ozymandias' song. But lichens are active destroyers, and not simply signs of time passing; for being both algae and fungi, they literally eat the rock. Their greyness is the greyness of anonymity; 'a common greyness silvers everything,' says Andrea, who has lost his hopes. The lichens have 'softened down the crisp-cut name and date'; the process sounds gentle, almost preferable to the spanking newness created by the stone-cutter's chisel; similarly the adjective 'prettiest' ('See, as the prettiest graves will do in time ... ') makes the grave – and the poet – part of a picturesque cemetery setting. Both diminutions are, however, the beginnings of roads to oblivion.

In the *Love* stanza, it is a victim speaking ('Now snows fall round me') and the ironic refrain of immortal love (*'Love me for ever!'*) echoes through her head (it is more probably a woman than a man). The last line of the stanza is a powerful echo, being the ninth line after eight lines in a *ababcbcbb* rhyme scheme. The *b* rhyme is with 'for ever,' and the ironic variation goes 'endeavour, sever,' then 'fever,' which breaks the rhyme somewhat as falling snows break the spring's ardour and the notion of immortal love slides into that of disease.

The first poem is a glancing one: its force is in its casualness, the very casualness of the visitor to 'our poet's' (another diminution, this local patronage) grave marking the decline of his fame. The poem is an aside, a comment on a tombstone; no attempt is made to develop a *sic transit gloria* theme any more heavily than this; the effort is to produce the kind of ironic understatement which Hardy likes to practise. In the second poem one of the principals speaks, and again the touch is kept light. So difficult is it to do this with the deserted woman (cf. *In a Year* where, despite the short-lined stanza and the force of the ending, the woman has just enough self-pity to draw her toward a melodramatic type) that the song is made very short and concise. The whole story is told in seven lines plus two lines of refrain, and such concision is possible by using the familiar connections of love with the seasons of the year ('So, the year's done with!'). It is a connection we have seen used in *The Flower's Name*, touched on in *The Lost Mistress*, and developed in the Ottima-Sebald scene and the prostitute's song in *Pippa Passes*.

In the latter, the pattern is gracefully used by a love-smitten young Englishman. He takes a lesson from his beloved's flowers: 'June reared that bunch of flowers you carry, / From seeds of April's sowing. / I plant a heartful now ...' Some seed will grow, and though she may not pluck, may not love, she may like. He can wait 'love's protracted growing' like the lover (less gullible) of Evelyn Hope: 'You'll look at least on love's remains, / A grave's one violet ... What's death? You'll love me yet!' But in *Earth's Immortalities* there is no consolation from the sweets of after-life; love, like the year, is over and done with.

Each of the poems touches delicately on imagery which Browning both before and after associated with mutability. In the first poem, change is marked by the persistent growth of grass, 'spite of the sexton's browsing horse,' and of lichens. Grass in its slow inexorable way obliterating the monument of a man, like the cognate image of lichen covering stone, is not a startling symbol of destruction by time. But it was pesistently used by Browning, and especially developed in his later poetry. He had already used it in *Sordello*: 'Ah, the slim castle! dwindled of late years, / But more mysterious; gone to ruin – trails / Of vine through every loop-hole' (II, 978–80). This is Sordello's Goito-Paradise revisited, and the ravages mark the similar damage to Sordello's spirit and the fact that he no longer can or should find a refuge here. A more traditional use of the image is in Browning's account of events after Sordello's death:

> I think grass grew
> Never so pleasant as in Valley Rù
> By San Zenon where Alberic in turn
> Saw his exasperated captors burn
> Seven children and their mother
>   ... 'mid the brake
> Wild o'er his castle on the pleasant knoll,
> You hear its one tower left, a belfry, toll –
> ...
> Chirrups the contumacious grasshopper,
> Rustles the lizard and the cushats chirre
> Above the ravage ...   (VI, 775–89)

The best-known development of the figure is, of course, in *Love Among the Ruins.* There are striking uses of it in *Fifine at the Fair* and *Clive*, and an extended development in *Red Cotton Night-Cap*

Country, subtitled *Turf and Tower*, where it is part of the central symbol. Long before, Elizabeth had made use of the contrast: 'The only greenness I used to have (before you brought your flowers) was as the grass growing in deserted streets, ... which brings a proof, in every increase, of the extending desolation' (*LRBEB*, I, 553; Mar. 24, 1846).

In the second poem change is marked by the revolution of the seasons. DeVane hazards a composition-date for the first poem of some time after October 1844, when Browning visited Shelley's grave; the comment on love 'was probably written as a companion-piece,' and the lines 'So, the year's done with' possibly suggest December 1844 as the date of their composition. On October 29, 1845, Elizabeth spoke of *Earth's Immortalities* as one of the 'new poems,' that is, poems she had not seen previously in manuscript. Whatever the date of composition of the second lyric (and I incline to place it in the spring or summer of 1845, for reasons stated below), its theme is a theme for discussion between Browning and Elizabeth long before she set eyes on the poem; and after its publication the refrain figures in their exchanges. One of the early points of dispute between the two was whether or not Browning was deceiving himself about the quality of his attachment; since Miss Barrett refused to allow him to declare what the attachment was, the dispute remained oblique, and was in any case a contest in generosities. In mid-summer of 1845 Elizabeth protested at being elevated by Browning to the eminence of teaching him: 'I do wish you w^d consider all this reasonably, & understand it as a third person would in a moment, & consent not to spoil the real pleasure I have & am about to have in your poetry, by nailing me up into a false position with your gold-headed nails of chivalry, which wont hold to the wall through this summer' (*LRBEB*, I, 125; July 16–17, 1845). Browning became as angry with her as he was ever to become during their courtship. 'I shall just say, at the beginning of a note as at the end, I am yours *ever*, and not till summer ends & my nails fall out, and my breath breaks bubbles, – ought you to write thus having restricted me as you once did, and do still? You tie me like a Shrove-Tuesday fowl to a stake and then pick the thickest cudgel out of your lot, and at my head it goes ... ' (ibid., I, 128; n.d., written between July 18 and July 21, 1845).

But with the declaration and conditional engagement in the fall, the mournful irony of the stanza could be turned to another use.

Elizabeth confessed that she had been persuaded of Browning's love when he said he could not name a reason for caring for her. 'If a fact includes its own cause .. why there it stands for ever – one of "earth's immortalities" ... ' (ibid., I, 265–6; Nov. 12, 1845). She picks up the poem again some five weeks later: 'Should I have said to you instead of it .. "*Love me for ever*"? Well then, .. I *do*' (ibid., I, 339; Dec. 21, 1845; the year's end no doubt brought the refrain to mind). Browning responded: '... just that I may forever, – certainly during our mortal "forever" – mix my love for you, and, as you suffer me to say, your love for me' (ibid., I, 343; Dec. 25, 1845). He repeated the phrase in an immediately subsequent note ('"Forever" and for ever I *do* love you' [ibid., I, 345; Dec. 27, 1845]). The sting of the song had been pulled; the year was safely done with. On the first day of the new year, Elizabeth could say that she contemplated the bouquet of her thoughts with joy: 'It is a nosegay of mystical flowers, looking strangely & brightly .. & keeping their May-dew through the Christmases – better even than *your* flowers' (ibid., I, 353; Jan. I, 1846). The seasons could be defied if one knew the way, and if natural flowers died with the snow, there were others that lived.

May-dew was an appropriate decoration for thoughts of love's beginnings; it also had the advantage of literal truth for Elizabeth. She and Browning had first met in person in the month of May. May was Browning's own month, he wrote, even before he had met Elizabeth ('My own month came; / 'T was a sunrise of blossoming and May' [*Sordello*, II, 296–7]). It was his own month because it included his birthday ('The 7th of May last was my birthday (your's is the 20th, tho' you did not say so at our parting dinner, when I spoke about May and birthdays!)' [*RBAD*, 33; May 22, 1842]). But the old birthday was to be abrogated by a new one. May and spring made the season for seeing Elizabeth: 'I will joyfully wait for the delight of your friendship, and the spring, and my Chapel-sight after all!' (*LRBEB*, I, 7; Jan. 13, 1845). 'Spring is to come, however!' (ibid., I, 12; Jan. 27, 1845). 'Mind that spring is coming, for all this snow' (ibid., I, 20; Feb. 11, 1845). 'Real warm Spring, dear Miss Barrett, and the birds know it; and in Spring I shall see you, surely see you ... tell me if Spring *be not* coming, come' (ibid., I, 25, 28; Feb. 26, 1845) – to which craftily traditional reading of the season, Elizabeth prudently replied: 'Yes, but, dear Mr. Browning, I want the spring according to the new "style" (mine), & not the old one of you

& the rest of the poets' (ibid., I, 29; Feb. 27, 1845). But in retrospect the spring (new style) is joyfully 'May & the day we met' (Elizabeth, ibid., I, 178; Aug. 31, 1845); 'I have this on my mind, on my heart, ever since that May morning,' writes Browning (ibid., I, 295; Nov. 28, 1845). That morning eclipsed the birthday morning. 'Nor think that I shall forget how tomorrow is the seventh of May .. your month as you call it somewhere .. in Sordello, I believe .. so that I knew before, you had a birthday there' (ibid., II, 683; May 6, 1846); 'Have you not forgotten that birthday? Do, my Ba, forget it – my day, as I told you, is the 20th – my true, happiest day' (ibid., II, 686; May 7, 1846). Nor is there any need for wistful back glances at that first spring: 'Would it not be perilous in some cases, – many cases – [Browning and Elizabeth, like other lovers, enjoyed contrasting their situation with that of others] to contrast the present with the very early Past – the first time, even when there is abundant fruit, – with the dewy springing and blossoming? One would confess to a regret at the vanishing of that charm, at least' (ibid., II, 676; Browning to Elizabeth, May 5, 1846). And May, like the mystical flowers of Christmas freshness, can be re-created: 'And it shall be *not* April when I read it [his heart] your letter – but June and May – if it tells me *you* are well' (ibid., II, 648; Browning to Elizabeth, Apr. 23, 1846).

May remained the time and symbol of love for Browning:

> Never the time and the place
>   And the loved one all together!
> This path – how soft to pace!
>   This May – what magic weather!

This poem was published in March 1883 when Browning was seventy, and the modulation in it from literal to symbolic May is as persuasive as in his youth: 'This path so soft to pace shall lead / Thro' the magic of May to herself indeed ... ' The associations of May with new life and love are what give point to the quiet poignant lyric of 1864, *May and Death*:

> I wish that when you died last May,
>   Charles, there had died along with you
> Three parts of spring's delightful things;
>   Ay, and, for me, the fourth part too.

But, above all, the symbolism of May marks the love lyrics of *Men and Women*. It marks, for example, *By the Fireside*; the point of looking ahead into life's November, and of placing the declaration of love in an autumn setting, is to mark the defiance of the seasons – and by extension in this poem and others, of time and change. The *By the Fireside* couple can anticipate with joy May's bleak antithesis, November, while the *Two in the Campagna* couple, surrounded by 'Rome and May,' remain apart. *A Lovers' Quarrel* turns on the seasonal contrast. In *Dramatic Lyrics* and *Dramatic Lyrics and Romances*, May also figures. The last lines of *Count Gismond*, which have helped to give rise to reinterpretations of the poem, no doubt play on the symbolism of spring: 'And have you brought my tercel back? / I just was telling Adela / How many birds it struck since May.' As May is the season of love, the usual connotations of May for Browning, even before he met Elizabeth, may strengthen the 'mask' reading of the poem. The time of loss of love in *The Lost Mistress* is spring, the contrast deliberately cruel. But May and spring are not prominent elsewhere: April is the month first mentioned in that most famous of spring songs 'Oh to be in England ... '

Love and fame (if fame may be considered the aim of 'a world of men') are the two poles of *Night and Morning*, one of Browning's finest linked pairs of lyrics. The contrast in mood has been well sketched by Ralph W. Condee (*Explicator* xii [4], item 23) : it is the contrast between the 'speaker's quickened, sensitive anticipation as he approaches the tryst, and his satisfied departure the next morning for the "world of men" that he needs'; the imagery of the first poem

> stresses tension, awareness, and anticipation ... the speaker is acutely sensitive to 'the yellow half-moon,' 'the startled little waves,' the 'fiery ringlets' ... he is sharply conscious of the 'warm sea, scented beach,' and of precisely 'three fields to cross.' The tap, the match-flame, the whisper, in lines 9–11, by their ellipsis of both syntax and sense ... create an anticipatory tension that is resolved by the lovers' embrace in the last line ... Here [in the second poem] is not expectancy, but flatness – broad effects rather than intense perception of detail, the bright glare of the sun on the water instead of the 'gray sea,' the dim light of a half-moon, and a match-flare. Here the imagery is purely visual, instead of calling on all the senses ... It is ... blunt and general instead of detailed, intense, and suggestive.

Mood, imagery, ellipsis: more than this. The rhyme contributes to the contrast, the rhyme of the second half (*abba*) being but an abbreviated version of the stanzaic form of the first (*abccba*). The night is over and done with; now is the time for a quick parting. Further, the two stanzas of the first part are not complete sentences: they are snatches of heightened perception, landmarks, just before two stages of the journey are reached, sea to land, land to beloved. In the quatrain that makes up the second poem, there are three main verbs; there is action, and it is sudden and decisive. It is also simple; the four lines are end-stopped. What has been dropped from the long stanza is the inner couplet, which was also a line run into the next; and what this couplet does for the long stanza may be seen by dropping it from the two long verses, thus bringing them much closer to the form of the second poem.

The two halves make up a brilliant contrast. In the first, the large expanses of the sea and mountain are only a grey and black background for what is near at hand and closely seen. In the second, the horizon widens out as far as eye can perceive; the sea seems to come suddenly around the cape. It is as if the sea had vanished after the lover travelled over it, left it, and put it out of his mind; now it returns, with its enormous claim. The mountain appears suddenly too, as the sun looks over its rim; in the night-scene we do not even realize it is a mountain, so much a backdrop is that 'long black land.' The night-scene is under the moon's domain, that feminine light of the sky, and the moon is not white and remote, pulling the gaze out into a starry universe, but large, yellow, and low, like some domestic lamp, or like a personal guide for the travelling lover. It lights up only a few waves at a time for the lover's eye: they seem to spring out of sleep, startled, like children from cribs; disturbed by the boat, they leap in fiery ringlets, and again the image is domestic: those ringlets belong in a cherished, protected world. In the second poem, the sun reigns. Unlike the moon he is not simply there, but rises and looks over the rim and alters the world. He does not shed a small, gentle glow, but acts, blazes out, makes a path. His long dazzling path of gold lies across the water, sun uniting with water as moon never did, beating down upon it in a golden glow, not waiting for the water to be disturbed and only then to catch the light. In the dim night the lover finds his own way: light seems to come with him, to surround him, making a circle of light like a flashlight in the dark. In the daylight world, the path of gold is laid out by another: dazzling and alluring, it beckons toward the horizons and the large world; its mood is imperative. The first poem narrows down and down: sea, land, beach, fields, farm, window, the beloved: the light narrows from the low moon to the circle of illumination cast by a match; the perception has narrowed down, and is lost, buried – as the speeding boat buries its prow in sand: 'a voice less loud, thro' its joys and fears, / Than the two hearts beating each to each!' In the second poem the movement is opposite, from the eye of the beholder out as far as may be seen. The first poem comes toward the woman and sees the universe in domestic and personal terms. The second moves rapidly away from her toward the sun ('him') and the 'world of men.'

This kind of imagery with this kind of opposition is used by Browning in later poems. I do not want to read back into *Night and Morning* the considerably more complex developments of *Love Among the Ruins*, or especially *Fifine at the Fair*, nor do I want to read forward into those poems the comparatively straightforward contrast here. But a glance at the later poems is instructive. In *Love Among the Ruins*, for instance, the two worlds have other important connotations. But the world of striving for glory, of competing and building and warring and ruling is, as in *Parting at Morning*, a world of gold and fire, a daylight world of brilliant light, a world of far horizons, and a world of sudden shooting, spurting action. And the world of love (also, which is important, a pastoral world) is one of dim colour and light, an evening world of fading sun, a world moving inward toward a central enclosure, a world of steady anticipating movement toward the beloved. The meeting in *Love Among the Ruins* is very like that in *Meeting at Night*: 'And a voice less loud, thro' its joys and fears, / Than the two hearts beating each to each!' '... Ere we rush, ere we extinguish sight and speech / Each on each.' *Love Among the Ruins* is also a meeting at night, but the speaker is more imaginative than that of the earlier lyric. The first man must wait for morning to hear the call of the outside world and he seems simply to accept its summons. The second hears it within himself and its ambiguous attractiveness agitates him.

The most interesting development of the *Night and Morning* pattern of imagery is in *Fifine at the Fair*. Only a full-scale treatment would do justice to the poem's subtlety, but the division is the same. The land represents one sort of life and allegiance; it focuses on village and house, the house into which Don Juan so nearly and finally walks at the end, before, with a sudden twist, he goes off. The sea represents another and opposing life: the gypsies are connected with the sea (their pennant stretches frenetically toward it in the wind) ; they have houses but houses on wheels, movable as boats. In the bright noonday sun, Don Juan, like the amphibian of the prologue, swims, stretched out between sun and sea. As night approaches, the sea begins to appear domestic; Don Juan turns literally and figuratively inland toward his home, and toward the image of the householder in the epilogue, who sits at home at night. 'How quickly night comes! Lo, already 't is the land / Turns sea-like; overcrept by grey, the plains expand, / Assume significance; while ocean dwindles, shrinks / Into a pettier bound' (lxxxiv).

There is a more explicit (and more removed) contrasting of the two worlds in *Dîs Aliter Visum*. Here the surrounding scene – sea, church, birds – should have spoken to the half-hearted suitor, says the girl long afterwards. And here we move into the kind of witnessing by nature which is not seen in Browning's poetry at the time of *Night and Morning*: 'Who made things plain in vain?' In the *Bells and Pomegranates* poems, prior enlightenment will enable an observer to penetrate some of the mysteries of nature (the Englishman in Italy can comprehend bird songs), and the Browning hero, or heroine especially, may be in a harmonious relation with nature (Pippa, Colombe, the late Duchess of Ferrara, the fleeing Duchess, presumably Brother Lawrence, the Englishman in Italy, the lady of *The Flower's Name*, and the speaker of *Sibrandus Schafnaburgensis*). But there is no suggestion here or elsewhere at this time that man is to read from the book of nature (except in *Sordello*; see pp. 200–2). What interests me in the later poem is the use of a phrase very like 'the need of a world of men' in connection with the outside world: ' "I rally, *need* my books and men" ' (italics mine). This is the man's supposed remark as sardonically fancied by the girl; perhaps the earlier 'need' implies something about the quality of that love. The same image, too, as in *Parting at Morning* and *Fifine at the Fair* is used to symbolize the outside world – the sea.

But it is important to remember that any interpretation which pulls *Night and Morning* into a 'this is good – this is bad' opposition does the poem injustice. Browning is not writing that kind of poem, but simply, in what must be the shortest possible space, indicating the

opposition of two worlds, 'the coolness which as duly follows flame'
(*Beatrice Signorini*). The use of the word 'need' in the second poem
means that the attachment is not of the Barrett-Browning quality.
But the lady may not be a Miss Barrett. That farmhouse pulling the
speaker so surely toward it at night may have to be broken from, may
even sometimes threaten like a Simone de Beauvoir domestic nightmare. Night and morning are parts of one day, and each is com-
plement as well as contrast with the other.

I have followed Browning's own emphasis in calling the 'scenes
and song-scraps' of *Bells and Pomegranates* practice for what is to
come.

> Songs, Spring thought perfection,
>   Summer criticizes:
> What in May escaped detection,
>   August, past surprises,
> Notes, and names each blunder.   (*Flute Music*)

The above group of love lyrics includes some of his most exquisite
work. But in *Men and Women* come lyrics in which all his experience
is focused. Each is shaped by a central viewpoint, a 'sight' related to
other 'sights' in Browning. These viewpoints are dramatic. And each
viewpoint is given its appropriate music – thought governing tune,
not vice versa. Browning's lyric achievement is yet to come in 1845.

III MEN AND WOMEN:

ATTAINMENT

7   ENCLOSURE

Men and Women, published in 1855, is Browning's most extensive
and impressive collection of poems. Its fifty poems include thirty that
he classified in 1863 as dramatic lyrics. I should like to move
directly into a consideration of these lyrics, grouping them sometimes
according to a dominant image, sometimes according to a common
theme, and often according to both. The logic of such grouping will
appear, I trust, as the argument proceeds.

The first dominant theme and image I have called 'enclosure,' a
theme and image significant in much of Browning's poetry from
Pauline to *Asolando*. If the thematic implications of enclosure have
sometimes been considered, the imagery of enclosure has not. For
this reason, I should like to look at Browning's enclosure imagery
outside *Men and Women* before examining it in certain lyrics of
that collection.

In *Pauline* the question of freedom is central. It is presented in
personal terms, but really conceived in metaphysical terms. This is why
Pauline, as Mill points out, is no more than a phantom character. She
is needed as imaginary listener, but her redemptive role is spurious.
The dialogue and action all remain within the young man's breast.
What organizes them is the speaker's gradual apprehension of the kind
of metaphysical freedom a man may have. He began, he says, bliss-
fully united with God; he assumed this condition natural and
inevitable, and allowed himself to follow his own inclination as if it
were divine; he awakes to find himself enslaved to himself; he abjures
this slavery and now, weakened, seeks a new freedom under God.
The sequence makes the familiar theological contrast between the
freedom of the believer and the enslavement of the man who supposes himself free from a master. Non-theocentric versions of the
same theme are also familiar.

In describing this process Browning uses several groups of images that illuminate not only the metaphysical but also the psychological condition of the speaker. These groups appear later in his poetry, but they are especially interesting seen in their unpolished early use here. The most prominent group is light imagery, which I have briefly discussed above (pp. 31–2). Browning also introduces, appropriately enough in a confession in which freedom is important, images of enclosure. These latter I would like to look at more closely.

The speaker's opening mood inclines him to seek refuge in the circle that Pauline's arms and face and loosened hair make. It is at once clear that, while Pauline may be presented in sensuous terms, what the speaker chiefly wants is to be cradled and protected by her ('these build up a screen / To shut me in with thee, and from all fear'). Thus enclosed, the speaker can open an inner enclosure, 'unlock the sleepless bood / Of fancies from my soul, their lurking-place,' and rid himself of his suppressed, debilitating anxieties. A similar image follows: 'the past is in its grave / Tho' its ghost haunts us; still this much is ours, / To cast away restraint, lest a worse thing / Wait for us in the dark' (39–42). The speaker then recalls the time of his first confession, the first spring morning after winter, bright with sunshine, like the brightness of his first singing. The same alliances of light and freedom, and of darkness and slavery, common enough alliances, are developed in several uncommon images. The speaker's soul has floated into the dim orb of self and now must follow that dim orb (the words are repeated) reflecting its shades and shapes. In his two nightmares, figures are chained to earth and lure and entrap radiant heavenly visitors. The first figure is 'a fiend in darkness chained for ever / Within some ocean-cave'; the second is more sinister because her enslavement is concealed, light surrounds her, and she lives propitiously by her water ('a young witch whose blue eyes, / As she stood naked by the river springs, / Drew down a god' [99–100, 112–14]). In the long Shelley passage, light imagery is very prominent. But it is important that Shelley is elevated and free. The speaker has stood with him 'as on a throne' (163) ; Shelley is a star.

When the speaker begins to analyse his nature and recall his former self, he says that in his early trust in God, 'I felt as one beloved, and so shut in / From fear' (300–1). The lines closely echo the opening lines quoted above ('to shut me in with thee, and from all fear'), and it is apparent the speaker seeks a return not only to God but also to his early security. The most interesting thing about *Pauline*, as Mill noted, is that no real alternative to the present or past states, no future is proposed or imagined. The imagery is all of returning, of re-approaching a happy state which need not have been forfeited. If this prodigal son returns, he returns weary and chastened, and to no banquet or festive garments. It is interesting to watch Browning break this pattern in *Paracelsus* and *Sordello*. Again the two chief characters have idyllic boyhoods; again they suppose themselves secure, then find they have betrayed themselves. But the latter two break out again, after a period of desperation, and move toward a new position. Sordello makes the more interesting parallel because he attempts a return to his boyhood existence.

When the *Pauline* speaker is wallowing in disillusionment, his soul becomes a temple with no God, self-enclosed. 'And thus I sought / To chain my spirit down which erst I freed / For flights to fame' (504–6) ; he would make his readers 'bow enslaved' (544) ; he begins to fear 'what dread may lurk in darkness' (550) – age, death. But 'I cannot chain my soul' (593), and the young man proudly expresses the insatiable romantic thirst for life which possesses him; a similar passion for knowledge he can control with difficulty ('it lies in me a chained thing' [631]). The word 'chain' reappears in the ensuing discussion of love and reason: reason is 'chainless' and thus the speaker's reason, though less than his love, has quelled 'love chained below' to this earth (641). The tour de force of his imaginary night-to-day journey ends in the English countryside:

> Hedgerows for me – those living hedgerows where
> The bushes close and clasp above and keep
> Thought in – I am concentrated – I feel;
> But my soul saddens when it looks beyond:
> I cannot be immortal, taste all joy.   (806–10)

This time the circle of enclosure is not formed by God or Pauline, but by a hedgerow. It is not a shelter but a circumscription; its advantage is to concentrate being. But when the speaker peeps beyond, he sees not a brood of fears, but a beckoning world. The terms of conflict have shifted into the romantic opposition between infinite thirst for life and necessary finitude. The speaker knows that part of his nature will always yearn for an omnivorous grasp of all life; he has said so in his self-analysis. More ominous, this yearning, pursued, is what has reduced him to self-enslavement and divided him from God. He begins to move toward a solution of his dilemma in familiar Browning fashion. He supposes that his soul is allowed to fulfil all its romantic aspirations; even then, it would not be satisfied ('commanding, for commanding [i.e. for the sake of commanding], sickens it'). This is exactly the process of thought in *Easter-Day*, and it is sufficiently satisfactory to the *Pauline* speaker to allow him to reconfirm his faithfulness to God.

This done, there is at once an easing of tension. Pauline no longer shelters the speaker but is beneath him, looking up. Her look is 'as I might kill her and be loved the more.' (It is intriguing to speculate on the psychological reaction that has produced this remark, and to recall the romantic tradition it follows. Mill is right to emphasize that the speaker is far from healed.) However, he can at least imagine some happier state, full of books and music with Pauline by his side; or the two may go hand in hand, but even here she must lead him 'as a child.' As for the sinister inner enclosure, his mind – 'I'll look within no more' (937). When he has recovered, he and Pauline will go

> like twin gods
> Of the infernal world, with scented lamp
> Over the dead, to call and to awake,
> Over the unshaped images which lie
> Within my mind's cave ...   (966–70)

The closing paragraph shows the still-present weakness. The speaker turns to Shelley for support, as he turned to Pauline at the poem's beginning (Shelley has considerably more life throughout). He wishes to lean on the poet, as one escaped from death 'would bind himself in bands of friends to feel / He lives indeed' (1022–3). Shelley must support him through the gloom and especially in the hour of his death: 'For I seem, dying, as one going in the dark / To fight a giant.' But the speaker is by no means ready yet for the isolation of a Childe Roland quest.

I have followed the enclosure imagery of *Pauline* in some detail because it sets a pattern for later imagery, notably in *Paracelsus*. There, also, is a happy childhood enclosure, literally the high-walled garden at Einsiedeln, and figuratively the love of Festus and Michal, and Paracelsus' confident faith. Paracelsus realizes quite rightly that he must break from this circle, but his break is essentially romantic. His attitude to mankind is in general Byronic, his prototype Prometheus. The past is scorned, the limits of knowledge will readily be reached. Of course his attitude is complex,[1] but romanticism like the *Pauline* speaker's possesses him more than he recognizes. When his quest fails, Paracelsus resigns himself to the small circle of Basel concerns, to crowd-pleasing, magic, and so on. If there are horizons, he is not interested in them. He is about to descend into the last and narrowest confinement, the grave, when he suddenly breaks out again. I have noted the imagery of this break: the transformation of cell to shrine; the burial of light within the gloom of death, light which will eventually emerge. If Paracelsus ends in a far more final enclosure than the *Pauline* speaker's, he will not remain there fearful of what lurks outside. He will re-emerge to conquer.

The reason for this may be seen in a shift in the light imagery of the two poems. In *Pauline*, light belongs without. It is associated with Shelley and Pauline and the clear sight the speaker cannot now possess. His mind remains a dark cave, whose darkness must be looked at no more. Like the fiend's ocean-cave, the only light penetrating it is another's; the speaker even feared once that light could not live in his presence. But in *Paracelsus* a little light belongs within:

> There is an inmost centre in us all,
> Where truth abides in fulness; and around,
> Wall upon wall, the gross flesh hems it in,
> This perfect, clear perception – which is truth.
> A baffling and perverting carnal mesh
> Binds it, and makes all error: and, to KNOW
> Rather consists in opening out a way
> Whence the imprisoned splendour may escape,
> Than in effecting entry for a light
> Supposed to be without.   (I, 728–37)

---

1 Cf. W.O. Raymond, 'Browning's Conception of Love as Represented in *Paracelsus*,' in *The Infinite Moment*, 156–75; and F.E.L. Priestley, 'The Ironic Pattern of Browning's *Paracelsus*,' *University of Toronto Quarterly* 34 (1964), 68–81

This Socratic interpretation Paracelsus later modifies. At the end, for instance, he would not speak of the gross flesh or the carnal mesh. Still, more attention is paid, even in the last book, to inner than to outer illumination.

The most interesting assumption in the above passage is that the inner light is to be associated with truth, and that truth is 'perfect, clear perception.' Perception is the word that in *Sordello* indicates the poet's perfect whole inspiration, which he must break into units of thought and word; when the reader apprehends these, he can begin to piece them together and reconstitute something of the original 'white light.' When Browning speaks to Elizabeth of his own moments of inspiration, from which poetry is made, he uses the same metaphor of light, and the light similarly is often shut in. The phrases are familiar: 'I ... give you truth broken into prismatic hues, and fear the pure white light, even if it is in me' (*LRBEB*,I, 7; Jan. 13, 1845); 'my inner power, which lives in me like the light in those crazy Mediterrean phares ... wherein the light is ever revolving in a dark gallery, bright and alive, and only after a weary interval leaps out, for a moment, from the one narrow chink, and then goes on with the *blind wall* [italics mine] between it and you ... what stuff, in the way of wood, I *could* make a great bonfire with, if I might only knock the whole clumsy top off my tower!' (ibid., I, 17–18; Feb. 11, 1845). ' "Reflection" is exactly what it names itself – a *re*-presentation, in scattered rays from every angle of incidence, of what first of all became present in a great light, a whole one. So tell me how these lights are born, if you can!' (ibid., I, 95; June 14, 1845). Browning is using the metaphor of light in both *Paracelsus* and *Sordello* fashion: first, as a constant inner power, and second as something intermittent (whether inner or outer he does not here elaborate: the apprehension of it is certainly inner). When Paracelsus uses the metaphor, he is not speaking of the creative process, of course. Nor do the Browning quotations above speak of the kind of truth that the *young* Paracelsus seeks. But Paracelsus' conception of knowledge is modified by his final comprehension of Aprile's significance, and in this modification the perceptions of artist and scholar come closer. In his dying vision, Paracelsus makes this clear: 'new perceptions must / Be born in me before I plunge therein [into death]' (v, 500–1); 'so glorious is our nature, so august / Man's inborn uninstructed impulses' (v, 619–20; cf. the favourable

use in *Pauline* of 'impulse'; Browning would not later retain such
a cheerful view of human nature); 'I knew, I felt, (perception
unexpressed, / Uncomprehended by our narrow thought ...) what
God is, what we are, / What life is' (v, 638–43; here, as in *Sordello*,
perception far exceeds thought, but is a genuine mode of knowledge);
'knowledge – not intuition, but the slow / Uncertain fruit of an
enhancing toil, / Strengthened by love' (v, 696–8).

The use of the metaphor in *Paracelsus* is also interesting because
of Browning's burial of truth. It is here enclosed within man, the
hidden light. In *Sordello*, the process becomes cosmic. Too certain
knowledge, says Browning (speaking in his own voice and in familiar
fashion) would mean a paralysis of the will, a blasting of the flower-
bud by too close exposure to the sun:

> Hence
> Must truth be casual truth, elicited
> In sparks so mean, at intervals dispread
> So rarely, that 't is like at no one time
> Of the world's story has not truth, the prime
> Of truth, the very truth, which, loosed, had hurled
> The world's course right, been really in the world
> – Content the while with some mean spark by dint
> Of some chance-blow, the solitary hint
> Of buried fire, which, rip earth's breast, would stream
> Sky-ward!   (vi, 184–94)

The burial of truth somehow within history, and the concept of
finding the 'very truth' in one spot if one knows how to search, as
well as the necessity of limiting truth – these things anticipate *The
Ring and the Book* where both image and theme are greatly developed. Moreover, the word 'dispread' used here recalls 'dispread,
dispart, disperse,' which describes what both Sordello's and Browning's poems do (cf. p. 45 above). There is a parallel scattering from
a central point, breaking from a whole, diffusing from a great light,
and work for the recipient in both the creative process and the
dissemination of truth.

One other use of enclosure is touched on in *Paracelsus*: its security.
For Paracelsus, it is a 'joy to see / The beings I love best, shut in so
well / From all rude chances like to be my lot' (i, 70–2). Of course,

as noted above, Festus and Michal do not actually inhabit the world
in which Paracelsus imagines them. Preservation from chance and
change Paracelsus naturally associates with a childhood haven.
(Sometimes the adult yearns for such refuge too: in *A Woman's
Last Word*, especially in *The Guardian Angel*, and later in *James
Lee's Wife*, this is pronounced – the three effects being very different.)

I have already noted the use in *Sordello* of some images of enclosure – the Goito-paradise, castle and grounds – and I shall return
to the 'font-tomb' later. Both Sordello and Paracelsus naturally make
use of such images because they think about the limiting of infinite
possibility by man's finite condition. Both end with their heroes ready
– too late, as it happens – to adapt themselves to the human condition
in ways not considered before. For both, the evolvement of this decision is a slow complicated struggle.

By the time of *Sordello* Browning has mapped out what will be
his chief images of enclosure: first, childhood security as in the arms
of a mother, or as in a childhood garden ('this / Sequestered nest! –
this kingdom, limited / Alone by one old populous green wall'
[*Paracelsus*, I, 35–7]) or a childhood house and environment; second,
the human body, and the body's final container, the grave; third,
the world itself. Cognate images of house, tower, cave, and so on,
are also used. Not only the images themselves, but different attitudes
toward them are indicated this early. First is simple acceptance of
such boundaries, with no interest in what lies beyond. This is the
attitude of the child and allows him his temporary bliss, as in *Pauline*,
Paracelsus, and *Sordello*. It is also the attitude of the animal and
insect world, Browning frequently asserts; their paddocks are marked
out for them, and they pursue their appointed lots whole-heartedly.
Sooner or later man begins to feel confined by such boundaries,
and he speculates on what lies beyond. He can attempt to remain in
childlike security (cf. Browning's remarks on giving one's will to
another, pp. 131–2 below; or Sordello's return, or the *Pauline* speaker's
or Miranda's actions), but once grown he will never find the old satisfaction there. He can attempt to fly entirely the hold these confinements have on him: this is Paracelsus' first step, and it is the romantic
reaction, precisely the one which the *Pauline* speaker could not
shake. Or he can submit to them in cynicism or weariness: this is
Paracelsus' reaction in Book IV, and it is the naturalistic reaction,
precisely the one which the *Pauline* speaker moved into before his first

confession. (It is also the reaction of Caliban, the exponent of 'natural theology in the island.') These last two reactions may be made two poles of an either-or, in the kind of thinking that, Browning believes, can only lead to disaster. This is the kind of thinking in which Gigadibs indulges. It is the kind of reaction (the poor man scarcely thinks) that finally kills Miranda. These, too, are the two poles between which Don Juan vacillates at the end of his poem, unable or unwilling to make some kind of connection that would move him into a new kind of thinking and out of his romantic dilemma. This is Aristophanes' view of himself and Euripides, one in the world as it is, the other far out of it.

For Browning himself, after *Pauline*, there were always two connected points of reference. This is what he explicitly says in *La Saisiaz* where he names them as himself and God. The names will do for the two reference points throughout Browning's poetry, though it is at once apparent that the significance of both alters. The connecting of these two points gives meaning to both the confinements of man and his instinctive endeavours to move beyond them. Browning would have considered these views in the end invalid without a metaphysical foundation, but his outline of men's reactions to confinement has a psychological consistency apart from such a foundation.

To attempt to connect the infinite and the finite (to use Browning's usual terms) means assuming an attitude of incessant tension. It will end, finally, not in the rejection of the finite, but in the converging of finite and infinite. It is man's desire for the finality and perfection of this state that makes him try to achieve on earth moments and pieces of something unchangeable and good: notably, in art and in love. Browning has a great sensitivity to this kind of yearning; otherwise he would not have written *Pauline, Paracelsus, Sordello* – and *Two in the Campagna* and *Women and Roses.*

Browning's use of the word infinite might encourage the question of how close the two infinites of romantic aspiration and the thirst for God come to each other. But in *Pauline* there is distinction in analysis and opposition in action between yearning after God and the restless appetite for all life. In *Paracelsus* the two are seen as part of a process, one fulfilling rather than cancelling the other. The sharpest opposition is in *Fifine at the Fair*, where Don Juan, clear-sighted, sees that he wants only the romantic infinite and not in the least the infinite that is something outside man and his world. He can argue his need for the latter, and nearly talk himself into accepting it. But at the last moment the romantic infinite beckons in the person of Fifine: one more possibility – maybe the last, who knows? – and Don Juan is off on his romantic round again. Here Browning's distinction between the two infinites is given an image: the romantic is a circle of points here on earth; in a circle, there are an infinite number of points, but a circle may also be another enclosure. The metaphysical infinite is one far-off point (Browning's star-image) and it is all a man can do to connect his own self here with such a point. The distinction is Don Juan's, and one of Browning's boldest and most successful strokes is to bring him to this kind of conclusion, then suddenly, without explanation, have him opt for his old life.

In *Fifine at the Fair* Browning begins, and speaks throughout most immediately, of Don Juan's attitude to women. What Don Juan makes of women is a symbol, the points of light of which he fashions a circle. Their attraction is their ability to illuminate his own being. He uses this to demonstrate to Elvire that she has nothing to fear from other females (and she at once, as so often in the poem, falls in with his lead by querying just how concrete is his relation with the others). Actually such attraction is deadly and unconquerable for Elvire, since Don Juan is mesmerized by himself reflected in others. It is not for nothing that he is made to love the reflecting water and use water images. Nor that he is intrigued by the legend of the double Helen, one the seeming real woman, existing in free bliss, observing her own *eidolon*.[2] Don Juan would like, and endeavours, to exist in this way himself; he would like Elvire to do so also (his peculiar loyalty to her is fascinating), and the words phantom and ghost are several times associated with her. He is intrigued also by the double life of the

---

2 Don Juan does not use the word *eidolon* (image). But Elizabeth Barrett had, much earlier, and her associations with the word make interesting reading à propos of *Fifine at the Fair*. She first speaks of 'the difference between the thing desired & the thing attained, between the idea in the writer's mind & the εἴδωλον cast off in his work' (*LRBEB*, 1, 9; Jan. 15, 1845). Later the word is applied personally, and in *Fifine* fashion: 'the εἴδωλον sits by the fire – the real Ba is cold at heart through wanting her letter ... I confess to being more than half jealous of the εἴδωλον in the gondola chair, who isn't the real Ba after all, & yet is set up there to do away with the necessity "at certain times" of writing to her' (*ibid.*, 1, 556; Mar. 24, 1846).

carnival actors, a modern variation of the Helen legend. (His own ability to view them doubly is seen at the beginning of the poem.)

Something of what is conceived in confessional and rather crude terms in *Pauline* may be seen developed in *Fifine at the Fair*. Don Juan like the Pauline speaker, feels a thirst for all experience, and becomes enslaved to himself. But he dares to persist where the *Pauline* speaker turns back. The latter fluctuates between images of constraint and freedom, but never conceives the sophisticated variation on them of Don Juan's split self. When the *Pauline* speaker's self is split, it is not between real self and emanation, actor and mask, but between corrupter and innocent. Don Juan also desires a woman who is chiefly mother (perhaps Browning's use of the word phantom in connection with Elvire derives from Mill's description of Pauline as a phantom). The alternative to Don Juan's romantic self-absorption is made essentially the same as in *Pauline, Paracelsus*, and *Sordello*. It is a religious alternative that connects man with a God who is other than himself and outside the circle of his concerns. In *Paracelsus* and *Sordello* the alternative is figuratively to break a circle. In *Pauline* where the religious alternative is derivative and the chief character numbed by psychological conflict, the alternative is to return to the maternal protection of the circle.[3]

In *Fifine at the Fair*, the alternative to Don Juan's present life is to break his circle, to concentrate on connecting the one point in it

3 In *Red Cotton Night-Cap Country* the chief character's derivative religious thinking is not a solution but a cause of psychological conflict, with mother on one side and mistress on the other; the result kills the man between. This is a more profound version of the *Pauline* situation, where the speaker's torment, when he is caught between the demands of this world and another, finds solution by abjuring one set of demands.

I call the *Pauline* speaker's religious thinking derivative, but Browning was far severer on youthful religiosity in general and himself in particular: 'I observe nowhere in youth, except in diseased and dying youth, the religious instinct: religious dogmas are accepted at that age undoubtingly, but they don't influence a child's actions at all – *that* business is done by quite other agents: it is curious to observe what practical atheism, so far as regards the God themselves affect to believe in, distinguishes ordinary children ... the real instinct is developed in mature years ... I possess at this minute every advantage that I had thirty five years ago ... and yet have outgrown all the considerations which used to manage, for better and worse, the wise person of my perfect remembrance and particular dislike' (*RBJW*, 73–5; Sept. 2, 1864).

which is himself with an outside point which is God. At least this is the image in Don Juan's final theorizing on his life. But as the action moves toward the end, and Don Juan translates theory into practical application, the imagery shifts. Don Juan will become, he says resignedly, a dull bourgeois householder, faithful in all ways to his wife alone, allowing himself no glances from his tower to the sea, confining himself to a placid village routine. Suddenly we are back at his house; his door looms ahead ready to shut him in, and never can Elvire, house, and village have appeared more like jail walls triply enclosing a hapless prisoner. One twist and Don Juan is off. What has happened in the poem's last sections is that Don Juan has moved from *Paracelsus* and *Sordello* enclosure imagery back to *Pauline* enclosure imagery, all the while remaining his sophisticated self. The circle to break from is no longer the circle of earthly points, that is, of Don Juan's women and self-absorption; this is the circle a man may make around himself to his own harm. Don Juan has altered it to the kind of circle that is made around a man by others, like the childhood circles from which Paracelsus and Sordello must break, and to which the *Pauline* speaker tries to return. Once Don Juan has put the alternatives in this way (and made Elvire again the confining wife, resembling some grasping mother), there is only one answer – Fifine.

If Don Juan's personal predilections are for a kind of romanticism, the alternative he works out, and finally rejects, may be considered a type of classicism. Browning's own alternative to Don Juan's self-enclosed romanticism is not, I think, essentially aesthetic or even ethical. Yet as Don Juan works out the alternative, it may also be seen as an ethical one, of the kind familiar in Babbitt or Santayana: 'classicism, the need for men to give allegiance to something, an unquestioned spiritual authority, outside themselves.'[4] I am less interested in working out this contrast than in noting how Don Juan's two reactions to enclosure imagery are like two reactions to classicism. When accepted, the 'classical' alternative seems to promise order and harmony in Don Juan's life, new insight through the discipline which his present whims do not allow him. But when rejected, the same alternative seems to offer only a stale restricted routine, a 'bourgeois' life (the convenient pejorative word: Don Juan the aristocrat and

4 R.A. Foakes, *The Romantic Assertion* (London, 1958), 12

the outcast gypsies leave such routine to the dullards between them).
Browning, of course, sees classicism as also a closed world, because
it lacks the metaphysical basis for belief in 'an unquestioned spiritual
authority,' that is, rejects a transcendent concept of authority though
it may accept an authority outside man's personal self. (But he is
something of a Renaissance man in his view of the classics: some
favourites are reread so that they foreshadow the coming of Christianity. Euripides, like Shelley, is made a Christian in spite of
himself.)

   Don Juan theorizes about art as well as women, and that Browning
had the aesthetic implications of his thinking in mind is made clear
by his reference to Byron. It has also been shown that Browning very
probably intended the poem as comment on Pater's aesthetic theories.[5]
Don Juan is a romantic in art as well as life and thus the more con-
vincing, to me, in life; his seductions are refined and reinforced by
nearly unanswerable argument, which makes up part of a connoisseur's careful mental stimulation. Attitudes to women and art
are frequently connected in Browning: in *My Last Duchess, The
Bishop Orders his Tomb, Andrea del Sarto, Fra Lippo Lippi, Women
and Roses,* and *Fifine at the Fair.* Browning did not publicly, but did
privately, connect his art and his love for Elizabeth Barrett Browning.
The kind of connection is interesting: for the Duke of Ferrara, the
Bishop, and sometimes Don Juan, the woman is an objet d'art; for
Fra Lippo Lippi, part of the multifarious life he paints (not at all
confused with or confined by her painted sister) ; for Andrea, there is
one woman, not swallowed by art as was the Duchess of Ferrara, but
who swallows his own best art. For Sordello, art and love are connected in Palma: he has to decide how he loves both her and what
she loves before he can write; without such a decision he is as impotent as Aprile. The *Pauline* poet likewise makes a certain connection
between love and art: with Pauline's help and under the shelter of
God's love, he will be able to write again.

   Art is a form of love for Don Juan, a form of self-love, since that
it the kind he cultivates. He is an artistic dilettante. He finishes a half-
completed Michelangelo statue, contemplates it, and smashes it
(or is this all figurative? – the significance is the same). He fights to

---

5 Section lxvii, 1119–25; Charlotte Crawford Watkins, 'The "Abstruser
   Themes" of Browning's *Fifine at the Fair*,' *PMLA* 74 (1959), 426–37

collect the best – a Raphael, an Elvire; but once possessed, the best
becomes background, and he needs titillation – Dore, Fifine. He plays
with art as with women: 'a poet never dreams: / We prose-folk
always do' (1524–5). Like the prologue's amphibian, Don Juan swims
when it is pleasant ('sometimes when the weather / Is blue, and
warm waves tempt'), as he dreams pleasantly with the prose-folk.
(In the sea, or poetry, 'all deeds they [heaven's inhabitants] do, we
dream,' though Don Juan later acknowledges that 'a poet never
dreams.' Is this also a comment on a possible difference between
creator and reader?) In the prologue the sea signifies poetry; Don
Juan's participation in it is fair-weather participation. Not for him
the hardship of loyalty, the isolation and darkness from which the
epilogue's speaker, the householder, suffers. His attitude to the sea is
half make-believe – like Byron's whose phrase Browning put in Don
Juan's mouth, and of whom Browning wrote:

> I never said or wrote a word against or about Byron's poetry or power
> in my life; but I did say, that, if he were in earnest and preferred
> being with the sea to associating with mankind, he would do well to stay
> with the sea's population; thereby simply taking him at his word,
> had it been honest – whereas it was altogether dishonest, seeing that
> nobody cared so much about the opinions of mankind.[6]

Most important, everything in Don Juan's life – women, art, dreams,
events, the sea – has one purpose: 'it did its duty, though: I felt it,
it felt me' (1101; this line precedes the Byron references). Purpose

6 To Miss A.E. Smith, in *Letters*, ed. Hood, 159; Aug. 16, 1873. But
   Browning admired much in Byron: 'Ba, Lord Byron is altogether in my
   affection again .. I have read on to the end, and am quite sure of the great
   qualities which the last ten or fifteen years had partially obscured. Only
   a little longer life and all would have been gloriously right again ... I
   always retained my first feeling for Byron in many respects ... I would at
   any time have gone to Finchley to see a curl of his hair or one of his gloves,
   I am sure – while Heaven knows that I could not get up enthusiasm
   enough to cross the room if at the other end of it all Wordsworth,
   Coleridge & Southey were condensed into the little China bottle yonder,
   after the Rosicrucian fashion .. they seem to "have their reward" and
   want nobody's love or faith. Just one of those trenchant opinions which
   I found fault with Byron for uttering, – as "proving nothing"' (*LRBEB*,
   II, 985–6; Aug. 22, 1846).

and phrase are repeated again and again: 'Now, there is one prime
point ... / One truth more true for me than any truth beside – /
To-wit, that I am I ...' (1063–5); 'I need to be proved true; and
nothing so confirms / One's faith in the prime point that one's alive,
not dead ...' (1155–6);

> Elvire, Fifine, 't is they
> Convince, – if little, much, no matter! – one degree
> The more, at least, convince unreasonable me
> That I am, anyhow, a truth, though all else seem
> And be not: if I dream, at least I know I dream.
> The falsity, beside, is fleeting: I can stand
> Still, and let truth come back, – your steadying touch of hand
> Assists me to remain self-centred, fixed amid
> All on the move.   (1355–63)

Three years earlier Browning had put into the Pope's mouth a like
phrase; he knows that 'I am I' but he knows 'I am I, *as* He is He'
(italics mine). I have already suggested that Don Juan cuts himself
off from the Pope's parallel, concentrates on making one circle of his
own. He defines himself solely in terms of himself: he feels, therefore
he is. That he does this in art as well as in life is highly important.
One kind of romanticism (or all?), Browning implies (as he implied
less elaborately in *Pauline, Paracelsus,* and *Sordello*), ends in a self-
enclosed circle. Don Juan's is more sophisticated than the earlier
speakers'; the self he defines is very interesting and his ingenious play
with the numerous images in his circle is likewise interesting. But
neither self nor image ever commits itself to act. Both attempt to
remain in perpetual self-created detachment, to have the perfect
round here and now, to keep free from mutability and pain, time
and death. Something in Browning from *Pauline* to *Fifine at the Fair*
made him fear and shun this kind of enclosure for man and poem
much more than obvious constrictions.

Browning's conception of romanticism, or his alternative to it, may
sound foreign to modern ears. But the image and theme he uses in
Fifine at the Fair (the circle of earthly points and the one far-off
point, and the question of where reality may be found) are closely
related to Northrop Frye's analysis of romanticism: 'What I see first
of all in Romanticism is the effect of a profound change ... in the

spatial projection of reality. This in turn leads to a different localizing of the various levels of that reality.'[7] Rosemond Tuve argues similarly: 'The seventeenth was almost the last century to succeed in looking within without falling in head first and being submerged – probably because its thinkers had as a governing conception not reality conceived as within the individual consciousness, but, rather the possibility of inner harmony with reality.'[8] What Don Juan argues and decides in *Fifine* is the localizing of reality, and he locates it where Frye states the Romantics locate it – within himself. His answer Browning was to protest against both in and outside lyric poetry, by statement and image, and of the latter frequently by enclosure images.

7 *Romanticism Reconsidered* (New York, 1963), 5
8 *A Reading of George Herbert* (London, 1952), 194

8   ENCLOSURE:

MEN AND WOMEN

I have moved from 1840 to 1871 in order to highlight some of the common patterns of Browning's enclosure imagery and their implications. Now I want to return to the years between and take note of Browning's use of this imagery then.

In the *Bells and Pomegranates* poems, such imagery seldom appears. It does play an important role in *Pippa Passes* in the settings of the four main scenes. Such settings are backdrops to action: it is the peculiar situations of the Four Happiest Ones that make it imperative they find their settings confining and break out of them. The setting of the third main scene, with Luigi and his mother in the ruined tower, their decisions, unknown to them, crucially conditioned by secret observers, is particularly well handled. Luigi's mother literally and figuratively tries to keep him inside the shelter of what she knows, what she judges is security. But the peril inside is as great as that outside. The real alternative is to perish with nothing done or with something done. All this is obvious at the literal level, but equally valid on the psychological level.

Again, in *My Last Duchess*, the duke's peculiar character makes enclosure imagery appropriate to his poem. He has shut up his duchess (in the grave or in a convent: Browning offered the two possibilities; cf. DeVane, *Handbook*, 109), just as he did Tasso. It is the point of choosing this particular duke that he did so ruthlessly dispose of both an eminent subordinate and a helpless wife.[1] The duke enjoys controlling things: shutting them up, like his wife and Tasso and the picture; or manipulating them, like the envoy; or

---

1 Cf. Louis S. Friedland, 'Ferrara and *My Last Duchess*,' *Studies in Philology* 33 (1936), 656–84, where heavy artillery is used to show conclusively that Ferrara's duke was the Este, Alfonso II. The Tasso connection is important and, curiously, often ignored.

taming them, as Neptune does the sea-horse. The duke's fellow-Renaissance figure, the Bishop of St Praxed's, centres his remarks on the grave that will soon enclose him. But he is irrepressible even in such a solemn exercise: he 'orders' a tomb and shuts himself in, his material and spiritual arrangements for tenancy all carefully made.

With *Easter-Day*, which turns on the significance of the infinite for the finite life, the early imagery of enclosure reappears, with the old contrast made explicit. The implications of the contrast begin to sound familiar:

> ... could you joint
> This flexile finite life once tight
> Into the fixed and infinite,
> You, *safe inside*, would spurn what's out,
> With carelessness enough, no doubt –
> Would spurn mere life ...   (50–5; italics mine)

The argument is like that of the *Epistle of Karshish*. Not since the *Pauline* speaker has Browning presented the sure protected life as a truly safe place, but he felt the ambiguous attraction there, and he continued to feel what might be the pleasures of absolute certainty. In *Easter-Day* Browning also begins to pay some attention to the wall that encloses, the wall which is most often a wall of time or a wall of sense in his work. Walls may be 'the utmost walls / Of time, about to tumble in / And end the world' (544–6). Or there may be just enough wall between this world and the next to pin a curtain on:

> '... the arras-folds that variegate
> The earth, God's antechamber, well!
> The wise, who waited there, could tell
> By these, what royalties in store
> Lay one step past the entrance-door.'   (751–5)

I noted above one of Browning's favourite contrasts: that of the confined beast, contented because born to be confined, with man. The contrast is made here: '"Man reckoned it [his world] immeasurable? / So thinks the lizard of his vault!"' (846–7). When the speaker is cut off from the infinite, he resolves to try the pleasures of his spacious enclosure; he will

'try how far my tethered strength
May crawl in this poor breadth and length.
Let me, since I can fly no more,
At least spin dervish-like about
(Till giddy rapture almost doubt
I fly) through circling sciences,
Philosophies and histories!
Should the whirl slacken there, then verse
Fining to music, shall asperse
Fresh and fresh fire-dew ...'   (876–85)

Browning would again contrast the earthbound creature with the flier. He had already made use of bird imagery, especially of soaring birds like the eagle and the lark. It is not so much their airy freedom as the direction of their flight that seems to matter. In *Two in the Campagna* the blind beetles are confined to their flower-cup; the thistle-down is blown freely, but is equally a subject (more, since its master is a wind whimsical as Setebos); the contrast is with vertical movement ('I yearn upward') toward a friendly star. The whirling-dervish figure also recalls *Women and Roses*, where the speaker desires, like the *Two in the Campagna* lover, to 'fix' something fast. 'Fixing' is usually auspicious in Browning, unless it is an attempt to fix all existence. (Johannes Agricola fixes his religion fast, and Porphyria's lover his love; it is interesting to remember that these are the two things the *Pauline* speaker also wishes to have entirely sure.) And the whole passage above again recalls Don Juan's circle, his dream of successive philosophies, and his passion for music.

Some twenty-two poems in the 1855 *Men and Women* centre on kinds of love, eighteen of these being later classified by Browning as lyrics. If there is a dominant subject in these love lyrics, it is the vision of some kind of hope, a vision that, whatever its variations, has an ultimate validity. Sometimes the speaker, as in *By the Fireside* and *My Star*, is allowed the vision; more often, he knows of it, even glimpses it, but cannot attain it. Such unhappy petitioners are the speakers of *Two in the Campagna, Women and Roses, A Serenade at the Villa, Love in a Life,* and *Any Wife to Any Husband.* (I also sometimes hear the *Up at a Villa* speaker as a mock-unhappy-petitioner, shut outside his only shining city by the high-taxing gates.) Sometimes the speaker is satisfied with the grace of striving, as in *The Last Ride Together, Misconceptions,* and *One Way of Love.* Sometimes with only a little effort grace could be achieved, as in *Andrea del Sarto* and *The Statue and the Bust.* Sometimes the exclusion seems to be merely temporary as in *A Lovers' Quarrel, Evelyn Hope,* and *In Three Days.* Where the question is of attainment in love, the appropriateness of enclosure imagery is plain. I want to begin by looking first at its use in *Andrea del Sarto* and *The Statue and the Bust.*

Andrea, like the woman of *A Woman's Last Word,* has confined himself, and like her he knows and half shuns the knowledge that he is shutting himself in: 'My youth, my hope, my art, being all toned down / To yonder sober pleasant Fiesole ... That length of convent-wall across the way / Holds the trees safer, huddled more inside ... So free we seem, so fettered fast we are! ... a man's reach should exceed his grasp ... I'm the weak-eyed bat no sun should tempt / Out of the grange whose four walls make his world ... come in, at last, / Inside the melancholy little house / We built to be so gay with.' It is Andrea's fancy that Lucrezia's 'soft hand is a woman of itself, / And mine the man's bared breast she curls inside,' but if Lucrezia momentarily curls, it is so that same soft hand can close over some money ('I'll ... shut the money into this small hand'). And a 'serpentining beauty, rounds on rounds' may please a man caught in its toils, but seems rather more snaky to the observer. Indeed Andrea can sometimes see Lucrezia as the hypnotizing trapper she is: '... the low voice my soul hears, as a bird / The fowler's pipe, and follows to the snare.'[2] Andrea, like another *Men and Women* speaker, mentions the number of his four walls, as if to emphasize how definite their confinement is. But if a grange's four walls can make a world, so can those 'four great walls in the New Jerusalem' of which Andrea covets one. All depends on what is inside the wall. (This is true of the other enumerator of walls: 'I ... go / Into thy tomb ... Seeing thy face

2 This line always sets up in my mind the echo of Elizabeth's first letter to Browning: 'I ask for only a sentence or two [on her poetry] ... not ... so as to teaze you – but in the humble, low voice, which is so excellent a thing in women – particularly when they go a-begging!' (*LRBEB,* I, 5; Jan. 11, 1845). Her authority is King Lear (v, iii, 273). The attribute may have seemed particularly comely to the nineteenth century; cf.: 'Jeanie had a voice low and sweetly toned, an admirable thing in women' (*The Heart of Midlothian,* chap. xxxvii).

on those four sides of it' [*Any Wife to Any Husband*, 103–7]. And cf.
Browning to Elizabeth: 'I could, would, *will* shut myself in four walls
of a room with you and never leave you and be most of all *then*
"a lord of infinite space"' [*LRBEB*, I, 253–4; Oct. 29, 1845]; and
'the dearest four walls that I ever have been enclosed by' [ibid., II,
944; Aug. 7, 1846].)

A similar pattern surrounds the similarly slothful lovers of *The
Statue and the Bust* (or does Andrea's infatuation more properly
come under the category of lust?). They are caught in the reader's
memory in their first and perpetual positions: she in the house,
framed by the window; he riding without, framed by the square.
This is their instant which is made eternity, and it is not the one they
would have chosen. They are allowed one face-to-face contact, then
back they go to their marionette poses, like unhappy variations on
Keats' urn figures. What is art there, caught forever in a thing of
beauty, becomes art here, caught in an ironic *memento mori*. For the
artist and the lover, as in *Women and Roses* or *Two in the Campagna*,
to strive after the fixing of one woman or the being fixed by a friendly
star is natural; but they strive first. These offers of grace are not
diurnal in Browning, and the lovers here had their revelation and
their chances. But they vanish off into some limbo, art substituting
for life. The pathos is that they voluntarily slide into the roles of
frozen observers; they are not forced, as the Duke of Ferrara forced
his last duchess into a painting and Don Juan forces Elvire into
various convenient forms, a painting included. When the *Statue and
the Bust* lovers constrict themselves into a statue and a bust, they are
only performing an exercise in preparation for dying. Both anticipate
the descent into a confinement narrower than that of their lifetime.
The lady's reflections may 'beguile / Dreary days which the dead
must spend / Down in their darkness under the aisle'; the duke will
manage to 'laugh in my tomb / At idleness which aspires [the
Paracelsian word] to strive.' Lady and duke have the least touch of
melancholy pleasure in picturing themselves entombed. They are as
fond of contemplating their poses as the Bishop of St Praxed's; alive
or dead, they have a grace (clear to all in the ballad-like drama of
their first meeting), but one wonders whether each sees the other, or
chiefly sees himself seeing the other. After all, even at the time of the
mock-morbid death fantasies, it is not too late; and it would have made
a fine Browning challenge to treat the elopement of the two timeworn

romance figures. But the lady avers that age is fatal: 'where is the use of the lip's red charm' and the hair, the brow, the blue-veined arm, unless to turn 'the earthly gift to an end divine?'

In the epilogue, the focus widens from the lovers whiling away eternity 'in the narrow room,' as they once whiled away time on earth, to the others who did not aspire and strive, and who, in a gigantic bank of candles, burn upward 'each to his point of bliss.' The still, cold, confined isolation is what the lovers chose in life: they are damped, so to speak. Their sin, says Browning, was the unlit lamp and the ungirt loin; and he shuts out this pair of foolish virgins from the Bridegroom's feast (the only bridegroom's feast is a mockery of the lovers' intentions, as the only lamp lit is the taper on the lady's wedding night).

Andrea and the *Statue and the Bust* lovers give themselves into confinement against their better judgment. They are thus closest to the passive, naturalist reaction to enclosure discussed above. When this happens in a love lyric, the result is a poem close to part of *Andrea del Sarto* in theme (the woman, like Andrea, loves her spouse unwisely), and with enclosure images of great psychological significance. The poem is *A Woman's Last Word*.

This is one poem whose title is not fully understood until the end. The 'last word' is not a dying word, but the last word in a dispute. Browning once wrote to Elizabeth that the last word was commonly claimed by those in the wrong, but he could also claim its use when he felt in the right.[3] Still, to have the last word was usually to be unpleasant, and Browning accused himself of such over-argument in the nerve-wracking final days of his engagement.[4] The right to the last word, he said much later, was a feminine right (perhaps bal-

---

3 'Nay – I *must* have last word – as all people in the wrong desire to have – and then, no more of the subject' (*LRBEB*, I, 80; May 26, 1845). The subject was the painful one of the destroyed letter.

    'Indeed, dearest, you shall not have *last word* as you think, – all the "risk" shall not be mine' (*LRBEB*, I, 545; Mar. 18, 1846).

4 'They [his letters] generally run in the vile fashion of a disputatious "last word"; "one word yet" – do not they?' (*LRBEB*, II, 1058; Sept. 10, 1846). Did Browning remember this remark when he wrote Elizabeth another epistle, *One Word More*, in a manuscript entitled 'A Last Word,' nine years later?

ancing 'the man's right of first speech' once mentioned to Elizabeth Barrett).[5]

The woman who utters this last word does not speak in the disputatious tradition. She is all too anxious to be conciliatory, as anxious as Andrea; '... I and thou / In debate, as birds are, / Hawk on bough!' But after evoking a mediaeval bird debate, she suddenly capitulates: 'Hush and hide the talking.' She is no analyst, and more than Andrea shies away from what goes on behind her words. How fully she faces, even in private, what she is doing, we do not know. Nor do we know whether some secret rebellion lingers. Probably the former, for on the surface the poem reads like the end to some lovers' quarrel. Browning uses phrases which recall his own *Lovers' Quarrel*, the point of which is that it is so unquarrelsome. The woman's wish here ('All be as before, Love') sounds like what the man in that poem wishes ('forgive me as before ... I shall have her'). Her 'what so wild as words are?' recalls his 'see a word, how it severeth!' And if her 'what so false as truth is, / False to thee?' is startling, still one 'truth' may be untypical ('not from the heart beneath ... what of a hasty word?').

But in stanza vii Browning makes clear what kind of last word this is:

As I ought
I will speak thy speech, Love,
      Think thy thought –
Meet, if thou require it,
      Both demands,
Laying flesh and spirit
      In thy hands.

Sordello, defeated in Mantua, was also finally reduced to deciding 'better think / Their thoughts and speak their speech, secure to slink / Back expeditiously to his safe place' (II, 835–7). The woman here yearns like him for a safe place and her stanzas are full of

5 'And now, please further observe, I am "feminine," if you are not, and bent consequently on having the last word ...' (*RBJW*, 52; July 28, 1864). *LRBEB*, I, 388; Jan. 15, 1846

enclosure imagery in which enclosure is seen unambiguously as shelter (unlike Andrea, who alternately accepts and inveighs against it). The oblivion of sleep is the safest place of all and the woman begins and ends with a plea for sleep. In both instances the word is ominously rhymed with 'weep.' Words are wild, and so 'hush and hide the talking, / Cheek on cheek!' Truth may be false, and so 'lest we lose our Edens' this Eve will not pry where the apple reddens – is it on a tree of knowledge? One effect of eating the apple was to be a transformation of men to gods. Whether this association plays in the woman's mind or not, what follows the Eden lines is an injunction that her husband 'be a god.' (Cf. elsewhere in Browning: ' "Worship not me, but God!" the angels urge: / That is love's grandeur: still, in pettier love / The nice eye can distinguish grade and grade' [*Red Cotton Night-Cap Country*, 4119–21].) He is to hold her in the double security first of a supernatural enchantment, then of a natural embrace. Thus both flesh and spirit will be laid in his hand. Meanwhile a safe place must also be found for sorrow ('I must bury sorrow / Out of sight').

The woman's use of Eden imagery is for a moment confusing. Is she to leap into sin, matrimonial dispute, in order that grace may abound? Why not remain in Eden bliss? But the woman is no unfallen Eve, much as she yearns for the peace of paradise (her desperate yearning is a mark of how remote peace is). It is already too late; contention, strife, and weeping have already occurred; she is into another dispensation. When Sordello returns to Goito, sick at heart over his Mantuan experience, he attempts a return to his childhood Eden; it is impossible. 'The confused shifting sort of Eden tale' (*Sordello*, IV, 304) has more than one implication. Browning used it later in *The Ring and the Book*, chiefly in order to ring ironic changes on it. Thus the Archbishop in Arezzi, as quoted by Pompilia, speaks of 'further probation by the apple and snake' and the Fisc of Pompilia's sudden acquisition of literacy after plucking the 'apple from the knowledge-tree' (IX, 450). The most protracted use is in *The Inn Album*, where tree, fruit, and snake figure in various elaborations. Elm-tree and beech-tree are different symbols; the husband appears as a snake (though he began as a 'prophet's rod' [2649]: the regression from Mosaic to Satanic snake and the sexual symbolism are striking) ; like Milton's tempter, 'he, waking, whispered to your sense asleep' (2732) ; another Eve will bruise this serpent, his wife hopes. These later uses concentrate on the conflict in the garden. What the woman in her last word tries to establish is a garden with no snake, and with the husband as god.

Throughout his life, Browning was fascinated and repelled by kinds of personal domination. Tyranny in civic or religious realms he detested; social and personal tyranny, often harder to battle, he equally abhorred. In his own relations he attempted scrupulously to avoid the least shadow of domination over anyone. Such sensitivity was naturally heightened during his courtship, but even before this time he had dealt with the subject of domination. King Victor, Djabal (unwillingly), Ottima, the Duke of Ferrara, Porphyria's lover, the duke with the fleeting duchess, the lady of *Time's Revenges*, De Lorge in *The Glove* – all attempt a personal tyranny and sometimes more. On religious tyranny there are *Johannes Agricola* and *The Confessional*, where Protestantism and Catholicism are pushed to such extremes that they become perverted. Of victims conquered by tyranny, the Pictor Ignotus is the chief spokesman (the woman of *The Confessional* will be broken but not conquered). The most pitiable victims are those conquered more from within than without: the prostitutes in *Pippa Passes*, the lost leader, the speaker in *Time's Revenges*, Chiappino.

Elizabeth Barrett's situation, as Browning came to know it, could only exacerbate his sensitivity to domination. When the quarrel over Pisa broke in the autumn of 1845, he could say little except that 'I truly wish *you* may never feel what I have to bear in looking on, quite powerless, and silent.' He then went on to counsel Elizabeth (she had asked for advice) not to give up forthwith, as was her inclination. The reasons he advances are theological, and it is probably on these principles that he ultimately based his hatred of all tyrannies. Needless to say, such reasoning would also tell with Elizabeth:

> I will tell you: all passive obedience and implicit submission of will and intellect is by far too easy ... to be the course prescribed by God to Man in this life of probation ... The partial indulgence, the proper exercise of one's faculties, there is the difficulty and problem for solution, set by that Providence which might have made the laws of Religion as indubitable as those of vitality ... there must go a great deal more of voluntary effort to this latter than is implied in the getting absolutely rid of it at once,

by adopting the direction of an infallible church, or private judgment of
another – for all our life is some form of religion, and all our action
some belief, and there is but one law, however modified, for the greater
and the less – In your case I do think you are called upon to do your
duty to yourself; that is, to God in the end ... Will it *not* be infinitely
harder to act so than to blindly adopt his pleasure, and die under it?
Who can *not* do that?   (*LRBEB*, I, 212–13; Sept. 25, 1845)

A few months later, Browning began to be visited by a repeated
dream, which is easy to read: 'I never *used* to dream unless indis-
posed, and rarely then – (of late I dream of you, but quite of late)
– and *those* nightmare dreams have invariably been of one sort –
I stand by (powerless to interpose by a word even) and see the inflic-
tion of tyranny on the unresisting – man or beast (generally the last)
– and I wake just in time not to die: let no one try this kind of experiment on me or mine!' (ibid., I, 399; Jan. 18, 1846). For himself,
'I should never be able to say "she shall dine on fish, or fruit," – "She
shall wear silk gloves or thread gloves" – even to exercise in fancy
that much "will over you" is revolting' (ibid., II, 815; June 26, 1846).

In *Men and Women* studies of tyranny are not prominent. Besides
A Woman's Last Word, there are *Life in a Love, A Light Woman,
Instans Tyrannus, The Heretic's Tragedy* (a far more lurid *Confessional*), *Mesmerism*, and the social tyranny touched on in *Respect-
ability*. But later come some of Browning's classic studies through the
characters of Caliban, Mr Sludge, Prince Hohenstiel-Schwangau,
Don Juan (indirectly), the mother of Miranda, and *Numpholeptos*.
The tyrant needs a victim, and often, as in *A Woman's Last Word*,
the victim interests Browning as much as his master. From the
enthralled speakers of *Time's Revenges* and *Numpholeptos* to the
gulled audiences of Mr Sludge, some part of the victim's self, more
or less conscious and controllable, betrays him.

Thus with the woman here, who, outwardly a pattern of submis-
sive wifeliness, hands flesh and spirit over to another. This is her last
word because she will henceforth 'speak thy speech, Love.' If this
means the end to contention and weeping, it also means the end
to striving as well as strife, Browning perhaps suggesting echoes of
his other uses of the word 'strive' in 'Let's contend no more, Love, /
Strive nor weep.' What the woman's husband is like, we have no
idea, except that he is apparently willing to accept her offer. How

conditional he has made his love on such an offer we do not know
either. But it is impossible to escape the ironic ring in the repeated
'and so fall asleep, *Love*, / *Loved* by thee' (italics mine).

The rhythm is one of the slowest in Browning; it is hard to read
the poem too slowly. The effect is of caught breath, and a subdued
sobbing seems to persist behind the calm words, a sobbing which
just breaks the surface at the end ('must a little weep, Love'). The
woman began by begging for an end to weeping but there is no end to
it in this direction. The images which occur to her are, first, bird
debate; second, a hunt, one creature stalking another; and third,
paradise. The change represents an advance in kind of life (animal
to human), but an increasing distance from the husband. From a
fellow-debater, the woman has changed to someone held by a god's
charm or an Eve with no decision to make. Between the two roles
comes the observation of one creature stalking another: it is not difficult to read the sequence.

What happens to enclosure imagery when bliss is attained may be
seen by looking at a contrasting poem, for enclosure imagery plays
a part in *By the Fireside*, the first enclosure being the nook mentioned
in the title. That Browning considered this domestic-hearth title
significant may be inferred from his use of it again in 1864 as title for
one of the *James Lee's Wife* poems. (Later, in *Two Poets of Croisic*,
he shows the kind of symbolic structure he can build on the fancies
thrown by a heart-fire.) In the first *By the Fireside*, the pleasures
of being shut in with memory are anticipated, as the present pleasure
of being shut in with Leonor is enjoyed. (The pleasure is like
that in *A Lovers' Quarrel*, with its winter ingle and its auspicious
November; it may be contrasted with the shunning of memory in
Andrea, *The Statue and the Bust*, and *A Woman's Last Word*.)
The *By the Fireside* speaker manipulates perspective, first projecting
himself into the future, then doubling back, his imaginary older self
moving back through memory to the present and to the precious past
and merging with his present self in contemplation of the present.
From home back to home: the movement is the circular one that Don
Juan nearly but not quite makes; but then he is never really inside
his house, never really a 'householder.' In *By the Fireside*, everything
radiates out from the central circle of husband, wife, and hearth-fire;
and this outward movement is the mark of the propitious love-affair
in Browning. Where the enclosure forces out or forces in, something

is wrong, and in *By the Fireside* walls are remarkably fluid. The walls of memory are tunnel-like, leading 'to a vista opening far and wide'; there appear to be two walls, 'the outside-frame, like your hazel-trees,' that is, inflexible; this may be the boundary of what happened. 'But the inside-archway widens fast': this is the wall shaped by the man who remembers, and it leads to a symbolic Italian scene. The scene proves to be that of the real union of husband and wife, the demolishing of 'the screen / So slight, so sure, 'twixt my love and her,' 'the mortal screen.' This barrier broken, no others remain: 'you, too, find without rebuff / Response your soul seeks many a time / Piercing its fine flesh-stuff.' Or in a metaphysical conceit: 'each is sucked / In each now: on, the new stream rolls.' In the moment of union, too, the world itself changes: the sharp details of the setting seem to become transparent; the world is seen as a stage. As in *Easter-Day* or *A Lovers' Quarrel*, its phenomena are so many properties, its walls hung with curtains. There is a sense of this even in 'the woods are round us, heaped and dim,' but later it is more explicit: 'hands unseen / Were hanging the night around us fast.' The following words, 'but we knew,' show that this hanging of night is also symbolic, the moment of union and the one star necessarily being followed by some separation and dusk; in this context, the light cast by the hearth-fire into the evening assumes significance. 'How the world is made for each of us,' adds the lover to 'the forests had done it'; the remark is meant literally (the world as forest-scene) and figuratively (the world which presents 'the moment'). But like Andrea, this speaker includes a new as well as an old world in his scheme of things. In both poems enclosure imagery appears – woman, house, world – and in both futures, enclosure imagery follows from what has gone before. Andrea sees the four great walls of the New Jerusalem, and in a burst of hope yearns for one for himself to paint, postponing his aspirations to the next world; then he subsides: 'So – still they overcome / Because there's still Lucrezia, –[6] as I choose.' In *By the Fireside* the speaker imagines a 'house not made with hands,' unlike his own literal house (and most unlike Andrea's solid-gold-mortared home, raised by the unhappy labour of his own hands). There he wishes only to continue his present bliss. In *The Statue and the Bust*, too, the future is read from the present. In *A Woman's Last Word*,

6 Cf. on the importance of punctuation, note 4, chapter 10

the woman attempts to pull some future paradise of peace and sleep into her present life; her concept of Eden and her use of it reflect her own pitiful need.

Woman, house, world: I have noted the use of these in *By the Fireside, Andrea,* and also *Fifine at the Fair.* Browning could use such enclosure images to take the weight of a whole poem, as in *A Serenade at the Villa. A Serenade* turns on these three enclosure images, which are arranged in three concentric circles. Outside all of them, because rejected by all, is the speaker, the serenader at the villa. First of the three is the world itself, which contains the second, the villa, which contains the third, the lady. Each of the three enclosures, with much resistance, sometimes pain, allows a tiny aperture to be forced through its wall and the least contact to be made with the outside – the outside of which the lover is the chief representative.

First is the world on an inauspicious night 'when there rose no moon at all' (the inversion emphasizes the negative), 'nor, to pierce the strained and tight / Tent of heaven, a planet small: / Life was dead and so was light.' A tent pierced by a ray of sun ('the canopy – [a streak / That pierced it, of the outside sun ...],' 'a sunbeam, that burst thro' the tent-roof') had been used by Browning in *Count Gismond* and *Saul* to mark out an arena for ordeal, the sun in both cases prophesying triumph. In *A Serenade* the whole sky is made a tent, pressing down on and suffocating the earth, and able to shut out light of any kind. The enclosing act makes of the earth a dead planet. Thus no night-life – fire-fly, glow-worm, cricket, or owl – makes a sight or sound; only the serenader's music breaks the silence. Under the heavy canopy the earth, not expired yet, 'turned in her sleep with pain,' as if protesting against the music. She 'sultrily suspired' and as if in answer to the rhythm of her breathing, 'in at heaven and out again, / Lightning! – where it broke the roof, / Bloodlike, some few drops of rain.' Like the serenader's lone song breaking the silence, the least rupture of the tight black universe is allowed. Literally, it is a hot sultry night, unable to clear the air with storm. But the few blood-like drops of rain suggest a stabbing lightning, wounding the body of the universe and adding to the cosmic pain. It recalls faintly the Old Testament plague of blood for rain. And it just suggests a sexual symbolism, the violation of an unwilling woman. (Whether this is deliberate or not, I do not know. The sexual symbolism is most appropriate to the poem, the lines are repeated

with variations in stanza ix, and similar symbolism is used in the
Ottima-Sebald scene of *Pippa Passes* with unmistakable sexual connotations. There the night also has a canopy [line 186] which descends
to press the lovers one against the other; the night is hot and humid
and portentous; the lightning, there no menace, repeatedly plunges
down to search out the lovers.[7])

In stanza iv the unfortunate serenader iterates a fraction of his
evening sentiment. 'O my love, my all, my one!' is the only invocation
allowed him, this serenade never being sung to the reader's ears nor
heard except as torment by the lady's. Browning enjoys reversing
what the reader might expect – in this case, because of the title, to
hear a serenade. By the end of stanza v, a new day is dawning with
pallid hemlock-flowers and numerous 'heavy hours' to pass; but
before dawn, 'I had passed away,' the double meaning again introducing death into the poem, along with the end of the serenader's
hopes. For some eight lines he can fancy a grateful or at least tolerant
reception to his song from inside the silent villa. Then the other
alternative takes over, and despite the speaker's fear of it ('Never
say ...'), it is more persuasive to him ('Never say – as something
bodes –'). This fancied reaction of the beloved lasts for nineteen
lines, and it picks up the nature imagery that the speaker's own observation had already found baleful. Now 'no moon succeeds the sun'
and to the verbs 'pierce' and 'broke' is added 'rent.' The few drops
are even more sinister than in the speaker's fancy; they 'show the
final storm begun,' and the repeated suggestion of death is deliberate,
as is seen by the lady's final lines, ' "Can't one even die in peace? /
As one shuts one's eyes on youth, / Is that face the last one sees?" '

Whether her death is literal or not, we do not know. Probably
not, but the ambiguity heightens the tension. A literal serenade
to a literal dying woman would be a trifle curious. What would the
lover's hopes be then? Or were they dashed by finding she was
dying? – or diminished into hoping his song assisted her ' "when life

7 Cf. the Pope in *The Ring and the Book*: 'As when a thundrous midnight,
  with black air / That burns, rain-drops that blister, breaks a spell, /
  Draws out the excessive virtue of some sheathed / Shut unsuspected
  flower that hoards and hides / Immensity of sweetness' (x, 1175-9). Here
  again, while the chief purpose is not to evoke it, the sexual symbolism is
  unmistakable, and appropriate to Pompilia's plight, the sexual complica-
  tions of which Browning does not ignore.

gropes / Feebly for the path where fell / Light last on the evening slopes" '? But the questions are inappropriate, death in some form attending the earth, the lover, and the lady that night. Her last lines explicitly mention death, bringing us back to the beginning of the poem where 'Life was dead and so was light.' The song is a violation of her peace, a 'plague,' beside which 'the taskmaster's curse' is preferable. The echoes are those of the Israelites' Egyptian bondage. They reinforce the rain-like-blood echo of stanza iii and suggest not only the burden of the mere serenade, but, faintly, its figurative likeness to some form of physical violation.

We end not with the earth's enclosure, with which the poem began, nor with the lady's complete rejection. At the end we return to the enclosure mentioned in the title, the villa, into whose grounds the lover has forced himself as the lightning forces its way through the tent of heaven, and the song to the lady's ears. But the villa is as inimical as earth or lady, and the lover now turns his attention unhappily to the strength of such enmity. The last stanza is a series of exclamatory sentences:

> Oh how dark your villa was,
>   Windows fast and obdurate!
> How the garden grudged me grass
>   Where I stood – the iron gate
> Ground its teeth to let me pass!

If the serenader's imagination is dramatic to the point of being over-wrought, still it carries the last stanza through effectively. The preceding verses have not given way to the exclamatory mood, and the imagery, while strong, is lightly handled. The poem can afford a *forte* ending, achieved by the hard *g*s and *r*s (a gr-r-r like the Spanish monk's sounds through line 3 and is picked up in the last line) ; by the iron of the gate, grinding like some frustrated Cerberus; by the darkness and fastness of the house, like that of the sky; by the rejection of the serenader by even the grass, the resistance of this pliable plant showing the lengths to which the enmity goes.

This is one of Browning's most effective uses of enclosure imagery, a use confined chiefly to the development of the three images themselves, and unrelated to any larger issue save whether the lady will love or not. The tone is of rejection without mitigation.

The poem represents a variation on the house imagery associated in *Men and Women* (usually considerably more happily) with the love lyrics. It also has something in common with *Childe Roland*. What is kept fanciful in this poem (the blight on earth, earth wounded, suggestions of death, the sinister dwelling) is given a dream-like reality in the other, with appropriate attending metaphysical validation. The tone of endurance rising to confrontation and climax is similar, but the battle here is never engaged and the tone hopeless.

A Lovers' Quarrel also uses images of house and world, the view of both also being determined by the lady. As in *A Serenade* lady and lover are separated and the two patterns pursued have certain similarities with important differences. This poem moves from dawn to an imagined, mystic midnight, not from sinister night to empty dawn. It moves, like *A Serenade*, from world to house, from nature to dwelling-place, with the difference here that nature is outwardly friendly and that the lover is inside the house. The sense of exclusion is as strong here as in *A Serenade*, but it is a former exclusion now longed for again in an exclusion which shut two people in a private place and kept out the outside world. If the high love of *By the Fireside* creates an exceptional harmony between lovers and the outside world, still Browning retains a sharp sense of the deliciousness of privacy: here its delights are recalled and anticipated; in the later *Never the Time and the Place* it is poignantly desired on any conditions. The quarrelling lover's house is not a *By the Fireside* dwelling, though it has affinities with that house. It centres on an 'ingle' with a fire (surely the 'ingle-glow' is both literal and figurative) and a man and woman. Its happy hour, in an anti-pastoral inversion, is also in the month that is the exact opposite from the conventional May–November. This union, too, enables the couple to read lessons from nature; at least, it is hinted that it might do so were it not at the moment broken: 'Each with a tale to tell / Could my Love but attend as well.' There is not here the perfect harmony with nature that the *By the Fireside* union bestowed; like the lovers' union, it is broken, but not very seriously. This lover, too, maintains his human independence and detachment from the rule of nature. Nature's springtime gifts he regards with irony (his beloved is absent) and impatience (they give his lady the support that would otherwise come from him). Natural beauty is, after all, only a hanging on the walls of a crypt.

Browning here plays with the images of house and world with a
whimsy that, like the speaker's own whimsy, is grounded in something
serious. The speaker first turns from the present delightful world
to the more delightful house of the past whose insulation and
independence from the world are stressed. But inside this enclosed
world are created vivid scenes, and, until the microcosm is pierced,
it can make fairy-tale worlds from the ingredients of the great world.
Like the *In a Gondola* lovers, these two show their excess of bliss
by playing games. With the arrow from the devil's bow, the lady
flees into the actual outside world. But this world, the lover pleads, is
really only another dwelling-place, in fact a crypt. Its spring beauties
are only 'hangings' on the walls of the crypt (the same image had
been used in *Easter-Day*, cf. p. 124 above; cf. also *By the Fireside*:
'hands unseen / Were hanging the night around us fast ...'). Let
November come, and the lady will see herself isolated in one cold
crypt, her lover in another: a November storm, a midnight, and
through the door, like a happy variation on the *Mesmerism* phantom,
she will return forever.

In the deliberate fairy-tale atmosphere created by the lovers'
high spirits, stanzas iv–x become a series of fantasies. The Emperor
takes to his 'gruesome side' a bride who 'powders her hair with gold'
and 'there they sit ermine-stoled.' The far-off Pampas is like a
picture-book; table-turning a game that turns into love-making, as
do the various play-acting poses. The inner world is filled with light
and colour and opulence, a defiance of winter and isolation. When
spring provides natural light and colour ('Oh, what a dawn of day!
... All is blue again') and opulence ('Heaps of the guelder-rose'),
the lover, alone, is not pleased. Outer desolation might renew the
old fantasy ('I would laugh like the valiant Thumb / Facing the
castle glum / And the giant's fee-faw-fum!'). The fairy-tale aura
is used consciously; we are not inside the tale as we are in *Childe
Roland*. This speaker is like the *Waring* speaker and his fantasies;
he approaches his love obliquely and without direct declaration.
Here we observe the lover seeing himself in past and future in
fairy-tale roles; seeing himself also, in the present, in the role of
'quarrelling lover.' It is this whimsical irony that disposes the reader
not to take the quarrel very seriously, for like many Browning poems
this one turns on not being quite what it says it is – or rather, on
being precisely what it says it is – a 'lovers' quarrel,' that is, a quarrel
modified by the noun which possesses it. A lovers' quarrel is not as

other people's: 'I have not had *every* love-luxury, I now find out ...
where is the proper, rationally to-be-expected – "*lovers' quarrel*?" '
(Browning to Elizabeth, *LRBEB*, 1, 262; Nov. 9, 1845). It is like
Browning to give this phrase as title to a lyric so much less quarrel-
some than more peaceably titled poems (*A Woman's Last Word,
Another Way of Love,* or *Andrea del Sarto,* which begins 'But do
not let us quarrel any more ...').[8]

The imagery here invites comparison with that of *Any Wife to
Any Husband,* for there, also, is a crypt. The lady, buried in such a
tomb, widowed that is, would shut the door on herself 'and sit, /
Seeing thy face on those four sides of it / The better that they are
so blank, I know!' But her husband in similar plight she fears would
seek some picture rather than 'a room's bare side'; or in nature
imagery, would kiss the 'hedge-rose-cup.' There is no eschewing
by him, as by the quarrelling lover, of wild roses. But of course
the quarrelling lover anticipates solace in his bare-walled prison.
Figurative death in the crypt of winter can easily be vanquished
with the right company. In the late, exquisite lyric *Never the
Time and the Place,* the same kind of association is used, but more
succinctly, and also more pointedly, death there being literal. Another
later lover also uses the simile of the bare-walled room; it is Don
Juan and he turns the figure to his own account. Like 'any husband'
he wants a Raphael (or Titian) for chief decoration of his room, but
also for diversion a few sketches; bare walls are not for him. At the
end of his poem, Don Juan resolves to enclose himself, in lines
reminiscent of the end of *A Lovers' Quarrel*: 'enter for good and all!
then fate bolt fast the door, / Shut you and me inside, never to wander
more!' Even the rhyme is the same.

In both *Men and Women* and the collected *Dramatic Lyrics, A
Lovers' Quarrel* follows *Love Among the Ruins,* and the difference
in attitudes toward the two beloveds is striking. Where the lovers are
separated, the man is possessed by thoughts of the woman. Where
the lover is on his way to a tryst, he does not reflect on the woman's

---

8 In *A Woman's Last Word,* the division between the couple is more like
   Elizabeth's associations with the phrase: 'Of such are "Lovers' quarrels"
   for the most part. The growth of power on one side .. & the struggle
   against it, by means legal & illegal, on the other' (*LRBEB*, II, 844; July 4,
   1846).

qualities at all. But this is because of the types of love represented. Once the quarrelling lovers are united, no exterior threat can reach them (it is a 'bubble born of breath,' not the winter wind, that disrupts their harmony). There is no need for a violent 'Shut them in' to exorcise the outer world. In *Love Among the Ruins,* 'rills' intersect and map out the hills, which otherwise would melt into 'undistinguished grey.' Here there are 'rillets,' but each has 'a tale to tell / Could my Love but attend as well.' As for grey, 'I'd as lief the blue were grey.' The imagined summer scene of *A Lovers' Quarrel* has affinities with the actual summer setting of *Love Among the Ruins.* Again there are 'miles and miles' of territory, but here 'miles and miles' of gold *and* green. Gold and green do not combat each other, with the green consuming the gold; for the gold is all natural – the sheen on the Pampas, the solid glow of sunflowers (not parasitic vines climbing over turrets, but independent sun-suffused plants). The animal in this landscape is not the sheep, but a wild horse who, instead of some lone ruined turret, breaks the miles and miles of grass; he leaps as in *Love Among the Ruins* only the buildings of the dead city leap. Such a vital, alive nature the two quarrelling lovers, when in harmony, could imagine, as in *By the Fireside* the two lovers could see.

Browning, in writing to Elizabeth, uses more than once the image of the private, magic room. It was a room literal as well as figurative for him: 'as for the room, the dearest four walls that I ever have been enclosed by ...' (*LRBEB*, II, 944; Aug. 7, 1846). In his first letter to Elizabeth, Browning had pictured her in a remote room: 'I feel as at some untoward passage in my travels – as if I had been close, so close, to some world's-wonder in chapel or crypt [i.e., to seeing Elizabeth], only a screen to push and I might have entered, but there was some slight ... and just-sufficient bar to admission ...' (ibid., I, 3–4; Jan. 10, 1845).[9] He uses an Arabian Nights variation on the figure in his proposal to Elizabeth: 'Will it help me to say that once in this Aladdin-cavern I knew I ought to stop for no heaps of jewel-fruit

---

9 Elizabeth replied rather timidly and with her usual defensive diffidence to Browning's less than felicitous second image: 'BUT .. you know .. if you had entered the "crypt," you might have caught cold, or been tired to death' (*LRBEB*, I, 5; Jan. 11, 1845). In the next letter Browning changed the figure to 'my Chapel-sight' (ibid., I, 7; Jan. 13, 1845).

on the trees from the very beginning, but go on to the lamp, *the* prize, the last and best of all?' (ibid., 1, 197; Sept. 16, 1845). He had already spoken in a like image of the delight inherent in the comparative secrecy of their visits:

> Indeed, tho' on other grounds I should be all so proud of being known for your friend by everybody, yet there's no denying the deep delight of playing the Eastern Jew's part here in this London – they go about, you know by travel-books, with the tokens of extreme destitution & misery, and steal by blind ways & by-paths to some blank dreary house, one obscure door in it – which being well shut behind them, they grope on thro' a dark corridor or so, and then, a blaze follows the lifting a curtain or the like, for they are in a palace-hall with fountains and light, and marble and gold, of which the envious are never to dream!
> (*LRBEB*, 1, 118; July 9, 1845)

Artist as well as lover has his private place. It was as a poet that Browning told Elizabeth he could retire from the reviewers' blows to 'a garden-full of rose-trees, and a soul-full of comforts' (ibid., 1, 18; Feb. 11, 1845). The poet of *How It Strikes a Contemporary* retires to a neat, frugal house, observable (like Browning's own poetic dwelling in *House*) through the window. The 'Eastern Jew's part' is eschewed by him:

> I found no truth in one report at least –
> That if you tracked him to his home, down lanes
> Beyond the Jewry, and as clean to pace,
> You found he ate his supper in a room
> Blazing with lights, four Titians on the wall,
> And twenty naked girls to change his plate!

Later, in the *Parleying with Smart*, the poet's inspired production is a chapel the reader may enter, and the language is reminiscent of Browning's first letter to Elizabeth: 'On and on I went ... Till lo, I push a door, sudden uplift / A hanging, enter, chance upon a shift / Indeed of scene! ... It was the Chapel' (30–6; cf. in the quotations above, 'only a screen to push,' 'a blaze follows the lifting a curtain or the like,' 'a chapel or crypt').

Of course the door that shuts in can also shut out. What is frustration in 'only a screen to push and I might have entered' is anguish in the shut door of *A Serenade*. When Browning dreamt during his courtship of losing Elizabeth through her death, he dreamt of a closed door in her poetry:

> I woke – late, or early – and, in one of those lucid moments when all things are thoroughly *perceived*,[10] ... seem to *apprehend*, comprehend entirely, for the first time, what would happen if I lost you – the whole sense of that *closed door* of Catarina's came on me at once, and it was *I* who said – not as quoting or adapting another's words, but spontaneously, unavoidably, '*In that door, you will not enter, I have*'[11] ..
> And, dearest, the
> Unwritten it must remain.   (*LRBEB*, I, 410; Jan. 22, 1846)

In a late poem, *Bad Dreams* II, a lover visits 'a chapel, says / My memory or betrays – / Closet-like, kept aloof ...' What makes the dream a nightmare is that, in such a setting and as horror-struck as Hawthorne's Goodman Brown, the lover witnesses his beloved in a demonic rite.

I have pursued the imagery of enclosure in several *Men and Women* lyrics of varying tone and theme. None is difficult to comprehend without examining this imagery or comparing it with that of other poems. But in the pair *Love in a Life* and *Life in a Love* Browning works almost solely with images of enclosure. We can approach these poems with some assurance, I think, only if we have in mind something of the background I have sketched above.

The two poems consist of one of those exercises in ingenious inversion of which Browning was so fond. Both are hunts, the first after a lady never sighted, the second a chase, and the difference is important. The first is a hunt through a house, the second unspecified in setting. The first has a dream-like persuasiveness: the single-minded search, the lady always going out as the seeker enters, the evidence of her recent presence (a magic evidence: cornice-wreaths

---

10   Cf. the remarks on the use of the word perception, pp. 33, 41, 112–13
11   'On the door you will not enter, / I have gazed too long: adieu! / Hope withdraws her peradventure; / Death is near me, – and not *you*' (*Catarina to Camoens*, 1–4). The last line is one of Elizabeth's unintentional ambiguities.

re-blossom, mirrors gleam without a direct image), the mounting pressure to find her because the day is waning, the sense that she never will be found. The tension is like that of other dream-like pursuits in *Men and Women,* the endeavour to seize something from the whirl of *Women and Roses,* the whole day spent in the quest like Childe Roland's dream-like day.

Browning's use of the house image is most effective. Speaker and lady inhabit the house together, and her presence is apparent. The house sets bounds to the search, yet the lady, like some ghost, cannot be located. The possibility of a deserted dwelling, never to be in-habited by flesh and blood haunts the poem. (In the most blissful of *Men and Women* love poems, *By the Fireside,* present pleasure comes from sitting silently indoors with the lady; she may be contemplated at any moment.) The house image is here the house of life as a dwelling for love (love in a life). The companion-poem inverts the image: love becomes the would-be encloser of life as 'I ... the loving' pursue 'you the loth.' (Cf. the like concept of 'art in a life' and 'life in an art' as applied to Sordello and Eglamor.) The relation of inside to outside is not what matters, as with the play on confinement and freedom in *Pauline,* or the 'old blind wall' in the *Prologue* to *Pacchiarotto.* Or, for that matter, in *Life in a Love,* where the question is one of escape versus seizure (the poem opens abruptly with 'Escape me? / Never –'). *Love in a Life* is a quest, not a chase. The problem is not that the lady abhors her lover: otherwise she could leave the house for the outdoors like the lady of her companion-poem, and otherwise her presence would hardly cause a cornice-wreath to blossom. The problem is that, like the lady of *Two in the Campagna,* she is elusive. ('Par ces derniers mots et la détente qu'ils me pro-curèrent, Swann supprima brusquement pour moi une de ces affreuses distances intérieures au terme desquelles une femme que nous aimons nous apparaît si lointaine.') The frightening thing here ('Heart, fear nothing, for heart, thou shalt find her –') – as in *Two in the Campagna* it is painful – is that necessity seems to decree the separate-ness, strive as love will.

The imagery of the house of life[12] as a house for lovers is used in the Barrett-Browning letters, the figure being introduced early in the

---

12 The figure itself is common; Elizabeth, for instance, makes use of it in sonnets iv and vi of *Sonnets from the Portuguese.*

correspondence by Elizabeth: 'Oh – this life, this life! There is comfort in it, they say, & I almost believe – but the brightest place in the house, is the leaning out of the window! – at least, for me'[13] (*LRBEB*, I, 31; Feb. 27, 1845). Browning was quick to respond: 'And pray you not to "lean out of the window" when my own foot is only on the stair – do wait a little for / Yours EVER, / R.B.' (ibid., I, 33; Mar. 1, 1845). Elizabeth continues with the figure in the next letter: 'Yes! I am satisfied to "take up" with the blind hopes[14] again, & have them in the house with me, for all that I sit by the window' (ibid., I, 34; Mar. 5, 1845). Browning this time picked up the image to reassure Elizabeth indirectly of his devotion to her: 'Of what use is talking? Only, do you stay here with me in the "House" these few short years' (ibid., I, 39; Mar. 11, 1845). But like other images, this one takes a happier turn when love is declared. Elizabeth's next use of the window is no longer sinister: 'Yet I have been idle lately, I confess, – leaning half out of some turret-window of the castle of Indolence & watching the new sunrise' (ibid., I, 263; Nov. 10, 1845). When a threat occurs, the image reverts to its sinister usage: 'Take away the motive .. & I am where I was – leaning out of the window again' (Elizabeth to Browning, ibid., I, 385; Jan. 13, 1846). But Browning soon rehabilitates and expands the image, using it in a fashion much closer to that in *Love in a Life*: 'I fancy myself meeting you on "the stairs" – and passages generally, and galleries (ah, those indeed! –) all, with their picturesque *accidents*, of landing-places, and spiral heights & depths, and sudden turns and visions of half open doors into what Quarles calls "mollitious chambers" – and above all, *landing-places* – they are my heart's delight – I would come upon you unaware on a landing-place in my next dream!' (ibid., I, 404; Jan. 19, 1846). The sense of accident pleases Browning in such a fancy, probably especially because he had no chance of encountering Elizabeth unexpectedly. The image is inverted in *Love in a Life*,

---

13 There had once been a literal danger in such a pose: 'We have had one chimney pulled down to prevent it from tumbling down; and have received especial injunction from the brick-layers not to lean too much out of the windows, for fear the walls should follow the destiny of the chimney' (*LEB*, I, 22; Sept. 7, 1833).

14 They were discussing *Prometheus*; Elizabeth's translation contained the line (250), 'I set blind hopes to inhabit in their house,' Prometheus' way of preventing mortals from premeditating death.

where the lover wants only to behold his mistress, but cannot. A sure assignment would please him, for in his house there seem to be no unexpected meetings, so that his sense of expectation threatens to deteriorate into panic.

An even more striking use is in a letter of April 6, 1846: 'Oh, how different it all *might* be! In this House of Life – where I go, you go, – where I ascend you run before, – where I descend, it is after you. Now, one might have a *piece* of Ba, but a very little of her, and make it up into a Lady and a Mistress, and find her a room ... and visit her there ... and then, – after a time, leave her there ... and go whither one liked – after, to me, the most melancholy fashion in the world' (ibid., II, 591–2). The action here is very like that in *Love in a Life*, except that in the poem the lady has fatally outdistanced her lover. And the possible contrast is not unlike that of *Life in a Love*. There too if the pursuer captured his lady he would have to cage her; if they shared a house freely, she would be out the door at the first opportunity. (The parallel is not at all exact, Browning's alternative in his letter being unlikely to devote a life to finding a bird for his cage.[15])

In this pair of lyrics Browning works out the dream-like threats latent in his figure of the pursuit. The pursuit is good, it is true, but some end to it is ardently desired, as it is also in *Childe Roland, Women and Roses*, and *Two in the Campagna*. The long pursuit in Browning frequently brings torment and weariness and above all the fear of perpetuity. In *Easter-Day* such a fear is dreamt to be real, and the speaker falls into despair. *Easter-Day* and Browning's quest poems and the potential sinister use of enclosure imagery should be kept in mind before we agree with DeVane that Browning advocated flexing moral muscles for the sake of exercise alone.[16] Even these two poems raise questions about such a theory. The two actions are

15 Later Elizabeth played with the image too, sometimes echoing Browning's usage: 'A long rambling letter, with nothing in it! – "Passages, that lead to nothing" – & staircases, too!' (*LRBEB*, II, 791; June 16, 1846). 'And now I am going to dream of you .. to meet you on some mystical landing place' (ibid., II, 813; June 23, 1846). 'If you heard me say "Robert," it was on a stair-landing in the House of Dreams – never anywhere else!' (ibid., II, 831; July 1, 1846).
16 DeVane, *Browning's Parleyings: The Autobiography of a Mind* (New Haven, 1927), 189: 'This building of moral muscle for no particular end ... is a characteristic conception of Browning's ...'

equally energetic and persistent; it is the goals that make the difference.

Browning here shows a fine apprehension of the dangers of intimacy – in the first poem to oneself, in the second to the lady. The dilemma is that the lover must pursue his lady in order to find her, yet she must be left free to wander. Otherwise, the quest deteriorates to a chase, an effort to trap her and stop all her movement. Somehow a balance must be found between separation and intrusion. The question is how to be close to the lady without inhibiting her; how to stand away so as not to smother her, yet not to lose her either; how to prevent the symbolic house from becoming either an empty shell or a cage.

Some of Browning's best-known lyrics in *Men and Women* remain, despite their prominence, enigmatic and disputed to some degree. The foregoing discussion may be useful for them too. For example, *Two in the Campagna* turns, it seems to me, on the several types of enclosure imagery: the closed circle of a naturalistic world; the infinite whirl of the 'romantic'; and the break from both kinds of enclosure granted by the 'fixing' of a friendly star.

Two in the Campagna like *Women and Roses* touches the limits of will and action. The two in the campagna begin as two and end as two, despite the effort of one. They remain in the plight described in *By the Fireside*: 'If two lives join, there is oft a scar, / They are one and one, with a shadowy third; / One near one is too far.' It is a little hard on the speaker to blame him for wanting too much, for not trusting the evidence of the 'good minute.' His good minute shows no signs of transforming itself into a 'moment one and infinite,' though he yearns as much as the *By the Fireside* lover for the absent magic:

> I would that you were all to me,
>   You that are just so much, no more.
> Nor yours nor mine, nor slave nor free!
>   Where does the fault lie? What the core
> O' the wound, since wound must be?
>
> I would I could adopt your will,
>   See with your eyes, and set my heart
> Beating by yours, and drink my fill
>   At your soul's springs, – your part my part
> In life, for good and all.
>
> No ...

In the other poem, this is precisely what has been attained:

> You must be just before, in fine,
>   See and make me see, for your part,
> New depths of the divine!

> But who could have expected this
>   When we two drew together first
> Just for the obvious human bliss,
>   To satisfy life's daily thirst
> With a thing men seldom miss?

The *Two in the Campagna* speaker is prepared to explore and to probe the core of the wound, but he always gets only so far. He is direct enough ('I wonder do you feel today') and honest enough, but to no avail.

It is of no avail despite the setting, which looks propitious: 'this morn of Rome and May.' The time and the place and the loved one do seem all together ('This path – how soft to pace! / This May – what perfect weather!'). Rome may be an ambivalent symbol, to be sure. And there is no path apparent; in any case the lovers are sitting and their spirits are doing the walking for them. They have sat for this purpose, and there Browning leaves them at the end as at the beginning: they have gone nowhere. Nor does the spirit get very far. Nearby a path is clear enough, like the tantalizing spider-thread running from fennel to weed; but from there 'everywhere on the grassy slope / I traced it.' And there is a good deal of slope. Like the *Love Among the Ruins* miles and miles of flourishing pastureland, there stretches the 'champaign with its endless fleece / Of feathery grasses everywhere.' Not even a tower breaks the horizon; disturbing ruin though it be, it would offer a goal toward which the lovers could aim their steps.

The tantalizing thought is simply 'why' – 'where does the fault lie?' It appears also to be something of a confession: 'Let us be unashamed of soul ... How is it under our control / To love or not to love?' In an image suggesting sensuality ('as earth lies bare to heaven above'), the lover is proposing a different unveiling than that of the body ('let us be unashamed of soul'). He does his best, he says; he wishes for the complete union of spirit; he knows the good minute but after the closeness he stands away. The minute does not seem fit to declare itself as in *By the Fireside* by giving validity to what has gone before and what will come after. There is no mysterious breaking through the mask of nature, no glimpse of her forces converging for some special purpose, as in *By the Fireside* and *Saul*. The natural world here is closer to the natural world in *Love Among the Ruins*: it offers a flourishing life of its own, but the speaker does not belong to it, and the flourishing seems to mock him. 'Mock' is too strong a word here; this speaker is not given to the uncomplicated sarcasms of the shepherd; what mocks him is his own thinking, the spider-webs. If nature does so, it is indirectly, by allowing her denizens the completion and satisfaction denied to him.

It is common for Browning to assert that the things of nature find their completion here on earth, as does man's body, but that man's spirit is incomplete at death. The natural cycle pursues and repeats one pattern (birth, youth, maturity, age, death) as does the physical man. The rest of man does not develop, live, and perish after this pattern, and from this Browning draws his own inferences. It is common for Browning, too, to signify the closed circle of the natural cycle by an enclosure in which some animal spends his days and fulfils his purpose, nose to ground. The variation on that figure here is one small orange flower-cup in which five beetles grope for their honey, feed, and refresh themselves as the lover is unable to refresh himself at the springs of his beloved. They are blind; they have no need to see or explore beyond their womb-like shelter. They live in a static universe like that inhabited by the three Fates in *Apollo and the Fates*, the Fates who also live on honey in their dark cavern. They do not even see the picture they themselves make, green, in an orange cup, near yellowing fennel, against the background of endless feathery grasses. The fennel too is working through her cycle and has now come to her seed-time. Together the scene makes up a springtime world of gold and green, like the Pampas imagined all gold and green in *A Lovers' Quarrel*.

It is a temptation to slip into such a world of 'silence and passion, joy and peace' and 'let nature have her way / While heaven looks from its towers.' Here the speaker is too intent on holding fast his tantalizing thread of thought to do so, but there is an appealing mood of surrender in stanza v, where the light wind that capriciously drives the thistleball at the end is regarded very differently as 'an everlasting

wash of air – Rome's ghost since her decease.' The air here sounds as
tempting as the washing sea to the Amphibian or to Don Juan; it
rolls across the earth, which here lies bare to heaven above, as in
'Amphibian' the sea and sky face each other with only swimmer and
butterfly between. To submit to the watery element 'while heaven
looks from its towers' is less painful than yearning after a lodestar in
that same heaven. To slip into the world of gold and green is easier
than plucking[1] a rose, loving it, and seeing the good minute go.

> Such life here, through such lengths of hours,
>   Such miracles performed in play,
> Such primal naked forms of flowers,
>   Such letting nature have her way
> While heaven looks from its towers!

Here is the natural cycle seen in action and at its most attractive: in
'silence and passion, joy and peace,' in colour, in due fruitful cycle.
There would be great peace in resigning the love-affair to what seems
inevitable instead of yearning after something more. For a moment
the lover sounds as if he is going to do this, as if the poem is going to
be a confession of accepted inadequacy. 'Such letting nature have her
way ... How is it under our control ...? I would that you were all
to me ... I would I could adopt your will ... No.' The speaker does not
for long surrender to this mood. What he ends with finally is pain,
not the acquiescence of letting nature have her way. The naturalist
reaction would be to feed on his rose as the beetles feed on honey-
meal. But the beetles are blind, and this speaker intent on perceiving
clearly.

What he sees clearly at hand and follows as far as his eye will go
is a maze of spider-threads. His problem is to grasp and pursue it.
I assume the spider-threads indicate a 'tantalizing' thought-pattern
of the speaker's own. It has been a persistent, bothersome thread, and
a mocking one – mocking partly because it sticks so closely without
being firm, partly because it breaks when grasped. When the speaker

---

1 The verb is common with *Men and Women* roses; cf. remarks on *Women
and Roses*, and Browning's 'these last please you, serve you best when
plucked – and "my life's rose" ...' (quoted note 8, chapter 11).

does sit down to concentrate on pursuing it, he gets only so far: it is as if his conscious articulate mind takes him only a short distance through the thought-pattern; then he loses touch. Touch, rather than sight, is the image used here. The kind of thought is that which may be felt ('for me, I touched a thought ...'). The speaker makes contact too with the woman who is the occasion of the thought ('hand in hand,' 'I kiss your cheek'); 'then (I) stand away.' The lovers are apart, the thread is gone too, the three now being separate after once being together ('hand in hand ... Help me to hold it'). The thread is 'off again! / The old trick!' The speaker may have tried tracing it before, or he may now see that the result of pursuing it is the same as breaking through it: the thread remains elusive.

The problem is that the spider-thoughts lead only so far before they come to unanswerable questions. 'What the core o' the wound?' Then they are found to break. What happens in the interval between first exploration and the discovery of the limits of thought is a different kind of movement. Instead of following the horizontal web, 'I yearn upward.' No vindication follows, and by the end the speaker's second plight seems worse than his first.

In *A Blot in the 'Scutcheon* a spider-web is made to indicate the connections between two people:

> Each day, each hour throws forth its silk-slight film
> Between the being tied to you by birth,
> And you, until those slender threads compose
> A web that shrouds her daily life of hopes
> And fears and fancies, all her life, from yours:
> So close you live and yet so far apart!
> And must I rend this web ...
> That makes her sacred?   (II, i, 195–203)

In *Two in the Campagna*, the two people are also hidden from each other, but if this makes the lady sacred it is not appropriate for the lover as it may be for the brother. The lover wishes to trace the slender threads, but like his connection with the lady, after a certain time they always break off. His threads do not make an orderly web. Nor do they seem spun anonymously by time, like those in *A Blot*, but associated with thought and mockery, and with something traceable

and understandable if not controllable. Like the lover of *Love in a
Life* and the lover and artist of *Women and Roses*, he seeks diligently,
humbly and passionately for what seems not too difficult to find, yet
always eludes. The inevitability of the 'old trick' repeating itself is
alike in all three poems. As long as the *Two in the Campagna* speaker
simply observes the threads, not caring whether they shroud, giving
himself to the moment as the grasses to the wind, he is all right. It is
when he breaks the horizontal line and passive mood that trouble
begins. 'Help me to hold it ... probe the core ... I yearn upward.' Then
the connection seems to snap and he is not even like the grass, waving
in the wind yet also rooted (like the gypsies' frenetic flag in *Fifine*);
not even holding a 'floating weft,' which, though partly subject to the
vagaries of the wind, is attached to plants. He becomes altogether a
disconnected thing, a thistleball.

What has happened? Does the thread seem to transform itself
into an altogether passive thistleball? – the speaker's thoughts seem
to scatter into random pieces, conditioned by whatever force blows
them one way or another? Did the speaker turn from thought to
action in yet another effort to have action clarify thought, and then
find that neither thought nor action seemed to lead beyond itself?
Both, probably. The change from spider-silk to thistle-down is an
unhappy one.[2] The speaker is now associated with plant fibres, part of
nature's reproductive cycle, rather than something spun by an agent.
He seems to himself by force and no longer by choice a passive plaything of circumstance. The whims of any light wind can now scud
him like froth or bubble along the endless grass. (Browning uses
thistleball and seafroth and bubble figures for the passive and the

2 Other associations are also unfelicitous. Browning makes the contrast with
roses in *The Inn Album*: 'nor means / To stop and munch one thistle in
this life / Till next life smother him with roses' (2528–30). Cf. the curse in
Genesis: 'Thorns also and thistles shall it bring forth to thee.' Cf. also
Elizabeth Barrett: 'If you are forced to refer me to those long ears, I must
deserve the thistles besides. The thistles are the corollary' (*LRBEB*, I, 338;
Dec. 21, 1845); 'it would be dreadful to suffer these miseries to sow
themselves about the world, like so much thistle-down .. the world, where
there are thistles enough already, to make fodder for its wild asses' (ibid.,
II, 856; July 7, 1846); or on how Romney is not 'responsible for all the
thistles blown on earth' (*Aurora Leigh*, 728).

ephemeral elsewhere.[3]) The thread is gone and there remains
only pain.

It is worth asking at this point whether tracing the spider-thoughts
would lead the speaker anywhere after all. He must begin with them;
they are all that he has to guide him in the pathless scene. But
frustration seems bound to attend his effort. The threads are 'everywhere,' that is, they constitute an infinite, but an infinite of eternal
extension, something different from the 'infinite passion' of the
last stanza. The effort to trace and connect the threads resembles
Don Juan's attempt to connect an infinite number of points into an
earthly circle. Similarly the yearning toward a friendly star, the connecting of an earthly point with a celestial, is precisely Don Juan's
image of aspiration toward a metaphysical infinite. It is dangerous to
read back some sixteen years from *Fifine*, but I have already noted
a similar pattern in earlier poetry. The problem here is not at all the
same as in *Fifine*, of course. This speaker does not eschew vertical
movement in order to pursue the horizontal on and on. Perhaps this is
all to the good.

'Where does the fault lie? What the core / O' the wound, since
wound must be?' No answer is given. In *By the Fireside*, the lady, who
might have left the screen, the shadowy third, between the two
lovers, makes the decisive motion that unites them. There is no indication here that the lady could do something about this plight: she
remains a rather shadowy second, motionless and speechless as far as
we know. She receives a kiss (I suppose it is not just recollection:
'already how am I so far / Out of that minute?'), but no response is

3 Cf.:
                    ... the demagogue,
      (Noisome air-bubble, buoyed up, borne along
      By kindred breath of knave and fool below,
      Whose hearts swell proudly as each puffing face
      Grows big, reflected in that glassy ball,
      Vacuity, just bellied out to break
      And righteously bespatter friends the first) ...
      (*Aristophanes' Apology*, 1695–1701)

Or:
      And yet esteem the silken company
      So much sky-scud, sea-froth, earth-thistledown.   (ibid., 918–19)

indicated. Surmises about her only lead away from the poem and its emphasis in the last stanza on pain and yearning. This is a knocking on the gate of heaven for a sign of grace, and why it does not come no one knows.

Yet the knocker persists. He knows something of the rose and reaches for the star; 'you may / Master the heavens before you study earth, / Make you familiar with the meteor's birth / Ere you descend to scrutinize the rose! / I say ... learn earth first ere presume / To teach heaven legislation' (*Parleying with Smart*, 241–56). This quotation is from a parleying with a poet, but presumably the same order of priorities applies to the lover.[4] For Caponsacchi longs for the 'small experiences of every day, / Concerns of the particular hearth and home: / To learn not only by a comet's rush / But a rose's birth, – not by the grandeur, God – / But the comfort, Christ' (2092–6). (Meteor and comet move and vanish, of course, unlike the steady star. But compare the remarks below on *My Star*.) This lover has begun well enough; but how is he to continue?

There is in the poem another kind of image which is neither enclosed circle nor endless horizontal extension, neither nature's force nor man's conscious ingenious thought; yet which is like both and touched by both. It is the image of the broken enclosure, and hence like the final alternative in *Paracelsus* and *Fifine*, and also like the vertical movement at the end of this poem. It is a delicate matter even to suggest that it functions in such a way, and it is worth repeating that this is a love poem, not a tract. Yet there are two shelters at the beginning, close to each other; they are womb-like flower-cup and a grave: 'it[the spider-thread] left / The yellowing fennel ... branching from the brickwork's cleft, / Some old tomb's ruin: yonder weed / Took up the floating weft.' It may be that only the grave will put an end to the aimless wind-driven wandering of the last stanza, and that among men only ghosts can live in 'silence and passion, joy and peace.' But the ghosts do not inhabit the shelter, whose purpose appears already served. Life, in fact, grows out of the house of death, with fennel 'branching from the brickwork's cleft.' It is as if nature

4 The personal and the creative are connected very briefly in an echo in *Two in the Campagna*: 'Catch your soul's warmth ... then the good minute goes'; 'for rhymes / To catch at and let go.'

had done her work, split the tomb and allowed the ghosts their freedom.

It seems scarcely an accident that Browning juxtaposes the two images of the closed, cyclical life of nature and the open-ended life of man in this poem which turns on the finite and the infinite. The juxtaposition is delicate: it has not the marked contrivance of the contrast (with a difference) in *Love Among the Ruins*. But it is definite and meant, I think, to suggest the difference Browning often saw between the two patterns. Compare, for example, with the blind beetle passage these lines from *Red Cotton Night-Cap Country*. Browning is speaking, in his own person, of Clara:

> With this proviso, let me study her
> Approvingly, the finished little piece!
> Born, bred, with just one instinct, – that of growth, –
> Her quality was, caterpillar-like,
> To all-unerringly select a leaf
> And without intermission feed her fill ...
> And 't is a sign (say entomologists)
> Of sickness, when the creature stops its meal
> One minute, either to look up at heaven,
> Or turn aside for change of aliment.   (4034–45)

The beetles to their meal then, and the lover to the pain of his yearning. The word is a forceful one: it is used twice here. It also appears in 'O Lyric Love' where Browning himself yearns upward 'thither where eyes, that cannot reach, yet yearn / For all hope,' and in *Sordello*:

> Next Age or no? Shall its Sordello try
> Clue after clue, and catch at last the clue
> I miss? – that's underneath my finger too,
> Twice, thrice a day, perhaps, – some yearning traced
> Deeper, some petty consequence embraced
> Closer!   (iii, 182–7)

But it is *Easter-Day*, which precedes this poem by at least five years, and which is an elaboration of the implications of the cleft tomb, that offers the speaker promise,

                their inheritance
Who chose the spirit's fugitive
Brief gleams, and yearned, 'This were to live
Indeed, if rays, completely pure
From flesh that dulls them could endure, –
Not shoot in meteor-light athwart
Our earth, to show how cold and swart
It lies beneath their fire, but stand
As stars do, destined to expand,
Prove veritable worlds, our home!'   (683–92)

The cleft tomb will be used much later by Browning in his
Parleying with Gerard de Lairesse. There the word used is sepulchre,
and as if that does not imply resurrection strongly enough, Browning
drives the point home:

             ... us ignobly common-sensed,
Purblind, while plain could proper optics view
In that old sepulchre by lightning split,
Whereof the lid bore carven, – any dolt
Imagine why, – Jove's very thunderbolt.   (69–73)

In *Two in the Campagna* there is no such obvious statement: the
ruined tomb with the cleft in which fennel can grow may hint at this
kind of association, but only obliquely. Yet the hint may be clear
enough, if oblique. Consider again the setting, the Campagna,

              that Rome
Out in the champaign, say, o'er-rioted
By verdure, ravage, and gay winds that war
Against strong sunshine settled to his sleep.
(*Red Cotton Night-Cap Country*, 3–6)

The Campagna, with its ruins, and its rolling grassland and sun and
wind, seemed to many possessed of its own haunting life:

It [the Campagna] was so bright & yet so sad, so still & yet so
charged, to the supersensuous ear, with the murmur of an
extinguished life, that you could only say that it was intensely

and adorably strange, could only impute to the whole overarched
scene an unsurpassed secret for bringing tears of appreciation
to no matter how ignorant – archaeologically ignorant – eyes.[5]

Harriet Hosmer, who accompanied the Brownings on some Campagna excursions, writes how its 'gentle undulations – as if nature, by
a sudden fantasy, had resolved her sea-green waves into sea-green
sward – recall that dim age when this portion of our planet, so rich
in human events, was still unprepared for the food of man.'[6] And
Browning must have meant to recall the old Rome: otherwise, how
explain that curious line 'Rome's ghost since her decease'? Rome was
not deceased then, nor is she now. The only deceased Rome was
classical Rome – and Browning associated classicism with a static,
enclosed, finished universe.[7]

But the Campagna is on the edge of the living Rome, the living
Rome of whose presence 'Rome's ghost since her decease' must also
remind us. Rome is a many-sided symbol, 'Rome – at once the Paradise, / The grave, the city, and the wilderness,' as Shelley has it.
Or Pope:

> See the wild waste of all-devouring years,
> How Rome her own sad sepulchre appears,
> With nodding arches, broken temples spread,
> The very tombs now vanish'd like their dead.

From the Campagna could be seen evidence of the living Rome.
'When from far off on the Campagna you see the colossal images of
the mitred saints along the top standing distinct against the sky, you
forget their coarse construction and their inflated draperies.'[8]
Elizabeth Barrett Browning, from the same distance, saw doctrine:

5 Henry James, 'Roman Rides' (1873), in his *Italian Hours* (Boston and
   New York, 1909), 218
6 *Letters and Memories*, ed. Cornelia Carr (New York, 1912), 110
7   The dead Greek lore lies buried in the urn
       Where who seeks fire finds ashes. Ghost, forsooth!
       What was the best Greece babbled of as truth?
       'A shade, a wretched nothing –'
       (*Parleying with Gerard de Lairesse*, 392–5)
8 Henry James, *Italian Hours*, 204

Over the dumb Campagna-sea,
  Out in the offing through mist and rain,
Saint Peter's Church heaves silently
  Like a mighty ship in pain,
  Facing the tempest with struggle and strain.
(*A View across the Roman Campagna*, 1861)

The Campagna, for those who knew it, may have suggested a contrast between classical and Christian.[9] For those who did not know the Campagna, the hint of such a contrast is in the poem. Classicism and Christianity, deceased Rome and living Rome, dead nature and living nature, the old tomb and the ruined tomb – Rome and May – but what Rome and what May?

Here a word of caution is again necessary: this is decidedly not a poem about classicism and Christianity. On the other hand, Browning gently insists on the background, and it is hard to avoid the implicit contrast, and not to relate it to the two contrasting responses of disappointed love. Browning's setting seems to me like those Renaissance paintings Panofsky describes (and Browning was steeped in Renaissance painting and iconography), where 'classical sarcophagi and ruins are shown in a Nativity.'[10] And Tischbein had, in 1787, painted a portrait of Goethe in the Campagna, with Goethe, contemplative, surrounded by broken stone carvings over which ivy grows.

But meanwhile no friendly star opens in *Easter-Day* fashion for this speaker. No doubt he should infer a pledge from his scattered good minutes. (One sprig of fennel is pledge of a whole fieldful, and of victory besides, in *Pheidippides*.[11]) But the reader cannot help

9 'Jean Paul had said that "the origin and character of the whole of modern poetry can be derived so easily from Christianity, that one could call romantic poetry just as well Christian," and had proceeded to contrast the sensuous finite world of antiquity with the spiritual infinity of Christianity' (René Wellek, *Confrontations: Studies in the Intellectual and Literary Relations between Germany, England, and the United States during the Nineteenth Century* [Princeton, 1965], 129.

10 Edwin Panofsky, *Studies in Iconology: Humanistic Themes in the Art of the Renaissance* (New York, 1962, first published 1939), 70

11 Though the traditional association is with flattery and deceit; see G.L. Kittredge, ed., *Hamlet* (Boston, 1939), note to IV, v, 180. Still, Browning

feeling for him, especially if in the dancing ring of Browning's men and women, he has met the speaker of *By the Fireside*. *Easter-Day* is dogmatics, but as so often (for instance at the end of *Ferishtah's Fancies* or *Apollo and the Fates*), after Browning has finished dogmatizing, he turns suddenly to the human reaction. In *Easter-Day*, those who yearn sound secure and faithful. In *Two in the Campagna*, seen from the opposite perspective, a man on earth knows only 'the pain of finite hearts that yearn.'

does not mention this association, as he well might have, when his carefully garnered Italian fennel-seeds produced some other plant (*LRBEB*, I, 110–11; July 1, 1845).

Love Among the Ruins, which opened the 1855 *Men and Women,*
has some of the same properties as *Two in the Campagna.* It is a poem
that once again places a pair of lovers on bare grassy landscape by
the remains of a dead city. But the premises and the problem are
much different.

A manuscript draft of *Love Among the Ruins* in the Houghton
Library at Harvard entitles the poem 'Sicilian Pastoral,' and certainly
the requisite properties for a pastoral scene are present. A shepherd
and his feeding flock slowly wend their homeward way in a drowsy
peaceful twilight; a tryst with a maiden is anticipated, a fair-haired
maiden waiting in a turret. The whole to take place on a pastureland
covering the ruins of a prosperous but corrupt city of which the
turret is the only visible remain. ('Lean neath stone pine the pastor
lies with his crook; young pricket by pricket's sister nibbleth on
returned viridities; amaid her rocking grasses the herb trinity shams
lowliness; skyup is of ever-grey.') It is all a fine set piece, and due
contrast may be drawn between the wicked city and the pure country,
the sinful dead and the virtuous living, worldly glory and private
love. This is what the poem is sometimes reduced to. There is only
one problem, and that is the speaker, who does not seem to appreciate
the scene as he ought.

The contrast in the title is obvious: love alive among the ruins,
the relics of the dead; the fresh and new among the old and enduring;
the good (pastoral love is always good) among the remains of the
not-so-good, the venial, the ambitious, the dishonest, the corrupt.
(The contrast simply of alive and dead was mentioned by Elizabeth
Barrett in her *Greek Christian Poets*: 'Wonderful it is to look back
fathoms down the great Past, thousands of years away – where whole
generations lie unmade to dust – where the sounding of their trum-
pets, and the rushing of their scythed chariots ... are more silent than

the dog breathing at our feet, or the fly's paces on our window-
pane.'[1]) No specific indication is given of precisely what ruins
Browning has in mind; it would seem that the ruins are a type, and a
composite of the remains of several ancient cities.[2]

The speaker begins with his pastureland, moving through it in a
slow, meandering rhythm to match the ambling sheep-pace and
gradually to stretch out and relax the mind as the land itself stretches
out 'where the quiet-coloured end of evening smiles / Miles and
miles ...' Browning uses an internal rhyme in only one other short
line, and there too the word is repeated ('ere we extinguish sight and
speech / Each on each' – a thud of colliding bodies). Here the effect
is to draw our eye out and along the extent of the pastureland, the
easier done because it is (except for the lovers) uninhabited. It is
sleepy pastoral landscape, with sheep half-asleep as they wander, and
it seems to be receiving an evening benison from the setting sun,
which smiles on the scene. The rhythm picks up with the city. It is
something of a fairy-tale city ('so they say'), which was 'great and
gay'; however peaceful the first three lines are, they cannot be
described as gay, and that the pasture is undistinguished by marks
of greatness, or of anything at all for that matter, the speaker will
make clear. The city was the capital, the centre of things, drawing
them together; councils came into the city, authority went out from
it. Now the site is all circumference and no centre, diffused and
dissipated. Except for the streams, the hills would slide into one
land-mass, like the indistinguishable waves of the sea, rolling and
bare. The city used to stretch into the sky, and in the second stanza the
contrast is not between centre and circle but horizontal and vertical.
'Domed and daring,' spires like fires: then even the buildings
seemed as alive as flame, unlike the most unfiery present scene where
the only fire is the quiet-coloured dying sun. The present is all too
earthy and somewhat watery; it is the past that shoots into the
air like fire.

In the third stanza the shepherd attempts some unpastoral
sarcasm: 'And such plenty and perfection, see, of grass / Never was! /
Such a carpet ...' The romantic city is exerting its spell. Now the

1 *Poetical Works of Elizabeth Barrett Browning* (London, 1897), hereafter
   cited as *Works*, 590
2 Cf. DeVane, *Handbook*, 212–13. See also the persuasive suggestion of a
   Spenser source by R.K.R. Thornton, *Notes and Queries* 15 (1968), 178–9

shepherd sees himself walking on a carpet of grass which is not springing lush from solid earth, but which embeds the lost city over which he travels. Underneath the verdure the city lies all the while, with its fire now dead, and with all its gold again returned underground. The fluid rolling hills have also become hollow. But in the second half of this stanza, the city, hitherto a fairy-tale type, shifts to a wicked urban type. Glory and shame (a familiar pairing in Browning) were the motives, 'and that glory and that shame alike, the gold / Bought and sold.'[3] Nevertheless the city continues to shed influence. If it is a Sodom or a Babylon, it is a glittering one.

Only a turret now shows the spot where once a tower stood, and it too has fallen prey to greenery, to parasitic vines that mark time and disuse. It is 'over-rooted ... overscored,' overcome altogether, this remnant of a building that once sprang as the spires shot. Fiery as those spires was the burning ring traced about the tower by racing chariots watched by king, minions, and dames. This present earth melts away altogether in the vision. The quiet colours become undistinguished grey as light vanishes and the hills slip into anonymity. The sun still smiles but now it 'smiles *to* leave' the flock 'in *such* peace,' its smile now no evening benison, but an enigmatic, silent leave-taking.

Then comes a new factor: a girl with some of the vitality of the old city in her eager eyes and some of the city's golden allure in her yellow hair. The current monarch, she looks out where the king looked – but no, the figure is wrong, for she does not command, but awaits her lover in order to come alive. Like some princess captive in a tower and under a spell, she is 'breathless, dumb / Till I come.' And in the speaker's mind, even after evoking his beloved's image, the imaginary city still exercises its magic, spreading out building after building – '– and then! / All the men!' What follows does not lend itself to ready comparison, as in the other stanzas; the two halves

3 Cf. *Aristophanes' Apology*:

> That gold and that prosperity drive man
> Out of his mind – those charioteers who hale
> Might-without-right behind them: face who can
> Fortune's reverse which time prepares, nor quail?
> – He who evades law and in lawlessness
> Delights him, – he has broken down his trust –
> The chariot, riches haled – now blackening in the dust!   (4363–9)

This is a translation from Euripides.

seem somewhat unconnected. The king looked far and wide; the lovers will look only at each other (or rather, what the lover says exactly is that she will look only at him), and they will then rush together and extinguish both sight and speech, 'each on each.' To the king, his dominions; to the lovers, their own enclosed and willingly circumscribed kingdom. But again, a disturbing element has been introduced ('– and then, / All the men!').[4] There is somehow awkwardness in thinking of those men who 'breathed joy and woe / Long ago.' Then there was the multitude, full of its passion and its goal; now there is one pair.

In the last stanza, the city jumps quite out of control. It sends out a million fighters; it shoots a pillar to the sky; it retains a thousand golden chariots. It also takes over all the stanza except the last line, for the second half is the somewhat puzzling disposal of the vision:

> O heart! oh blood that freezes, blood that burns!
>   Earth's returns
> For whole centuries of folly, noise and sin!
>   Shut them in,
> With their triumphs and their glories and the rest!
>   Love is best.

Suddenly the earth takes over after all the fire and all the unearthly spurts of growth: the city is returned to its safe underground tomb, with triumphs, glories, *and the rest*.

Love is best then, better than the gold and glories of the past. In *Night and Morning*, that enigmatic little pair of lyrics, somewhat similar imagery is used, but no indication is given there of who the lovers are or what their situation, or even what the conclusion is. In *Fifine at the Fair*, like imagery of land, village, house represents domestic virtues and the sea the romantic call of adventure, the usage

4 Cf. Park Honan, *Browning's Characters* (New Haven, Yale University Press, 1961), 'Punctuation,' 284–91, on the importance of Browning's punctuation. The dash before 'and then' is meant to convey something. Cf. also: 'Even now it is on my mind that the printers have omitted a dash (–) after 'mount' – as if I fancied the name could be 'Mount Ben – something' – whereas I wanted Southron to *feel* after the name, with a couple of hesitations' (to J.D. Williams, Jan. 11, 1884; the poem is *Donald* holograph letter, courtesy of the Humanities Research Center, The University of Texas at Austin).

there being very complex. Here the path of gold is the burning ring
of the gold chariots or the brazen pillars' spurt toward the sky.
The city's movement is swift, aggressive, shooting, and daring. But
it has all been domesticated now: the king's tower is a lovers'
meeting-place; shepherd and flock merely saunter; the city's gold is
reflected only in the girl's muted yellow hair;[5] the magic city has been
converted into a cellar above which sheep may safely graze.

It has been shut in with considerable vehemence, however, and
the fact that it must be shut in and pushed down, active ghost that it
is, shows how alive it has become for the speaker. Why does it grow
out of all proportion in the last stanza, and why is the speaker so
agitated? Is it a yearning for the path of gold that produces his
irony and his disgust with the undistinguished grey and perfection of
the grass? If so, why does he not sell the flock and march off to the
big city with his golden girl? Perhaps there is some compulsion to
stay, but this is never hinted and takes us wildly astray. What is more
than hinted is the intense agitation over the idea of the city and
its inhabitants.

Here is the place to come back to the shepherd's stereotypes, both
of city and of men. For the speaker does tend to think in stereotypes
and some of them tend to break down. The pastoral archetype turns
ironic and mysterious. The city is in the first stanza a casual contrast
like an idle thought stumbled on as the shepherd goes to his beloved.
By the last stanza the sound is fortissimo, the city has grown up
through the ground to the sky and out to the horizon, the vehemence
approaches anguish. Curious things happen to the men too: they
breathe joy and woe; then what explains them is lust of glory and
dread of shame, either one for sale; then their lives are reduced
to folly, noise, and sin. If the description of the city is exaggerated,
may not that of the men also be? Even the shepherd's lady is
conceived in rather stereotyped terms: 'a girl with eager eyes and
yellow hair.' Such emphatic contrived contrast suits very well the
young shepherd's pattern of thinking. His sarcasms on the plenitude
of grass are heavy; his final dismissal, though no solution, is loudly
assertive. He seems unlikely to spend a day sitting on the campagna
musing on spider-threads. Nor do we hear much about his anticipated good minute. Indeed the attitude of a swain who says coolly

5 Cf. p. 87 above, on other gold-yellow contrasts

that his lady is 'breathless, dumb / Till I come' is interesting. The love among the ruins seems not to have mitigated the anguish, but merely to have suppressed it.

The lover does not pay much attention to his lady though he is on his way to a meeting. Perhaps I am being perverse: he is thinking of something else. But oddly enough the closer he comes to his beloved, the greater his vehemence grows, as if the city posed a direct personal threat to the lovers. When they meet they will extinguish sight and speech, and this includes the mental sight of the city, which so torments the young swain. Shut in by an embrace, he will be able to shut out the city. The noise as he approaches the turret is like the din surrounding Childe Roland as he comes close to the dark tower. Abruptly, with the last three lines, it is cut.

The city has proved altogether too lively for the simple tags assigned to it. There is more to those men than those motives will account for. Once they were as alive as the shepherd now is, and as joyful as he will be when he meets the girl with yellow hair. For the moment he stands apart and he sees one pair alive in the turret above a multitude dead under the carpet of grass. The grass that has grown over all the city's fire and gold will some day grow over the lovers' own vitality. His agitation grows, I think, from the same passion that animates the *Lament for Bion*: 'Alas, when the mallows and green parsley and curly-tendrilled anise perish in the garden, they live once more and grow up another year; but we men ...'

Grass or plant, especially when it grows over the artefacts and monuments of man, the latter usually stone, is a frequent symbol in Browning of the pasage of time and the persistence of the natural cycle. (Cf. pp. 95–6 above on *Earth's Immortalities: Fame*.) In *Red Cotton Night-Cap Country*, sub-titled *Turf and Towers*, turf represents changeable things, the finite; and rock and tower, what seems durable. When vegetation covers ruins, 'little life begins where great life ends' (1046). In *The Inn Album*, as in *Love Among the Ruins*, grass may prove different from what it first appears: '... the grass which grows so thick, he thinks, / Only to pillow him is product just / Of what lies festering beneath!' (2284–6). In *Clive* a crumbling castle may be climbed by any tourist:

Towers – the heap he kicks now! turrets – just the measure of his cane!
... Observe moreover – (same similitude again) –
Such a castle seldom crumbles by sheer stress of cannonade:

'T is when foes are foiled and fighting's finished that vile rains invade,
Grass o'ergrows, o'ergrows till night-birds congregating find no holes
Fit to build in like the topmost sockets made for banner-poles.
So Clive crumbled slow in London, crashed at last.   (53–9)

In *Fifine at the Fair*, section lxxxix, there is a tower overgrown by a
creeper-branch: the poem's imagery is complex, but notable among
the creeper's characteristics is its consciousness of purpose (a
flirtatious Fifine purpose, the creeper being invested with incredible
sexuality).

The tower itself is a fairly frequent image in Browning, its use
being varied and complex. Here it is enough to observe that besides
obvious connotations this turret is a remnant of the vertical aspiring
city so unlike the flat passive grass. (Cf. these two patterns in
Two in the Campagna, the latter there being the one that is
discarded; the question here is how much the shepherd's love has
in common with the flat passive landscape with which he associates
it.) The tower is also a place of observation. Elizabeth Barrett
more than once uses it in this sense: 'To make a promise is one thing,
& to keep it quite another: & the conclusion you see "as from a
tower"' (*LRBEB*, I, 291; Nov. 24, 1845). 'M. Milsand will not
[approve of *Aurora Leigh*], I prophesy; "seeing as from a tower the
end of all"' (*LEB*, II, 242; [Nov., 1856]). In *Aurora Leigh* 'towers of
observation' (849) are for sight. So too is the tower in *Fifine at the
Fair*, the sight being of ambiguous value. Soo too is the tower at the
end of *Red Cotton Night-Cap Country*, the sight proving fatal for
Miranda. In *Love Among the Ruins* the king surveyed his domains
from the tower; perhaps it is important that lover and beloved
'extinguish sight and speech' (and do so 'each on each') in the
turret that remains.

I do not want to press the Bion theme unduly hard. It seems to
me unmistakably present, but under the surface of the shepherd's
thinking. The lyric that centres on the Bion theme, and it is a not
infrequent theme in Browning,[6] is *A Toccata of Galuppi's*. Here

---

6 In the *Parleying with Gerard de Lairesse*, Browning cites the *Lament for
Bion*: 'Spring repeats / That miracle the Greek Bard sadly greets: /
"Spring for the tree and herb – no Spring for us!"' (422–4). DeVane
suggests (*Parleyings*, 251) that the passage 'seems to be Browning's para-
phrase of the *Iliad*, VI, 146–149'; but Homer here stresses the likeness
between trees and the generations of man, not the difference.

what we are left with is simply what the title says: love among the ruins, that is, a contrast. The contrast turns into a conflict as the speaker muses; the conflict becomes an impasse; in a way not immediately apparent to him, this threatens his love; he is impelled to deal forcibly if not persuasively with it; he does so by suppressing one contending half. It is not, after all, surprising that the shepherd does not concentrate on his lady as he approaches her: the poem is about a threat to her and the kind of relation is clearly not one in which she could be of use in meeting the threat. A girl who waits, breathless and dumb, to be awakened by her lover may please his vanity, but is little help in meeting danger with him. That this remark is not irrelevant is, I think, shown by the role Leonor plays in *By the Fireside*. (Browning had a great distaste for passive women: cf. *A Woman's Last Word*, even the woman of *Two in the Campagna*, the girl here; he managed to describe their malleable devotion as 'a kind of love' in *Red Cotton Night-Cap Country*, but it is ranked far below the love of a Leonor or a Lyric Love, and his active women are made far more attractive than his passive ones.) The girl with yellow hair will be as protected by her shepherd as she is now sheltered in her turret; left as peaceful as the dumb sheep he also protects, and shepherds to their fold. The city grows wildly in the last stanza because the speaker knows something must be done with it. Either he or his yellow-haired girl makes it impossible for him to begin speaking thus to her: 'I wonder do you feel today / As I have felt ...' Could he do so, the results might not be as subtle as those in *Two in the Campagna*, but they might also stay closer to reality.

The Bion theme may induce elegy or feeling 'chilly and grown old,' as in *A Toccata of Galuppi's*. Or the contrast may, as often in Browning, be used as a springboard from which to draw implications about the ordained differences between man and the rest of nature. The difficulty in *Love Among the Ruins* is that the dead city belongs to both orders, that is, of humanity and of nature. In death, it seems to have reverted entirely to nature, to have been consumed back into the soil; but there were also 'all the men.' Yet Browning could also put into the mouth of his characters the view that the dead should be left to bury their dead: in effect, this is what happens in *By the Fireside*. The fact that the dead so bother the speaker of *Love Among the Ruins*, and of *A Toccata of Galuppi's*, is meant to show something of these speakers' present lives, especially their

unprobed or unresolved assumptions. In *By the Fireside* such
things are easily disposed of. In *Two in the Campagna* the case is
more interesting, for some of the same potential conflict is there, but
a resolution is not permitted. Nonetheless the speaker is honest and
clear-sighted, and he knows that his answer to what problems the
past may have must be found in the present. The whole Bion theme
of *A Toccata of Galuppi's* could be developed from the 'Rome and
May' of the first stanza. But the *Two in the Campagna* speaker pulls
the two conflicting patterns of imagery into relation with his present
as shepherd and scientist do not. They remain with the pattern, the
shepherd finally altering it to his own needs, the scientist reacting
with a mood. The pattern remains unresolved and seems unresolv-
able. In *Two in the Campagna* the speaker is not subordinated to
the pattern. If he cannot trace the spider-thread, neither does it trap
him. He sees his alternatives too clearly and returns to his thread
too doggedly for that. If his conflict is unresolved, it is not unresolv-
able – if grace would but descend. He has followed the thread of
his thoughts as far as it will lead him: he now needs the confirmation
of action. But the other two speakers, as far as we can see, have
just grasped the thread.

Sometimes the attitude of Browning's characters is not merely,
let the dead bury their dead, but, it is better for them to die. This
may be seen in Festus' early speech (Paracelsus later has a very different view of the past):

> Why turn aside from her [wisdom]
> To visit ... ruins where she paused but would not stay,
> Old ravaged cities that, renouncing her,
> She called an endless curse on, so it came.   (I, 404–10)

But the city that is loved can never be so dismissed: 'Beautiful
Florence at a word laid low / – (Not in her domes and towers and
palaces, / Not even in a dream, that outrage!)' (*Luria*, IV, 259–61).
A moment later, Luria, though enraged against Florence, resolves
to take as his model the sun, who does not scorch the earth when
the earth does not understand him, but simply drops out of the
sky, as the sun drops smiling out of the shepherd's day. The closest
likeness to the *Love Among the Ruins* setting comes in a later poem,
Aristophanes' Apology, where Balaustion pictures the destruction of
Athens, also a much-loved city, but deserving obliteration:

> Let hill and plain
> Become a waste, a grassy pasture-ground
> Where sheep may wander, grazing goats depend
> From shapeless crags once columns! so at last
> Shall peace inhabit there, and peace enough.   (5535–9)

'The solitary pastures ... our sheep ... the hills ... such peace ...
undistinguished grey': the scenes are very like. May not the shepherd
be adopting Balaustion's attitude, assigning the city to the oblivion
it merits? But Balaustion has known and loved and fought for her
city; she is aware how 'all the men' have betrayed it. More important,
she re-creates imaginatively an ideal Athens, which she pictures in
the sungilt clouds seen from her fugitive boat; so Sordello also kept
an ideal Rome to place against the contemporary one. The problem,
to return to familiar Browning categories, is to relate the two. But
the shepherd has no second city, only the pastoral landscape and his
love-affair; only the city he shuts in, not an aetherial one. He guesses
there is some resolution to be found in the present, and he is right.
But it will not be found by trying to eliminate the past. This is what
Paracelsus tried to do, and concluded finally that he had been scorning
the finite. This is what the shepherd also attempts to do: to suppress
the achievements of the city, and the question of whether its way of
life is really an adequate reason for its being so dead. 'Love is best,'
he cries, having gradually eliminated love from his imagined city.

   And yet: 'The other day I took up a book two centuries old in
which "glory," "soldiering," "rushing to conquer" and the rest, were
most thoroughly "believed in" – and if by some miracle the writer
had conceived and described some unbeliever, unable to "rush to
conquer the Parthians" &c, it would have been as tho' you found
a green bough inside a truss of straw' (*LRBEB*, II, 710; Browning
to Elizabeth, May 17, 1846; the remark is a propos of 'the Young
England imbeciles,' who 'hold that "belief" is the admirable point –
in what, they judge comparatively immaterial!'). And yet again,
on the other side: 'I hear you reproach ... "their end was a crime." –
Oh, a crime will do / As well, I reply, to serve for a test, / As a
virtue ... Let a man contend to the uttermost / For his life's set
prize, be it what it will!' The difficulty is, of course, that *Love Among
the Ruins* is dramatic. It is not 'proved' one thing or the other by
outside references, although these raise pertinent questions about

the shepherd's attitudes. Browning in some poems presents arguments very close to those he might have offered in his own person. He also in some poems works out problems close to his own: hunting out the fallacies, showing the consequences of certain positions. The result is that the reader often tends to forget that Browning can and does present attitudes which he is neither for nor against. In *Men and Women* Browning writes some lyrics for which both sympathy and judgement are necessary; in which the dramatic pose is perfectly achieved and maintained. Browning has told us not to read him into these poems. If we cite related lines in other poetry, or remarks in letters, it must be with care. To hear Browning pronouncing 'love is best' is to make of the poem what he tells us not to make. To see the shepherd with some detachment is to recognize that Browning simply leaves him in the contrast of the title – in love among the ruins. To take over the shepherd's categories without seeing how they are shaped and limited robs the poem of much richness. To assume the categories are Browning's own is merely a piece of foolishness, as a glance at other poems shows.

A Toccata of Galuppi's is *Love Among the Ruins* with the terms shifted. Past and present confront each other by means of Galuppi's toccata, which both evokes and judges for a present listener a version of the eighteenth-century Venice in which it was created. Love now belongs not to the present but to the past. Of its quality we know little except that it is emphatically not pastoral arcadian love, and that it inspires a Catullan hyperbole of passion. Galuppi's strictures on it are, on the surface, precisely those of the young shepherd on the buried city, if the sins condemned are different. The speaker is the new element. It is his mind that brings Galuppi alive again, yet he is also spectator to Galuppi's several comments. The first and last stanzas show him detaching himself from the Galuppi world, however, so that a distance is achieved that is not attempted in *Love Among the Ruins*. The dead city and its critic are here seen through the eyes of a third party. His vocation – he is a scientist – makes his detachment appropriate; besides, he is not, like the shepherd, a lover whose love involves him in the dispute at hand.

The most immediate effect of the poem is what its title says it is: a toccata. The rhythm is light (a toccata is a 'touch-piece') but steady and persistent. Its faint beat may hasten or retard or simply

accompany the thought, but always regulates it like the quiet
ticking of a clock. For a poem in which the passage of time is
important, the effect is a happy one. Rhythm suits theme too: no
crisis, anguish, vehemence; no crescendos or fortissimos. The first
stanza introduces us to the toccata and sets the tempo; it continues
until the end, with the last stanza distancing the Venetian picture
like the approaching resolution at the music's end. But there is no real
resolution. The music approaches its end without affirmation; the
clock simply stops and the delicate rhythm is left haunting the
air, complete yet cut off. No heavy Weltschmerz can be assigned to
'I feel chilly and grown old'; but the sombre sentiment (like the
'heavy mind' in stanza i) is probably more memorable when in light
toccata form than if accompanied by drums and cymbals.

The speaker is a scientist who is also sensitive to musical effect.
His role as scientist is not stressed; but it does enable Browning briefly
to set up a scene with the scientist trying to 'triumph o'er a
secret wrung from nature's close reserve,' but being diverted from
his work by Galuppi's haunting music. The music does not mock
his work, but raises different questions from those he pursues by
avocation – metaphysical questions involving the nature whose
secrets he investigates, and questions Browning frequently raised in
connection with nature. The scientist has met these questions before.
When the poem opens he is retracing their inspiration, as if the
toccata is being re-played. Suspense is minimized: we are not
experiencing freshly as we do with the shepherd, but repeating an
experience whose final effect we know ('But although I take your
meaning, 't is with such a heavy mind!'). Theme and rhythm alike
will offer no shocks. Yet scientist, like musician, gives the impression
of being open-eyed and evading nothing: it is the scientist's business
to face facts, including the fact of this kind of question. 'I can hardly
misconceive you, it would prove me deaf and blind': Browning's
favourite seeing-and-hearing pair are again used to indicate perception, and the contrast with the shepherd's extinguishing of sight
and sound comes to mind.

The toccata first re-animates Venice, casually and deftly as the
buried city is first re-animated in *Love Among the Ruins*. 'What, they
lived once thus at Venice ...?' – and a Venice stereotype springs
to life as readily as Don Juan's dream-Venice. Canals – Shylock –
Doge wedding Adriatic: some explicators of the poem have inferred

that the speaker is unsophisticated because his Venice is a Venice
of conventional tourist landmarks and associations (cf. DeVane,
Handbook, 221). But the inference seems to me curious. The
speaker sketches a stylized Venice with stylized inhabitants who all
lead a certain sort of life. This is because the questions Galuppi's music
raises do not depend on detailed, close knowledge of eighteenth-
century Venetian life – perhaps this is the reason Browning makes
the speaker say he has never visited the city. Indeed Galuppi's
music evokes only tentative fancies. The only assertions the speaker
makes are that certain landmarks exist. The rest of the Venetian
background is created by questions, tentative interrogations appropriate to the tentative suggestiveness of the toccata and to its chilly
insinuations. It is true that Browning thought Venetian manners
of the time were in general decadent.[7] It is unlikely that he or this
speaker thought every Venetian behaved like those in the poem, or
thought like those in the poem. The Venetian lovers' first response
to the music is not historical: it is precisely the speaker's own
(' "Must we die?" '). Their answer to the question is different from
his – or rather from his lack of an answer, for he simply sees and
feels the question. They lose themselves in each other, like the lovers
among the ruins. The growth and confirmation of the passion that
is both diversion from the question and the lovers' only answer to it is
described in musical terms. It is as if Galuppi both accompanies
and directs their doll-like movements and tender conventionalities –
or perhaps as if their movements and conversation inspire both
Galuppi's stylized music and its ironic questioning. Such interweaving
produces considerable irony, always delicate. The fact that the
speaker hears in Galuppi both conventional Venice and an ironic
questioning of even the most conventional Venice seems to me to
show he is far from unsophisticated.

For the speaker reduces his Venetians to their common factor,
that is, the common factor of well-born Venetian grace. I have
said that the *Love Among the Ruins* speaker is unsophisticated and
thinks in stereotypes. This speaker pictures Venice in stereotypes, but

7 'As for what Burke wrote of Venice and its manners before the Revolution,
– I am pretty sure, – from what knowledge I have from no few sources,
memoirs, &c – that he was in the right' (*Letters of the Brownings to
George Barrett*, 323; Feb. 24, 1889).

there is no indication he uses these stereotypes as a basis for judgment. Quite the contrary. He creates his dead city as the shepherd does, but dispassionately. Its figures are slight and graceful, its women magnificent, its aspirations simply personal ones. It is hardly as imposing as the buried city of *Love Among the Ruins*, though this is in large part because of this speaker's detachment. What coincides precisely in the two poems is a moral judgement on an a-moral way of life: 'Earth's returns / For whole centuries of folly, noise and sin! ... Love is best.' ' "Venice spent what Venice earned ... mirth and folly were the crop: / What of soul was left, I wonder, when the kissing had to stop?" ' But the first heavy-handed moralism is affirmed by the shepherd, the second set aside by the scientist. In *Love Among the Ruins*, Browning refrains from telling us anything about the quality of the shepherd's love; the answers to the poem's questions are not found there. It provides no shadow of an answer, within the poem, to why earth should not also shut in love – with wisdom, silence, goodness, as well as folly, noise, and sin. What I called the Bion theme in that poem is kept under the surface. The shepherd assumes and loudly asserts that his love makes him essentially different from and better than the dead city-dwellers. What earth will return for him, he forbears considering.

In *A Toccata of Galuppi's* the Bion theme is dominant. It is developed through a vegetable-animal imagery that is associated with the Venetians. The Bion theme distinguishes the vegetable and human cycles of nature. The shepherd implies his city-dwellers deserve to be consumed by greedy grass, to be part of the vegetable cycle, while he does not. The scientist is offered by Galuppi the same division between self and past (' "Butterflies may dread extinction, – you'll not die, it cannot be!" '), but refuses such a gambit ('I want the heart to scold. / Dear dead women, with such hair, too – what's become of all the gold / Used to hang and brush their bosoms? I feel chilly and grown old'). Whatever the judgment on souls, this speaker's heart is with the beautiful empty Venetian women.

The vegetable-animal imagery begins with them: 'On her neck the small face buoyant, like a bell-flower on its bed, / O'er the breast's superb abundance where a man might base his head' (it was a bell-flower, a campanula, in which a bee swung when Ottima and Sebald declared their love). The figure here conveys delicacy and movement, together with ampleness and strength, and provides a quick powerful sketch of female allure. But later the image is given other implications: 'As for Venice and her people, merely born to bloom and drop, / Here on earth they bore their fruitage, mirth and folly were the crop.' One effect of the speaker's memorable image at the end of the poem is to transfer the women back from the realm of the bellflower born to bloom and drop, from a vegetable cycle, to a human cycle, or closer to a human cycle. The gold hair yet surviving in their coffins (Browning was to write a poem *Gold Hair*, on such buried beauty), and remembered as brushing live breasts – such an image affords a certain grief that the flower born to bloom and drop does not.

The parallel animal image to this vegetable one is the butterfly: ' "Butterflies may dread extinction, – you'll not die ..." ' Whether Browning meant Galuppi's image to remind the reader of the traditional butterfly-psyche association (used, for example, by Jules of Phene's newly awakened soul), I do not know, though I doubt this. If he did, the association would only reinforce the speaker's quiet protest against Galuppi (by implying the Venetians had discernible souls, after all), as well as increasing the irony. Galuppi himself is given the image of the other insect in the poem, a cricket. He is said twice to 'creak' his refrain (the second time sounds like the insect's name: 'so you creak it'), the cricket's persistence having something in common with the toccata's. The cricket is persistent in more ways than one, for he has survived burnt-out Venice: Galuppi's music, once impatiently heard out by flirting Venetians, has outlasted them all. Cricket still creaks while butterfly has flown his brief day. The cricket is given as setting a burned house, so that he can twice echo 'dust and ashes.' The house and phrase pick up the earlier image of intense activity – 'balls and masks begun at midnight, burning ever to mid-day' – which is now burnt out. And the phrase, literally applicable to the burnt house, symbolically and chiefly evokes death. It is little wonder that the speaker, hearing the insect's mordant surviving mockery, and remembering the bright gold now entombed in cold earth, himself seems to lose vitality: 'I feel chilly and grown old.'[8]

8 Note the similar use of 'chill' in a similar shift of feeling at the end of another poem, *Ferishtah's Fancies' Epilogue* (25–8):

> Only, at heart's utmost joy and triumph, terror
> Sudden turns the blood to ice: a chill wind disencharms
> All the late enchantment! What if all be error –
> If the halo irised round my head were, Love, thine arms?

Man versus nature, or man as a thing of nature; city versus country: what gives shape to some of Browning's finest lyrics can also provide the framework for an irreverent spoof. *Up at a Villa* offers a comic variation on more than one other lyric. In the collected *Dramatic Lyrics*, it follows *Love Among the Ruins* and *A Lovers' Quarrel*, and is followed by *A Toccata of Galuppi's*. Like *Love Among the Ruins* and *A Lovers' Quarrel*, it exhibits an anti-pastoral streak, and like *A Toccata of Galuppi's*, it is a musical poem. By the end we realize that the poem's rhythm is the bang-whang-whang and tootle-te-tootle of the town band in procession as surely as we realize *A Toccata*'s rhythm is based on Galuppi. By the end, too, we are likely to opt for country rather than city; as in *Love Among the Ruins*, the monologue has a somewhat different effect from what the speaker intends, though the irony of *Up at a Villa* is of the simplest sort.

The 'quality' of the Italian speaker might be inferred from the first short stanza: a thumping rhythm, stimulating, unavoidable, obvious; repetition (money, money; house, house; such a life, such a life), which simulates the town patter, announces the three focal points of the speaker's concerns, and has the predictable repetition of town life; the point of departure – money; the location of 'such a life' – at the window, as a spectator. None of this needs to be taken very seriously, but it is amusing to see Browning playing variations on persistent imagery of his own. The stance at the window, for example, is not infrequent in Browning and is often significant. Or the speaker avers in the second stanza that the city offers 'something to see, by Bacchus, something to hear, at least' – surely a variation on Browning's favourite seeing-and-hearing pair (here the speaker wants something 'to take the eye' not something the eye takes in).

The circumscription and control of town and houses are obvious, as is the chief threat of the country – its unpredictability. The speaker, being a happy parasite on others' actions, wants the actions to remain controlled, to observe their own due channels so he may safely watch from the shore. Thus the natural in the city is only simulated. The fountain provides a mechanical variation of the dancing stream in *A Lovers' Quarrel*, as do the horses of the wild, leaping horse in the same poem. Even the ladies are contrived: one is the statue in the fountain, who is oblivious to scrutiny of her state of nature (is her weed sash a comic variety of the weed sash at the beginning of the *Purgatorio*, which symbolizes humility?). The other is the 'smiling and smart' (a happy alliterative pair) Mary, in a pink gauze gown 'all spangles,'[9] who is oblivious to seven swords stuck in her heart. Both nymph and virgin have been thoroughly urbanized.

So sure is Browning of his touch, and of this character, that he puts into his mouth one of his most effective natural descriptions, that of the wild tulip shooting up with its 'thin clear bubble of blood.' Of course, it is a weed, and has no business growing among the wheat. And the thin clear bubble of blood has something slightly sinister about it. The Italian dislikes anything so human as blood: when three liberal thieves are shot, it is a news item, not a bloody execution, while a statue of Mary could have any number of swords stuck in her bloodless heart. (Another Italian, a deadly one, also disliked the spot of red summoned all too readily to his last Duchess' cheek.) Children pick and sell the wild tulip, a sylvan picture unlikely to soften the speaker's heart. And the nearness of the sound of 'pick' to 'prick' in following the word 'bubble' seems suddenly to deflate the tulip. Nonetheless, Browning does not grant the speaker a second such vivid picture; when he concedes that some think fire-flies pretty, he swiftly adds a reference to stinking hemp.

The clattering rhythm of the processional, *'bang-whang-whang goes the drum, tootle-te-tootle the fife,'* is repeated, and the poem closes on it. It is amusing to speculate whether the inspiration for the Italian person of quality might have been Browning's baby son, a devotee of the town, and especially the town band. 'We took a villa a mile and a half from the town, a villa situated on a windy hill (called "poggio al vento"), with magnificent views from all the windows ...' (*LEB*, I, 458; Sept. 24, 1850). 'We both of us grew rather pathetical on leaving our Sienese villa, and shrank from parting with the pig' (ibid., I, 463; Nov. 13, 1850). 'He [Pen] would change all your trees (except the apple trees), he says, for the Austrian band at any moment. He is rather a town baby ...' (ibid., I, 458; Sept. [1850]).

9 Browning had used and would use spangles as appropriate decorations for brash public entertainers. 'The poorest Man of letters (if *really* of letters) I ever knew is of far higher talent than the best actor I ever expect to know: nor is there one spangle too many, one rouge-smutch too much, on their outside man' (to Christopher Dowson, in *Letters*, ed. Hood, 9; Mar. 10 [1844]). Cf., too, the spangles worn by Fifine, which are mentioned more than once, and connected with the poem's sun imagery.

DeVane identifies the Italian's villa with this 1850 villa of the Brownings from Elizabeth's descriptions to her sisters (*Handbook*, 215), but does not mention Pen as possible source (and mental age?) of the speaker.

Much later, 'bang drum and blow fife' is all the literary critics manage to do (*Pacchiarotto*, 482), a possible retort against the critic who said all Browning's poetry was 'bang-whang-whang.' Fife and drum also figure in Don Juan's band: 'Bateleurs, baladines! We shall not miss the show! / They pace and promenade; they presently will dance: / What good were else i' the drum and fife? O pleasant land of France!' (12–14). The Italian person of quality is a very distant cousin indeed from Don Juan. Still, both are seekers after amusement, if one is very sophisticated; both can glamorize what is shoddy, if one does so knowingly; both are fascinated by a lady in spangles, if one knows the worth of all her glitter. Most important, both are observers not actors, tasters not eaters.

I began this examination of *Men and Women* lyrics by considering enclosure imagery, and the use of one type of such imagery in *Love Among the Ruins* and *A Toccata of Galuppi's* is obvious. At the end of both poems, the living confront the confined dead. For the shepherd, whom they threaten, the dead are to be shut in. For the scientist, whom they move, the dead come briefly alive in strands of long gold hair. But the buried gold of the dead city and of the dead Venetian beauties is equally vanished. Neither speaker offers an alternative strong enough to pull his poem's focus away from the dead, enclosed world that intrigues him. The *Two in the Campagna* speaker does; his poem ends with an impasse, but the focus is on the living man and his pain. Despite his impotence, he is freer than his two fellow-speakers. In both *Love Among the Ruins* and *A Toccata of Galuppi's* it is the dead who prove more vital than the living and who condition the responses of the living.

11 WOMEN AND ROSES

Women and Roses achieves its haunting effect, first, because it is a dream poem – neither a dream-vision like those in *Christmas-Eve* and *Easter-Day* nor a dream-like poem such as *Childe Roland*, but a present dream. Its first line draws us into the enclosure of the sleeper's experience ('I dream of a red-rose tree'), and we participate with the dreamer throughout rather than observe him (as we observe, for instance, the self-declared pain of the *Two in the Campagna* speaker). The main focus of the poem is on the women and the roses they encircle. Browning achieves this focus, at least in part, by telling us nothing at all about the speaker. We are invited to look or at least to glance at most of the lyric speakers of *Men and Women*; that is, we are reminded these are dramatic lyrics, as they were specifically to be called in the 1863 collection. But sometimes the speaker tells us so little of himself, or of people or concerns that interest him, that we move close to the non-dramatic lyric, and often close to the most enigmatic, because the most simple, of Browning's poems. In such poems (*My Star* is another) it is helpful to pay close attention to patterns of imagery within and without the poem. *Women and Roses* is about time, about past, present, and future, yet it does not suggest the passing of time. In the dream that is the poem, past and present and future seem frozen, and the roses not in time, though they are symbols of times. Thus the poem at once is and is not in the tradition of *Gather ye rosebuds* or *Mignonne allons voir*. The difference in focus is especially clear when the poem is compared with one using similar images in the service of the theme of transience; the poem is by Lorenzo de Medici:

Into a little close of mine I went,
    One morning when the sun with his fresh light
    Was rising all refulgent and unshent.

Rose-trees are planted there in order bright.
   Whereto I turned charmed eyes, and long did stay,
   Taking my fill of that new-found delight.
Red and white roses bloomed upon the spray;
   One opened, leaf by leaf, to greet the morn,
Shyly, at first, then in sweet disarray;
Another, yet a youngling, newly born,
   Scarce struggled from the bud, and there were some
   Whose petals closed them from the air forlorn;
Another fell, and showered the grass with bloom;
   Thus I beheld the roses down and die,
   And one short hour their loveliness consume ...[1]

Women and Roses is one of the most implacable of Browning's dream-poems. There is no glimpse or hint of hope, not one aperture in the whirling circles from which the speaker longs to seize and fix something. Haunted by the same oppressive sense of inevitability that marks *Love in a Life*, most of *Childe Roland*, *A Serenade*, and somewhat less *Two in the Campagna*, this poem excludes more relentlessly. The vision is not glimpsed or imagined, as in those poems, but seen entirely. The sight reduces the speaker to a passion of would-be service, if only one woman would stoop out from her circle and allow him to possess her. The passion could find expression in love for contemporary woman, or in art for past or future beauties. But it is all as useless as the pleas in *Numpholeptos*; the women whirl on, unheeding, their circles unbroken. Browning does not often treat the femme fatale, but he can do so memorably, especially with the indirect treatment in this poem and in *Numpholeptos*.

The circles are of past, present, and future women, whirling around a blown, a blooming, and a budding rose respectively. Here the movement, the dance, as well as the closed circle, exclude the speaker. The walls of such a poem as *A Serenade* are combined with the quest of a poem like *Love in a Life*. That the moving circles remain in view, centred on three roses of a rooted rose-tree, only adds to the frustration. They look available, and the speaker is in their field of vision. But there is not even the satisfaction of an angry response, as in *A Serenade*.

1 Translated by J.A. Symonds, in *The Renaissance in Italy: Italian Literature* (London, 1881), I, 329

The circle is part of Browning's complex of enclosure imagery, with the added advantage of the attributes of mystery and perfection. (Browning makes no mention of these attributes, but does invest his circling women with the essence of both mystery and perfection.) It is common to note the numerous connotations of the circle in remarks on the ring's meaning for *The Ring and the Book*. The simple attribute of perfect geometrical form is usual in Browning's poetry and letters; Elizabeth uses 'the perfect round' in 1846 and Browning echoes it in 1864 in *Abt Vogler*.[2] Yet at the same time Browning and Elizabeth speak of the perfect round of their year of love – and in a phrase that may have suggested Elizabeth's – Browning can speak of a dead circle of perfection ('times of comparative standing still, rounded in their impotent completeness' [*LRBEB*, II, 710; May 17, 1846]). The circle, like all the enclosure imagery, and like most other Browning imagery, may be viewed in two ways. In *Women and Roses*, it may suggest perfection and mystery, but decidedly does suggest exclusion. The exclusiveness which love, or friendship, may create between two people is mentioned in a Browning letter that uses an image like the central one of *Women and Roses*: 'Burn anybody's *real* letters, well & good: they move & live – the thoughts, feelings, & expressions even, – in a self-imposed circle limiting the experience of two persons only – *there* is the standard, and to *that* the appeal – how should a third person know? His presence breaks the line, so to speak, and lets in a whole tract of country on the originally inclosed spot ...' (ibid., I, 463; Feb. 15, 1846). But here, as in the happy love lyrics, the view is from within.

The circle is not only something to be contemplated or encircled by. It may also be traced, and Browning in a letter to Elizabeth says he can go round and round his love, in an ecstasy of new dis-

2 'And now as the year has rounded itself to "the perfect round" ...' (*LRBEB*, II, 714; May 19, 1846); Browning's reply speaks of 'our golden year' (ibid., II, 715; May 20, 1846). Cf. also: 'Oh, my happiness / Rounds to the full' (*Return of the Druses*, III, 100–1); 'matchless circle' (*Luria*, IV, 223); 'since your note would not round to the perfection of kindness and comfort' (*LRBEB*, I, 175; Aug. 29, 1845). Cf. Elizabeth later in expressions which sound like *Abt Vogler* but which echo her spiritualism: 'But this world is a fragment – or, rather, a segment – and it will be rounded presently, to the completer satisfaction' (*LEB*, II, 234–5); June 17, 1856). 'But the life here is only half the apple – a cut out of the apple, I should say, merely meant to suggest the perfect round of fruit' (ibid., II, 289; [Aug. 10, 1858]).

coveries, and in a path like the women's in *Women and Roses*. The important thing is that he is making the circle, not being shut outside by it. In one use of the figure, Browning pictures himself circling a flower of like shape to the rose and with its own tradition of symbolism, the lotus.[3]

If there is a circle lovers can make, there is likewise a circle of conceptions the artist can approach, and Browning makes use of this figure elsewhere than in *Men and Women*. In *Sordello*, for example, one of the most interesting images is the mysterious stone font with a circle of maidens holding its centre basin (cf. in *Women and Roses* the 'women ... / Sculptured in stone'). Sordello visits it surely as night comes, 'constant as eve' (the phrase is repeated). After Mantua he abandons his poetry to the font. At the end he is buried there, the stone receptacle now becoming a font-tomb in name and deed for him, as before it was in deed only for his poetry. The circle of maidens is neither friendly nor sinister, but remote; yet it gives Sordello sustenance. Its mythical women, its name and functions, suggest that it plays symbolically the same role as Palma, that it is a focal point for both love and art, which are connected for Sordello, as they also are for the *Women and Roses* speaker. If the devotion given the stone maidens is adolescent, and is replaced by love for the living Palma, still these women come closer to the *Ewig-Weibliche*, holders of the beginning and the end of Sordello. Their connections with both love and art, their existence before and after Sordello, their remoteness and at the same time their persistence – all suggest they may be forerunners of the *Women and Roses* figures.

Browning could also speak of his own dramatic characters as a moving circle, 'this dancing ring of men and women,' here a circle surrounding him from which he must slip away to write the 'R.B.'

---

3 'I ... end, and begin, going round and round in my circle of discovery, – *My* lotos-blossom! because they *loved* the lotos, were lotos-lovers, – λωτοῦ τ' ἔρωτες, as Euripides writes in the Τρωάδες' (*LRBEB*, I, 443; Feb. 8, 1846). Cf. also: 'I have a flower here ... which must be turned and turned, the side to the light changing in a little time to the *leafy* side, where all the fans lean and spread .. so I turn your name to me, that side I have not last seen (ibid., I, 329–30; Dec. 19, 1845). 'My thoughts have turned round and round it [Browning's letter] ever since' (Elizabeth, ibid., I, 254; Nov. 1, 1845). 'All my soul follows you, love! – encircles you' (ibid., I, 425; Jan. 28, 1846).

poem. ('I have some Romances and Lyrics, all dramatic, to dispatch, and *then*, I shall stoop of a sudden under and out of this dancing ring of men & women hand in hand; and stand still awhile, should my eyes dazzle, – and when that's over, they will be gone and you will be there, *pas vrai?*' [ibid., i, 26; Feb. 26, 1845].) If the circle here is to be escaped from (the characters are not fleeing images, but are already embodied), still it has the same hypnotic effect as the moving circle in *Women and Roses*. And if the 'dazzle' clause echoes *The Duchess of Malfi*, the antique women of *Women and Roses* also move in a 'dazzling drift.' (Cf. too Browning's remark: 'In Luria, I alter "little circle" to "circling faces" – which is more like what I meant' [ibid., ii, 598; Apr. 7, 1846].) The most interesting parallels to *Women and Roses* are, however, the elusive images haunting the *Pauline* speaker and Aprile, and to these I shall return.

Sometimes, as in *Easter-Day*, the whirling circle implies futility rather than frustration. Browning avoids such connotations here, for the speaker is not part of the circle. He longs to 'fix' some part of its flux, but he himself is not whirled about meanwhile, like the dreamer of *Easter-Day* or the lover at the end of *Two in the Campagna*. Browning elsewhere used the figure of the whole of life as a whirling circle from which man longs to seize something permanent. In *Two Poets of Croisic*, for instance, life is a race, with rounds: 'the drunken reel ... round him, left and right, / One dance ... ever 'mid the whirling fear, / Let, through the tumult, break the poet's face / Radiant' (1251–72). Earlier, in the *Epilogue* to *Dramatis Personae* Browning had used a whirlpool figure, which he expounds: 'when you see ... nature dance / About each man of us, retire, advance, / As though the pageant's end were to enhance / His worth ...' (87–90). There too, 'one Face' becomes the one stable thing, becomes in fact 'my universe that feels and knows,' while nature whirls on her way.

If the circle is the perfect shape, the rose is said to be the perfect flower, and each of the three circles of women guards its appropriate rose. Roses in *Men and Women* and thereafter are associated both with women and love, and also with artistic creation, but only in this poem are the two associations united, the speaker making his appeal both as man and as artist. Before *Men and Women*, Browning makes little or no use of roses, and twice relegates them to second place because they are too obvious a flower. Or rather, roses are ignored not

before *Men and Women*, but before Elizabeth Barrett, for the love
letters contain numerous references to them.

They were, first and literally, the most frequent flowers of Browning's regular bouquets for Elizabeth.[4] But before her first rose was
dispatched in a letter, Browning had described his private place of
reflection as a rose-garden: he can return, after adverse reviews, to
'a garden-full of rose-trees, and a soul-full of comforts' (*LRBEB*, I,
18; Feb. 11, 1845). For Elizabeth, 'the laburnum trees & rose trees are
plucked up by the roots' (ibid., I, 35; Mar. 5, 1845; cf. the Isaiah
variation later: 'only *I* know what was behind ... the long wilderness
... without the blossoming rose' [ibid., I, 376; Jan. 10, 1846]). Browning
let the image go, except for one example from her poetry that could
say more than he was permitted to say directly ('if I wished to "make
you vain," if having "found the Bower"[5] I did really address myself to
the wise business of spoiling its rose-roof ...' [ibid., I, 100; June 22,
1845]). The image does not reappear until early the next year, but
from then through the spring season there is a profusion of reference.
Browning twice used another example from Elizabeth's poetry. The
repeated quotation is interesting: as in *Women and Roses*, the double
usage belong to a rose-tree; it is applied both to the wonder of creation
and, three months later, to Elizabeth herself. 'May but *you* as surely
go perfecting – by continuing – the work begun so wonderfully –
"a rose-tree that beareth seven-times seven" '[6] (ibid., I, 439; Feb. 6,
1846); '... *my* flower-show [the sight of her], my "rose tree that beareth
seven times seven" ' (ibid., II, 715; May 20, 1846[7]).

Other allusions abound. On March 25, in reply to Elizabeth's

4 Elizabeth or Browning refers to Browning's roses in *LRBEB*, I, 96 (the
   season's first rose, sent in a letter, June 14, 1845), 97 (June 16), 99
   (June 19), 108 (June 30), 110 ('How good you are to my roses – they
   are not of my making, to be sure,' July 1), 120 (July 11), 141 (Aug. 12),
   147–8 (Aug. 8); II, 702 (May 15, 1846), 706 (May 16), 762 (June 7),
   784 (June 14). On March 26, 1846, Browning speaks of planting seven
   rose-trees; on April 5 of planting a dozen more.
5 Cf. Elizabeth Barrett's poem, *The Lost Bower*
6 Cf. Elizabeth Barrett's poem, *The Lay of the Brown Rosary*, 383
7 Two days later, by coincidence, Elizabeth 'had a rose tree sent to me by
   somebody [a woman] who has laid close siege to me this long while.' Then,
   'the sender of the rose tree sent to-day a great heliotrope – so, presently,
   you will have to seek me in a wood' (*LRBEB*, II, 719, 738; May 21
   and 28, 1846).

remarks on his flowers: 'God knows my life is for you to take as you take flowers: – these last please you, serve you best when plucked – and "my life's rose" .... if I dared profane *that* expression I would say, – you have but, to "stoop" for it'[8] (ibid., I, 557; Mar. 25, 1846). On March 26, 'you are *entirely* what I love – not just a rose plucked off with an inch of stalk, but presented as a rose should be, with a green world of boughs round, – all about you is "to my heart" – (*to my mind*, as they phrase it)' (ibid., I, 563). On March 27, Browning plants rose-trees whose 'first blossoms ... will go to dearest Ba who first taught me what a rose really *was*, how sweet it might become with superadded memories of the room and the chair and the vase' (ibid., I, 566). Two of the flowers Elizabeth sent as tokens of her excursions were roses: 'the eglantine ... shall be "*dog*-rose" for Flushie's sake! ... I fancy you proposing to give *me* a golden Papal rose and gift for a King, instead of this [cf. the contrast between gold and natural rose in *A Pretty Woman* and in the Pope's monologue (1027–98 *passim*)]' (ibid., II, 769; June 9, 1846; cf. also ibid., II, 818; June 26, 1846). Other poets' roses are associated with Elizabeth too.[9] As for her, Browning's flowers are a continuing witness to him when he is gone. 'You always, you know (*do* you know?), leave your presence with me in the flowers' (ibid., II, 803; June 21, 1846). 'What a luring thought you leave with me in the flowers! How I look at them as a sign of you, left behind – your footstep in the ground! It has been so from the beginning' (ibid., II, 980; Aug. 21, 1846).

It is hardly surprising, then, even after Browning's earlier ignoring of the flower, that fifteen of *Men and Women*'s fifty poems use the rose, several centrally.

The three kinds of women in *Women and Roses* are past, present, and future women. Woman past has been 'faded for ages,' and is

---

8 Cf. Elizabeth Barrett's poem, *A Thought for a Lonely Death-Bed*: 'But stoop Thyself to gather my life's rose, / And smile away my mortal to Divine!' Browning had already used the word stoop in interesting ways before this poem appeared, but Elizabeth's use might have started the chain of associations that links stooping with the divine in Browning from 1855 on.

9 '"And the roses which thou strowest, all the cheerful way thou goest, would direct to follow thee," as Shirley sings – and every now and then the full sense of the sweetness *collects* itself and overcomes me entirely, as now' (ibid., II, 725; May 24, 1846).

perhaps 'sculptured in stone,' perhaps 'on the poet's pages.' She hence has a 'pallid breast,' moves 'like a dance of snow'; her rose-leaf is bleached. She is like a statue ('you, great shapes of the antique[10] time'), and she is above the petitioner, like some high, still, marble creature ('stoop, since I cannot climb'). But there is life buried there, literally and figuratively, 'hearts that beat 'neath each pallid breast.' The speaker would break his own living heart at a famed woman's feet, prostrating himself, could he but bring her alive, set her blood going. ('How shall I fix you, fire you, freeze you ...?' Cf. *Love Among the Ruins,* line 79, also about dead, buried, once famed people: 'Oh heart! oh blood that freezes, blood that burns!' I take it, however, that this line refers to the speaker's as well as the dead's life-blood.)

Woman present is very near the speaker. The cup of her rose is ruby, the heart nectar. The bee that ignored woman past is 'sucked in' by such a flower, and the speaker longs for similar bliss. The bee 'drops from a statue's plinth,' as if he came in sudden dream-like movement from the remote, statuesque antique woman to a live, nearby woman. (Cf. also Jules' contrast in *Pippa Passes* between statue and live woman; there too the live woman is a flower, and is contrasted with a dead flower. Cf., too, of course, the live woman who transforms herself into a statue in *The Statue and the Bust,* and who fancies 'the rose would blow when the storm passed by ... both perceived they had dreamed a dream; / Which hovered as dreams do, still above.') Woman present is no woman or faded rose to adore from beneath, to re-awaken. She is a cup to be drunk or to be immersed in. 'So will I bury me while burning, / Quench like him [the bee] at a plunge my yearning.' There is no need to try the extremities of firing and freezing on this woman. She is already composed of the elements of fire and water (like Evelyn Hope, 'the good stars ... / Made you of spirit, fire and dew'; the fire-water combination is a favourite of Browning's), of ruby and nectar, and is fit match and solace for the burning suitor who longs to quench his ardour. The bee buried in the cup of a flower had served Browning before as an image of passionate love: a bee sways in a 'campanula chalice' (170) when Ottima and Sebald declare their love; the 'bee's kiss' of *In a Gondola*

10 Cf. Elizabeth Barrett: 'Why should we go back to the antique moulds .. classical moulds, as they are so improperly called?' (*LRBEB,* 1, 43; Mar. 20, 1845)

is 'as if you entered gay / My heart ... a bud ... its shattered cup / Over your head ...' (56–62).

But in a letter to Elizabeth, concerning her emendations of *The Flight of the Duchess*, Browning used the figure to suggest creative vitality ('wherever was a bud, even, in that strip of May-bloom, a live musical bee hangs now' [*LRBEB*, I, 135; July 25, 1845]). In the *Men and Women* poem on Keats, *Popularity*, the symbolism of art and ardour are combined felicitously. There the bee' goes singing to her groom,' like the Spouse to Solomon, whose presence is 'most like the centre-spike of gold / Which burns deep in the blue-bell's womb.' But Solomon's and the flower's blue is fancied to derive from the mysterious Phoenician dye, symbol of Keats' creative uniqueness. And the 'ardours manifold' of the bee move back through the ardours of the Song of Songs to suggest the creative passion of Keats, which the reader approaches by drinking the wine, and seeing the amazing colour, of the poetry. In *Women and Roses*, artist's and lover's passions are in separate stanzas, but meet in one man, who speaks first as lover, then as artist, but never explicitly excludes the artist from the lover. To possess the essence of woman, through some means, perhaps both, is his dearest desire. In stanzas v and vi, as in *Popularity*, both colour and drink are stressed. And the fire-water likeness may perhaps be seen in the gold-blue contrast of Solomon and bluebell, the gold burning, but the cool blue coming from the sea. In a similar flower, the opened rose, the speaker of *Women and Roses* would choose to be 'prisoned.'[11] In *Two in the Campagna*, the yearning and striving of the lover resemble the yearning and striving here. In both poems, the will goes only so far. There the beloved is also symbolized by the rose, which the lover can possess only so far and no farther. 'I kiss your cheek, / Catch your soul's warmth, – I pluck the rose ... then the good minute goes.' He remains outside his flower, which grants him only what the outside viewer may have; there is no immersion in its cup, though 'I would I could ... drink my fill / At your soul's springs.'

Woman future is not above or beside, but afar. To reach her, the bee's ardours do not suffice; 'new wings' are necessary. She is a rose

11 Cf. Browning's anecdote: 'this one wished, if he might get his wish, "to have a nine gallon cask of strong ale set running that minute and his own mouth to be *tied* under it" – the exquisiteness of the delight was to be in the security upon security, – the being "tied". Now, Ba says I shall not be "chained" if she can help!' (*LRBEB*, I, 510; Mar. 3, 1846).

of a new order, a new day ('first streak of a new morn'), a paradisal
rose ('dear rose without a thorn'). She will arise 'from the dust where
our flesh moulders' and 'with the cycle's change.' The artist would be
God in this paradise; he would shape an Eve from our dust, thus
being both creator and material; he would be over her – could he but
approach her. But she remains circling her rosebud, cold, unlike
ardent present woman; but also clear, not dazzling, like cold burned-
out past woman. Her element is the air ('wings, lend wings for the
cold, the clear!'); she is distant. She is not earthbound, buried under
stone like woman past, nor of live, moving fire and water like woman
present, but belongs outside this world.

Sixteen years later another Browning character intrigued by both
love and art mapped out womankind in three types. Don Juan chooses
Helen, Cleopatra, and the Saint as his typical women. They are not
quite woman past, present, and future; Cleopatra breaks the pattern,
and the women are supplemented by two very present women, Fifine
and Elvire (whose imagery connects them with Cleopatra and the
Saint respectively). But the three types here have something in
common with the three *Women and Roses* types. Helen would be the
obvious example of the woman of antique time. Like the high statuesque shapes of *Women and Roses*, she appears in 'prominent and
mighty form.' She demands that her adorers prostrate themselves,
and whiteness is associated with her (she is like a moon, and her brow
sheds candour). Both these qualities she shares with another classical
woman: the impervious nymph of *Numpholeptos*, whose victim longs
to pull her from Helen to Cleopatra, from past to present feminine
imagery. Cleopatra does not command her adorers but entices them;
she is witch rather than goddess, and bids them to drink her wine.
The Saint is as cold and far as future woman. She is on a church
steeple, high in the air; she is cold by nature and knee-deep in snow.
She also 'conquers what is near,' as Don Juan, connoisseur in sensuality, unexpectedly awards her the eminence over the other two. He
does this not by imagining new beauty, as did the *Women and Roses*
speaker, but by turning the Saint toward woman present. The moment
of turning, he says, when the Saint first suspects she needs earth as
well as heaven, when a faint flush begins to touch the snowy whiteness,
is worth all the contrived ingenuities of amateur sensualists.[12]

12 This is a refinement on the practice of the narrator in Kierkegaard's

The chief impression of *Women and Roses* is not of the essence of women or roses, but of their elusiveness. I have noted in chapter 1 how the *Pauline* speaker and Aprile are tormented by the elusiveness of the images their fancy presents. For them the dilemma is romantic: seize one and the others fade, the infinite choice is gone. But the *Women and Roses* speaker is ready to accept any woman and none will leave the magic circle. The *Pauline* passage describing similar frustration uses similar diction: 'dazzled by my wealth' (880), 'all so floated, nought was fixed and firm' (882). Compare, in *Women and Roses*, 'a dazzling drift,' '... go / Floating the women,' 'how shall I fix you?' So also does Aprile: '... dazzled by shapes, ... / Shapes clustered there to rule thee, not obey ... bright to thy despair? / Didst thou ne'er gaze on each by turns, and ne'er / Resolve to single out one ... those spells ... that charmed so long / Thine eyes, float fast, confuse thee, bear thee off, / As whirling snow-drifts blind a man ...' Again compare, in *Women and Roses*, 'great shapes of the antique time' and 'Round and round, like a dance of snow / In a dazzling drift, as its guardians, go / Floating the women ...' The two early artistic dilemmas are romantic: the artists must choose, bind themselves to the specific, the finite. This is a theme informing Browning's three early poems, and in his plays and *Bells and Pomegranates* poems, the importance of the specific act is stressed. The man of words rather than action (Djabal, Chiappino), the man of over-hasty action (Trasham), the small triggers that set off certain actions (*Pippa Passes*), the pleasure in action (*Cavalier Tunes, How They Brought the Good News*), the heroic act (*Incident of the French Camp*), the saintly act (*The Boy and the Angel*) : except for the love-poems, nearly every 1842 and 1845 poem centres on an important act. In *Men and Women* virtually none of the lyrics or dramatic monologues does so, and not all the romances (I am using Browning's 1863 classification). In *Men and Women* Browning touches the limits of both action and will: the speaker who puts forth all effort but can go only so far appears more than once (in *Women and Roses, Two in the Campagna, Love in a Life*; cf. also *Childe Roland, A Serenade,*

Diary of a Seducer. That seducer trains his protégé for one perfect night, then abandons her so as not to ruin his aesthetic experience. Don Juan's supreme moment is the first betrayal of passion – but he puts the sentiment in Fifine's mouth; he is unlikely to be so disciplined in practice.

Life in a Love). Where bliss descends, it is a gift: the recipient does his utmost and perhaps something happens, perhaps not (*By the Fireside, Saul,* and also *Childe Roland*).

In *Women and Roses*, the speaker does his utmost to fulfil a variation of Don Juan's injunction to join one point of a circle with one point outside; here the outside point is the artist, and the inner world would be what he created if he could. In *Fifine at the Fair* the outside point is God (Don Juan is not specific about what kind); the inner, man (Don Juan). The parallel of the two kinds of creation appears elsewhere in Browning, as a glance back at Aprile's dying words and forward to *The Ring and the Book* shows. But it is quite clear from *Women and Roses* itself: 'I will make an Eve, be the artist that began her, / Shaped her to his mind!' This, however, is an Eve who will not be incarnated, and the speaker a god whose material will not respond and rejects him. Will and act are not here synonymous. Is this why, thirteen years later, Browning speaks of the artistic as 'mimic creation' (*Ring and the Book,* I, 740), since 'Inalienable, the arch-prerogative / Which turns thought, act' (I, 720–1)? (Cf. also *Abt Vogler*: 'a flash of the will that can.') In '*Transcendentalism,*' also a *Men and Women* poem, what the will, the conscious endeavour, produces is books about the meanings of the rose. It is the mage 'who made things Boehme wrote about ... And in there breaks the sudden rose herself ...' The mystery of artistic creation Browning had already associated with the mage, and in *The Ring and the Book,* after the remarks quoted above, comes an example to parallel the artist: the mage. But after the mage comes Elisha, for Browning is offering a different parallel to artistic creation than the creation of an Eve. He calls it resuscitation, and the word, as well as the opening imagery of *The Ring and the Book,* suggest the parallel is resurrection, a second type of creation. For the first creation, will and power suffice. For the second, will, and love, may not. Why is a mystery, as is the reason the women do not respond to the man's and artist's will and love in *Women and Roses.*

12 ROSE AND STAR

The imagery of roses suddenly and somewhat surprisingly comes into prominence in *Men and Women* – surprisingly because Browning has twice rejected the rose image. In *Sordello* it is too obvious a sweetness to symbolize his rare poetry; in *The Flower's Name* it is too flaunting for the lover's delicate passion. The new prominence of the rose begins with its personal associations with Elizabeth Barrett. But the image has a variety of significance in *Men and Women*. In some poems, Browning seems to be offering variations of traditional associations. The most obvious is *The Heretic's Tragedy*, where biblical and secular roses are ironically juxtaposed as the image is pressed into macabre service. *A Pretty Woman* is clearly a 'gather ye rosebuds' poem ('Must you gather?'). '*Transcendentalism*,' as Browning says in a footnote prepared for Mrs Orr,[1] uses the traditional tale of the rose invented by a mage. All in all, the rose figures in fifteen of *Men and Women*'s fifty poems, and in some – *One Way of Love, Another Way of Love, Women and Roses*, besides the three above – it is central.

In many of these, the rose image is simple, general, and traditional, the rose acting, as in Browning's earlier usage, as a portmanteau symbol signifying enticing sweetness, usually love, perhaps youth. Sometimes the rose is part of a roses-and-wine extension, for as in *Popularity* the fully savoured flower offers nectar as well as colour and odour. In the *Women and Roses* dream the two go together. In *Any Wife to Any Husband* they will be sought together: '"if a man would press his lips to lips / Fresh as the wilding hedge-rose-cup

---

1 Mrs Alexandra Orr, *Handbook to the Works of Robert Browning* (London, 6th ed., 1923; cf. preface, p. vii), 213. 'The special feat imputed to him was recorded of other magicians in the Middle Ages ... [by] many other authorities.'

there slips / The dew-drop out of, must it be by stealth?"' In another
conventional combination, rose and grape combine to signify delights
that the guilty duellist of *Before* will never enjoy. Yet because they
are suffused by the haunted man's guilt, the conventional flower and
fruit assume a more than natural meaning and can no longer be taken
for granted. As in a dream, what seems ordinary becomes terrifying
when it is shown not to be so. Thus earth's composure also becomes
'terrible.' (Thus, also, into what seems an everyday scene described in
conventional manner comes such a *Waste Land* picture as 'What's
the leopard-dog-thing, constant at his side, / A leer and lie in every
eye of its obsequious hide?')

Where the rose signifies love, Browning implies the quality of the
love by what happens to the flower. In both *One Way of Love* and
Another Way of Love failure in love is anticipated though not certain.
The speakers announce how they will cope with it. The first, a man,
will shred his rose at the beloved's feet; if he is ignored, he can still
find the resource to rejoice with lovers who succeed. His rose,
mutilated, is witness in its destruction to his self-forgetting passion.
The second speaker, a woman, has no intention of sacrificing her rose.
If her lover is bored with her rose bower, she threatens to alter its
flowers. Presumably they have before been common garden variety,
for they can be converted either to thornless redness and sweetness
– for another man, says the lady – or to very prickly thorniness, to
teach this recalcitrant lover a lesson. The lady, unlike her fellow-
speaker, preserves her rose intact, indeed uses it as a weapon. To be
sure, it is not rejection that threatens her love, but something more
incensing – boredom. *Another Way of Love* seems to grow out of the
various possibilities that the rose metaphor offers. June, the month of
roses, is 'past the full' but 'the best of her roses' has yet to blow. The
lady offers the rose to a reluctant swain who has become bored with
mere 'sweetness and redness.' She promises him some thorns to
enliven their intercourse – but no enjoyment of a later, thornless rose,
'delicious as trickles / Of wine.' Again, the metaphor of drinking is
made to crown the bliss of the rose. Or, the lady threatens in a suddenly savage image, June may use June-lightning, which rids roses of
spiders and stops 'the fresh film-work.'

The companion-piece, *One Way of Love*, is less interested in the
possibilities of its rose image as either weapon or bribe. The speaker
displays the familiar prodigal devotion of some Browning lovers, and

it is in keeping with his self-abnegation that he focuses on his lady and not on the power of his love. It is worth considering whether the Browning lovers who revel in expanding their images and stress the sensation of their experience are not often deficient in love. Thus with this pair of poems, with the husband of *Any Wife*, and later with Don Juan (who presents a superb sustained rose-and-lily contrast). In Browning's highest love, the image seems not to match or to take over the experience; it is less identified with love and more peripheral to it. In this way Browning manages to suggest a private indescribable realm of bliss. He had used this manner already in the song 'Nay, but you' ... and in *The Flower's Name*. In *Men and Women* none of the quarrelling lover's fertile image-making is used to produce a metaphor of the quality of love. In *By the Fireside* nothing can describe the quality of love except its near-miraculous consequences. In *One Word More* the moon, with public and private sides, is an admirable image of the beloved. It is better, in a Browning lyric, to be tongue-tied rather than garrulous (he felt for the Tasso admirer who could say only 'O tu' – cf. note 9, chapter 6), to keep one's eye on the lady, to avoid conventional comparisons or pretty images or clever ingenuities. In the late *Poetics* it is the 'foolish' who are made to say '"Flower she is, my rose."' The speaker himself, in good Shakespearean tradition, chides, '"Hush, rose, blush! no balm like breath!" ... / What is she? Her human self, – no lower word will serve.' Elizabeth, it will be remembered, was not called a rose, but 'taught me what a rose really was.'

Browning thus tends to free his highest lovers from the development or even use of conventional images. The speaker of *A Lovers' Quarrel*, whose imagery invites comparison with 'any husband's,' eschews enjoyment of wild or other roses. 'Any husband' can fulfil his role superbly, always provided he has his garden-rose, his wife, to cherish; the obvious duty gone, he accepts what another flower offers in order to fill the vacuum. The lover turns conventional imagery upside down; the husband (says his wife) is incapable of this, dew and wild roses meaning only one thing – drink and pluck. One man is master of his image, the other mastered by it. One man is active and distinct from the natural world, the other passive and immersed in it. It need hardly be said that Browning's own sympathies are with the former.

The *Statue and the Bust* lovers once anticipated how

> The rose would blow when the storm passed by.
> Meantime they could profit in winter's dearth
> By store of fruits that supplant the rose:
> The world and its ways have a certain worth.

To create 'in the worst of a storm's uproar' flowers of their own, as does the quarrelling lover, is beyond the capacity of this conventional pair.

In *A Pretty Woman* it is the woman rather than love which is associated with the rose, and implications about her are read from her flower symbol. She is a natural (in Irving Babbitt's most pejorative sense) object. Like Fifine she is bewitching, but has no soul. Like Galuppi's soul-less flower-like Venetians, she is 'born to bloom and drop.' Or rather, to bloom and drop or to be plucked: a man has the choice of grasping or glancing. In both poems, the inevitability of 'born to' is taken for granted. The rhyme rings ironically throughout *A Pretty Woman*; it is a mocking fun-rhyme, as if the subject can hardly be considered a serious one. Yet the rhyme, like the rose-metaphor, turns its obviousness back on itself and the reader is made to question the facility of both. The pretty woman is 'dewy' and 'fresh' like 'any husband's' hedge-rose, and the permanence of love is similarly not meant for her, indeed would be destructive of her particular grace. (The various uses of the word 'grace' in the poem would repay notice.) Best not to pick this rose-bud. But – 'Must you gather?' Then, 'Smell, kiss, wear it – at last, throw away!'

In *Two in the Campagna* and *Master Hugues* the rose image again has traditional connotations, but in each poem it is part of a wider scheme of imagery that gives it a certain weight. In *Two in the Campagna* it is associated with the good minute of love; when the speaker is no longer a man with a rose but himself becomes a thistleball, it is as if he has slipped in ballad fashion from rose to thorn. Rose and star are both symbols of the desirable in this poem, and the combination also appears in *Master Hugues*. The position of 'stars and roses' is paralleled in this poem by 'truth and nature.' But although the star as symbol of truth and the rose as symbol of nature accord with Browning's usage elsewhere, the parallel is not made explicit. More interesting is the repeated combination of spider-web, rose, and star in *Two in the Campagna* and *Master Hugues*. (If lightning may be considered the lady's appropriate celestial parallel for a star in

Another Way of Love, then the rose, star, and spider trio is used there too.) But the lover's web is not the musician's, though they may be related. The lover's is not the web of past, dead traditions that obscures the life of the present. Master Hugues' web may, however, be spun from the same kind of reflections as the lover's – reflections that derive no sustenance from outside the self and remain sterile for all their ingenuity.

If such reflections produced poetry rather than Master Hugues' music, it would surely be poetry like the *Transcendentalism* of Browning's cautionary tale of that name. And in this poem the alternative is symbolized by the rose miraculously created by the mage. Again, as in *Women and Roses* the rose is made to symbolize the vital centre of creative art (here actual, there only potential). But neither the dreamt roses of *Women and Roses* nor the magic rose of '*Transcendentalism*' grows naturally from any soil, for Browning continues to stress the mystery of the creative process.

In the above poems, where the rose is a natural object it symbolizes the sweets of nature. The love it images is that of eros, of the realm of nature, the 'obvious human bliss.' The poetry it symbolizes is that of images and melody and youth, the boy-poet's natural production. In love, as in the making of poetry (cf. *Sordello*), or indeed as in all life (cf. *Rabbi ben Ezra* or the *Parleying with Smart*, which both use rose contrasted with star imagery), the natural comes first in sequence and is to be enjoyed. In *By the Fireside* a happy enough union precedes the extraordinary one. When men stop with the natural, Browning often grows impatient with them, especially in *Men and Women*. Later a wry acceptance of limited existences can be seen; here is the rose that is Clara in *Red Cotton Night-Cap Country*:

> And what a flower of flowers he chanced on now!
> To primrose, polyanthus I prefer
> As illustration, from the fancy-fact
> That out of simple came the composite
> By culture ...[2]
> Social manure had raised a rarity.
> Clara de Millefleurs (note the happy name)
> Blazed in the full-blown glory of her Spring.   (1502–14)

2 Could Browning have recalled the flowers of an early bouquet to

It is worth stressing that Browning found the natural good in itself, for in the discussions of *Love Among the Ruins* and *A Toccata of Galuppi's* I noted the implicit questions Browning asks the man who tries to read meaning from nature's cycle. There, as above, the happiest position is neither immersion in nature nor disdain of her, but independence of her while enjoying the legitimate sweets she offers. *Fra Lippo Lippi* is commonly cited in this connection. There are other interesting examples. In two later poems, women in much mental anguish begin the road to recovery by first recovering nature. The earth, by its simple normality, seems almost to minister to them when they are nearly maddened:

> Oh, good gigantic smile o' the brown old earth,
>   This autumn morning! How he sets his bones
> To bask i' the sun, and thrusts out knees and feet.
> (*James Lee's Wife: Among the Rocks*)

> I heard again a human lucid laugh
> All trust, no fear; again saw earth pursue
> Its narrow busy way amid small cares,
> Smaller contentments, much weeds, some few flowers, –
> Never suspicious of a thunderbolt
> Avenging presently each daisy's death.
> I recognized the beech-tree, knew the thrush
> Repeated his old music-phrase, – all right,
> How wrong was I, then!   (*Inn Album*, 1804–12)

It is a human agent that finally heals each woman, but nature has induced a calm and a perspective that are the prelude to health.

In the two examples above, nature acts upon characters, a nature that is different and apart from their private tormented worlds. To be sure, each character is ready to find in the natural scene what will be restorative for her. But the outer scene is much less an extension of the mind's landscape than in many Browning poems. James Lee's

Elizabeth? 'A friend of mine – one of the greatest poets in England too – brought me primroses and polyanthuses the other day, as they are grown in Surrey!' (*LEB*, 1, 277; [Feb.-Mar., 1846]).

wife had previously observed a nature strongly coloured by her own torment. As she relaxes, so does the natural scene she sees. It becomes separate from her, the human and natural worlds following their distinct though related courses. The lover among the ruins also observed a nature coloured by his own reflections. So does the *By the Fireside* speaker, but he, more felicitous in love than the shepherd, has a landscape which, it is suggested, is also separate from himself and his beloved.

I have been relying on the contexts of the above remarks to supply the meaning of the multi-significant word nature. Needless to say, the meaning may vary extensively for different Browning characters. The speakers in *The Ring and the Book*, for instance, make very diverse comments about nature and her laws; this is one touchstone by which we read their characters. Yet, as suggested above, I do not think such variation implies Browning was relativist, or that his landscapes are all inner ones writ large.

Browning likes to contrast those in harmony with nature and those enthralled by a false artificiality. The two dukes of *Bells and Pomegranates* and their two duchesses (the late and the fleeing ones) are examples. So are Cleon and Karshish in *Men and Women*. Cleon assumes his elaborations on nature constitute superiority:

> The wild flower was the larger; I have dashed
> Rose-blood upon its petals, pricked its cup's
> Honey with wine, and driven its seed to fruit,
> And show a better flower if not so large.   (147–50)

Karshish does curious things with nature, but respects her and grants her place. (For him incarnation in the natural, though nearly inconceivable, has amazing implications. For Cleon the Greek, the idea is foolishness.) Another *Men and Women* character in harmony with nature, Fra Lippo Lippi, strews his monologue with nonsense-verses, all amatory and all flowery: broom, quince, thyme, rose, clove, pine, and peach. The blossoms are wild and domestic, herb and fruit, large and small, colourful and inconspicuous – an eclectic group. But when the time comes to paint a penitential picture, it will be of a 'bowery, flowery angel-brood, / Lilies and vestments and white faces,' and its fragrance will be like shaved iris-root, of a sweet indoors fragility. No pungency or colour or outdoors earthiness and vitality here. There is in Browning a good deal of instinctive trust in this kind of vitality. Such trust, taken in isolation from the rest of Browning, provides the basis for such neo-classical attacks on him as Santayana's, Babbitt's, and Douglas Bush's.

Ruskin must have been among the first to charge Browning (directly or indirectly, and of course not as a neo-classicist) of liking nature for its mere animation. We have Browning's reply, though not Ruskin's charge:

> Lastly, you know what you say very energetically & observably about modern poets being 'without God in the world' 'an inherent & continual habit of thought which Scott shares with the moderns in general, being the instinctive sense of the divine presence, not formed into distinct belief – it creates no perfect form, does not apprehend distinctly any Divine being or operation, but only an animation (slightly credited) in the object, of nature – this feeling (you sum up) is quite universal with us.' Now, here I will take a liberty you would give me more difficultly elsewhere. I look at this as requiring answer, if answer be to give, – and, for one, & as poor an one as you please, speak for myself out of the 'universally habituated.' Of all my things, the single chance I have had of speaking in my own person – not dramatically – has been in a few words in the course of 'Sordello' – a poem never *forgotten*, for a good reason, but printed sixteen years ago – here it is, – I am rolling its clots out into one flat – so I at once ask myself – knowing what my faith was, & immeasurably deeper is – 'Did I then, if I needed to notice a natural object, really withhold my tributary two-mites tho' they do but make a farthing?' – I dip for & find these passages – now; do read them.

> > By this, the hermit-bee has stopped
> > His day's toil at Goito: the new-cropped
> > Dead vine-leaf answers, now 't is eve, he bit,
> > Twirled so, and filed all day: the mansion's fit,
> > God counselled for. As easy guess the word
> > That passed betwixt them, and become the third
> > To (*God and*) the soft small unfrighted bee, as tax
> > Him with one fault.

(*Alberic Romano was*) tied on to a wild horse, was trailed
To death through raunce and bramble-bush. I take
God's part and testify that 'mid the brake
Wild o'er his castle on the pleasant knoll,
You hear its one tower left, a belfry, toll – ...
Chirrups the contumacious grasshopper,
Rustles the lizard and the cushats chirre
Above the ravage.

Lo, on a heathy brown and nameless hill
By sparkling Asolo, in mist and chill,
Morning just up, higher and higher runs
A child barefoot and rosy. See! the sun's
On the square castle's inner-court's low wall
Like the chine of some extinct animal
Half turned to earth and flowers; and through the haze
(Save where some slender patches of grey maize
Are to be overleaped) that boy has crossed
The whole hill-side of dew and powder-frost
Matting the balm and mountain camomile.
Up and up goes he, singing all the while
Some unintelligible words to beat
The lark, God's poet, swooning at his feet,
So worsted is he at 'the few fine locks
Stained like pale honey oozed from topmost rocks
Sun-blanched the livelong summer,' – all that's left
Of the Goito lay!

Now, I think you will not object to me the poor quality of my verse any
more than you would deny a man's Christianity because he prayed in
broken English – I know & can mend the bad English poetry here – but
I am free of your graver reproach, I hope. This is certainly the first
time in my whole life that I ever quoted a line of my own – but you write
to me in the fullness of the days and I want to stand no worse with you
than must be ... I can only speak to that [Ruskin's] goodness and bid
you try and know me before you make up your mind – I aim widely
and want more than a glance to take in all I endeavor at, hit or miss.
With your letter came one from Carlyle – I hide his gold words as if

I had stolen them, as I partly have, – but he looks to what suits his
own sight in what I show. So God makes him, you & me.   (*A Letter
from Robert Browning to John Ruskin*; Feb. 1, 1856)

Browning's view of nature is, then, in intent at least, an orthodox
theological view. It must have been affected by the Romantics: perhaps the vitalism in his nature derives from theirs. But his reaction
to nature's vitalism in the classics, as seen in the *Parleying with
Gerard de Lairesse*, is surely also his reaction to nature's vitalism in
Romantic poetry. It is a reaction essentially the same as that in the
letter to Ruskin. Browning's view of nature probably comes closest
to Blake's, among the Romantics, no doubt because of the biblical influence on both. At least Browning's infernal and redeemed
natures seem close to Blake; of a distinct nature, existing apart from
man's vision (or lack of it), there is little or nothing in Blake.

Browning's paradisal nature may be seen in the speaking nature
at the end of *Saul* or the star become a familiar possession in *My Star*
or the thornless rose that the *Women and Roses* speaker imagines
but cannot create or the magic rose of poetry in '*Transcendentalism.*'
But such phenomena do not derive from a force immanent in
nature. Rather there is a sense of miracle happening, of grace
bestowed, whether beatific or in the more immediate areas of art
or human love. Such grace once granted, the receiver becomes
master of nature. His nature imagery does not become apocalyptic,
but he does sense what it might be to have the lion lie down with
the lamb or a star to play with. This kind of nature imagery, of some
earthly paradise, I noted in Pippa's songs (more conventional or
realistic nature imagery appears in the scenes themselves). The
imagery of some earthly paradise, of what Browning calls a 'mystic
land,' also appears intermittently in his letters to Elizabeth Barrett.

'One of these days,' he wrote in an early, often-cited letter to her,
'I shall describe a country I have seen in my soul only, fruits, flowers,
birds and all' (*LRBEB*, 1, 47; Apr. 15, 1845). His love for Elizabeth
could be symbolized by her precious vanished garden in *The Lost
Bower*.[3] The 'mystic land of the four rivers' appears later (ibid., 1,

---

3 'One must give no clue, of a silk's breadth, to the "*Bower*" yet. One day!'
    (*LRBEB*, 1, 242; Oct. 20, 1845).

531; Mar. 11, 1846) and shortly afterwards the Bower image is merged into what became the favourite image for Browning and Elizabeth's future private realm of bliss – the Siren's isle.[4] Elizabeth acknowledges Browning's power to create 'that Dreamland which is your especial dominion' (ibid., II, 696; May 11, 1846), a land no doubt like 'that far land we dream about / Where every man is his own architect' (*Red Cotton Night-Cap Country*, 2021–2). Even in the letters, it is interesting to note, the favourite Siren's isle figure[5] is associated not only with love but also with art. Indeed the figure of the Siren must have particularly pleased Browning because of its double association with feminine allure and with singing; as in *One Word More* and 'O Lyric Love,' he liked Ba to be 'my dearest siren, and muse, and Mistress, and ... something beyond all' (*LRBEB*, II, 725; May 24, 1846); 'I *know* and could prove you are as much my Poet as my Mistress' (ibid., II, 638; Apr. 19, 1846).[6] Even beyond art, the image could be 'the serene spot attained, the solid siren's isle amid the sea' where a man may possess his soul; 'but he [Haydon] would put out to sea again, after a breathing time, I suppose: though even a smaller strip of land was enough to maintain Blake, for one instance, in power and glory thro' the poor, fleeting "sixty years" ' (ibid., II, 861; July 9, 1846). The old references in *Paracelsus* and *Sordello* and by Jules in *Pippa Passes* to a happy island in some far sea come to mind at once.

If nature may be earthly or paradisal, she may also be infernal. Browning rarely uses such imagery, but can do so memorably. Such

4 'Come, some good out of those old conventions, in which you lost faith after the Bower's disappearance – (it was carried by the singing angels, like the House at Loretto, to the Siren's Isle where we shall find it preserved in a beauty "very rare and absolute") – is it not right you should be my Lady, my Queen?' (*LRBEB*, I, 543; Mar. 17, 1846).

5 Browning mentions the Siren in the *Letters*, I, 352, 414, 419, 423, 425, 443, 493, 520, 543, 559, 566; II, 605, 606, 631, 655, 697–8, 725, 861.

6 Jay Macpherson notes the tradition of the good Siren, as for example in the invocation to Sabrina (878–82): 'And the songs of Sirens sweet, / By dead Parthenope's dear tomb.' She remarks how, in the move from Renaissance to Romantic, the good Siren departs ('Narcissus or the Pastoral of Solitude: Some Conventions of Nineteenth-Century Romance' [PH D thesis, University of Toronto, 1964], 148). In the Barrett-Browning letters may be found a private remnant of the old tradition.

use, I think, gives much of its power to *Childe Roland*. In some
poems nature appears menacing because she is a meaningless cycle
upon which man whirls away his life. (One of the few classical
myths Browning treated was that of Ixion on the wheel; it is the fear
that this may be the real pattern of earthly life that oppresses such
speakers as *A Toccata*'s.) In *Childe Roland* nature is not a deadly
cycle, but has stopped. Grass, which is omnivorous in *Love Among
the Ruins*, is here scant and likened to hair on a diseased body.
The animal in the poem is 'past service.' Things have happened
in the landscape but happen no longer, for life is nearly petrified.
Rivers do not act normally, but snake about like some animate
creature. (When nature's phenomena take on functions that usually
belong to something else, we know we are out of this world, for
better or for worse. In the lyric snatch on Thamuris in *Aristophanes'
Apology*, this happens in a paradisal fashion. In fact, point for
point the scene is nearly the precise opposite of *Childe Roland*'s.)
All is arrested and comatose in this deathly, dream-like atmosphere,
until the shattering horn at the end, which brings us back to the
title, and to Shakespeare's stray line to which this dream has been
prologue. Suddenly we emerge into the familiar world again, where
choice and change and action are possible.

I have moved from *Women and Roses* through a discussion of rose,
and thence nature imagery. I wish now to return to a poem that,
like *Women and Roses*, has to do with both love and art – *My Star*.
     The question of the poem's significance is, however, disputed,
for the lyric consists of nothing but an elaboration of its central image.
C. Willard Smith in *Browning's Star-Imagery* (Princeton, 1941,
151–2) associates *My Star* with Browning's poetic inspiration. The
more common association is with Elizabeth Barrett (cf. DeVane,
Handbook, 227), and to this latter interpretation I also incline, if
one must ask the question which it answers. But the two associations
may not be mutually exclusive.
     The most interesting thing about the poem is, I think, not precisely
what the star signifies, but its domestication. The poem begins
'All that I know / Of a certain star,' but it appears that the speaker
knows a good deal: 'mine has opened its soul to me.' Nonetheless
his friends cannot see the star, so that the speaker's intimate knowledge is of its private aspects, and these private aspects must be

reportable but not demonstrable. Friends have to go by this witness's testimony.

In both *The Ring and the Book* and *Parleying with Smart* occur passages in which a speaker chooses the intimacy and accessibility of the rose to the grandeur and distance of a shooting star. For Caponsacchi the context is love: he would prefer to learn from human love of divine love rather than simply dreaming of the former. For Browning in the *Parleying* the context is all life with special reference to poetry: man must know earth, the rose, before heaven, the star, in order to have something to learn from. Rose and comet are the images of the first poem, rose and meteor of the second. In *Two in the Campagna* the lover wishes to connect the rose he partially knows with a star – which will not favour him. In *Women and Roses* it is the roses that will not favour the speaker – roses that seem as accessible as any other flowers, but prove as remote as some star, and like stars are the centres of revolving satellites. The context of the former poem is love, of the latter love and artistic creation.

The star of *My Star* moves like comet or meteor. Movement is one of its chief attributes, colour being the other. The star makes colour move, throws 'darts' of it like a spar, 'dartling' colour. Or 'it stops like a bird; like a flower, hangs furled.' It moves, that is, like some earthly thing; it is a tamed star. And its colours, red and blue, while legitimate star colours, are also more earthly than white or silver. What happens in the poem is, I think, that star and rose images combine. The star, in opening its soul to the man who loves it, becomes as intimate, close, and colourful as the rose. It opens out like the star at the end of the *Dramatis Personae Epilogue* or in St John's vision in *A Death in the Desert,* and unlike the closed circles of *Women and Roses.* As in the blissful order of things imagined by Caponsacchi, by Browning, and by the *Two in the Campagna* speaker, star and flower both have place; happier still, the two become one so that the 'finite heart' need no longer yearn to be fixed by some friendly star. In this poem the speaker is sure of his star, 'my star.' He can afford to watch its movement and colour in perfect security, and to let it rush about in its own way.

If Smith's connecting of the *My Star* imagery with poetic inspiration is persuasive, the connections with Elizabeth Barrett are even more cogent. First, of course, are the mutual associations from the Barrett-Browning letters: Browning is to Elizabeth the poet of 'the

Lyre and the Crown,' her association being drawn from the Preface to *Paracelsus*.[7] But as for herself, 'my own star, my own particular star, the star I was born under, [is] the star *Wormwood* ... on the opposite side of the heavens from the constellations of "the Lyre & the Crown" ' (*LRBEB*, I, 126; July 16–17, 1845).[8] What Elizabeth reads from their stars is the certainty of Browning becoming disillusioned with her. But Browning sees something different: 'Dearest, I believed in your glorious genius and knew it for a true star from the movement I saw it, – long before I had the blessing of knowing it was MY star, with my fortune and futurity in it' (ibid., I, 261; Nov. 9, 1845). What is interesting here is not only the title of Browning's *Men and Women* lyric, with the possessive capitalized, but the associations by both Browning and Elizabeth of the star image with the beloved and also with the beloved's creative capacity.

The precious possessive is later emphasized again by Browning: 'it was as if someone had said "but that star [Elizabeth] is your own" ' (ibid., II, 823; June 28, 1846). He had earlier entered a caveat: 'I do not *expect*, – as a foolish fanciful boy might, that on the sudden application of "Hymen's torch" (to give the old simile one chance more), – our happiness will blaze out apparent to the whole world lying in darkness, like a wondrous "Catherine-wheel," now all blue, now red ... I trust a long life of real work' (ibid., II, 587; Apr. 4, 1846).

Celestial imagery and the imagery of birds and of red and blue reappear in other lines of Browning. In 'O Lyric Love' they are as closely associated with Elizabeth as the star and red-blue images above, and, most important, with Elizabeth in her double capacity as Lyric and Love. The dead Elizabeth is there half angel and half bird; like the star, she is of celestial origin, and now celestial habitation, but when alive she dropped earthward, bird-like, to assist man. Red is connected with the human,[9] blue with the heavenly.

---

7 'Were my scenes stars, it must be his [the reader's] co-operating fancy which, supplying all chasms, shall connect the scattered lights into one constellation – a Lyre or a Crown.'

8 Cf. ' "a dropped star / Makes bitter waters, says a Book I've read" ' (*Aurora Leigh*, v, 917–18). The idea haunted Elizabeth: 'what if it should be the crossing of my bad star? *You* of the "Crown" and the "Lyre" to seek the influences from the "chair of Cassiopeia" ' (*LRBEB*, I, 386; Jan. 13, 1846).

9 Cf. H.N. Fairchild, 'Browning's Pomegranate Heart,' *Modern Language*

In *James Lee's Wife* red and blue are used in a passage of colour
and movement like that in *My Star* and are associated with love.[10]
Perhaps Browning's use, in *My Star*, of the star darting red and blue
like some Catherine-wheel was meant to indicate to Elizabeth
how such a love as his could blaze forth – in private if not to the
whole dark world. It could also be an answer to one of her moments
of despondency. She once wrote to Browning: 'I see the new light
which Reichenbach [a German chemist] shows pouring forth visibly
from these chrystals tossed out. But when you say that the blue, I see,
is red, and that the little chrystals are the fixed stars of the Heavens,
how am I to think of you but that you are deluded .. mistaken? –
& in *what*? in love itself?' (ibid., II, 640; Apr. 21, 1846). In *My Star*
a 'fixed star of Heaven' can also be a little blue or red light, an
adored beloved also a cherished one; and perhaps a great white
light, in a moment of happy inspiration, a darting red and blue.

My Star is then, I believe, about both love and art, as is *Women
and Roses*. It is also the blissful opposite of that haunting poem.
In *Women and Roses* the speaker longs to 'fix' just one woman.
So in *Two in the Campagna* the speaker longs to be fixed by a
friendly star. Both yearn for safety and steadfastness, for security
against the women's remoteness or the wind's caprice. To be rooted
and fastened and still seems the highest bliss to each. But the
speaker of *My Star* has attained such bliss, and has learned not to
cling to his security. There is no need for him of the inturned *Pauline*
attitude, where the fearful speaker hides in the enclosure of the
beloved's arm. The same sense of joyous freedom that lightens
By the Fireside and informs part of *A Lovers' Quarrel* prevails in
this little poem. This lover has no fear of losing his little star.

Notes 66 (1951), 265–6. Mr Fairchild does not mention Browning's
association of pomegranates with good works in the explanation of
'bells and pomegranates.' The association would be appropriate for this
context too.

10 Browning was, of course, fond of the combination, and of the separate
colours: 'when reds and blues were indeed red and blue' (*The Ring and
the Book*, I, 62) ; 'I confess to a Chinese love for bright red – the very
names "vermilion" "scarlet" warm me, – yet in this cold climate nobody
wears red to comfort one's eye save soldiers and fox hunters, and old
women fresh from a Parish Christmas Distribution of cloaks. To dress
in floating loose crimson silk, I almost understand being a Cardinal'
(*LRBEB*, I, 500; Feb. 27, 1846).

He makes no effort to chase or imprison it. The sense of freedom
in this poem, and in the two just mentioned, is the alternative to the
quest of *Love in a Life* and the hunt of *Life in a Love*. Once grace
is attained, in this secular realm of eros, as well as in the religious
context I have outlined for *Pauline*, the man so blessed moves beyond
the alternatives of the fixed and the fluctuating, capture or loss.
As in *By the Fireside* the enclosures of self, home, and world abolish
themselves.

13 TIME AND SPACE:

BY THE FIRESIDE

Both the *Pauline* speaker and Paracelsus want the benefits of time without the disadvantages. The *Pauline* speaker wants the permanent security of his old place in God's care and his literal protection in Pauline's arms. He must come back to these shelters, and thus the change that is part of time is necessary for his rehabilitation. That he detests having to go through such a process is clear from his emphasis that apostasy need not have happened. With Paracelsus, change is connected with the finite mutable world that is so unsatisfactory to the seeker after the infinite. Yet he will, he assumes, in the course of time change definitively man's knowledge and thence the world; he will change the record of the sages' imperfect achievement, alter the past. Sordello, too, wants the advantages of change, the incarnation of Palma for instance, but time offers him unpleasantnesses as well. The mere physical changes of time displease the *Pauline* poet in his unregenerate days: suicide at the prime of life is his answer to this problem. Paracelsus though worn dies comparatively young, and both Aprile and Sordello very young. Early death is not a Browning obsession, but to reserve a final revelation until just before death certainly solves various plot problems. Luigi's appetite for death may be romantic and jejune. Still, death in youth, besides offering pathos automatically, does get rid of the challenge of time. Thamuris or Chatterton provided instances; even Shelley had the advantage both of tangible and potential achievement, so that Browning can fashion of his future what he will; he does the same thing with Byron (cf. note 6, chapter 7).

In *Bells and Pomegranates* time is not regarded sombrely, not even the time that inevitably brings death. In fact, death itself is not regarded very sombrely. *Bells and Pomegranates* contains the best example of a sensuous death-wish, developed in a mood of languor, *In a Gondola*. But it is not the only poem of the collections in which death is sensuously apprehended. Porphyria's lover, with his long yellow-hair noose and his arrangement of his beloved's corpse, may be macabre but makes his murder picturesque. So does *The Laboratory* speaker. The Bishop of St Praxed's slides into sensuous death like the *In a Gondola* lover. And if Waring's assassination of the Czar is a political murder, it is still as colourful as that of Porphyria's lover '... kerchiefwise unfold his sash / Which, softness' self, is yet the stuff / To hold fast where a steel chain snaps, / And leave the grand white neck no gash' [116–19]). (Strangulation seems to intrigue Browning in these years: Luigi advises, 'Walk in – straight up to him; you have no knife: / Be prompt, how should he scream?' And of course the grisly lines on Metternich come to mind.) Or death may be not only met, but reached for with gallantry as in *Cavalier Tunes* and *Incident of the French Camp*, or dealt out with gusto as in *Count Gismond*. Even Artemis makes of Hippolytus' funeral pyre a gravely sensuous thing, partly because the reader knows he is to be revived. There are also whimsical burials, of Sibrandus Schafnaburgensis' book and of the claret flask.

Nor does time intrude very seriously. In *The Flower's Name*, there is no pain in the knowledge that the magic moment must fade. *Time's Revenges* are not really the revenges of time but of coincidence. (A spurns friend B's love, and is spurned in turn by lady C; if C were in love with B and rejected by him, the triangle would be complete in *L'Enclos* fashion; in *A Light Woman* Browning does close the triangle.) When the Duchess of *The Flight of the Duchess* finds herself caught in a miserable marriage, she flees to some mystically apprehended existence with the gypsies, her bliss practically guaranteed. Only in *Earth's Immortalities* is the theme of the vicissitudes of time touched on, and the touch is very light, ironic, even a little enigmatic.

In *Men and Women* there is little interest in the mundane effects of time and change. Much more dominant is the vision of some kind of hope. Sometimes the speaker is allowed the fulfilment of his vision; more often he knows of it, may glimpse it, but cannot attain it. Hardly any of the *Men and Women* poems are concerned with the possibly debilitating effects of time. Time is the metaphysical destroyer of life and love in *Love Among the Ruins* and *A Toccata*, but only through death, that is by destroying the lovers. Both poems contain the assertion (which satisfies neither speaker) that destruction applies only to certain kinds of life and love. Saul is less sanguine about this (as is Cleon) and another kind of suggestion is made in both poems. The challenge of time in both, however, remains the challenge of death. In *By the Fireside* the challenge of time is surely and cheerfully answered ('old age seems blest instead'). Even in *Any Wife to Any Husband,* time could do no harm, only providing the wife could remain alive. Where time is seen as menacing through erosion rather than annihilation, the poems move towards melodrama. *In a Year* and *Another Way of Love* have unsatisfactory, deserting males; no reason for dissatisfaction is given.

Easeful death, however, is no longer an escape from the vicissitudes of time; the vision, of art or love, or, behind them, some beatific vision, redeems time. Death at the pinnacle of love may be joyful in *In a Balcony*; elsewhere in *Men and Women,* death may be very unpleasant (as in *A Heretic's Tragedy* and *The Patriot*) or a cause for some sorrow (*Any Wife*). Comfort is found in poems like *Karshish, Saul,* and *By the Fireside.* But nowhere does time's fatal mirror offer serious menace. It is in *Dramatis Personae* that Browning turns his attention to the attritions of time.

In Three Days should, I think, be ranked with *My Star, The Guardian Angel,* and *By the Fireside* as a poem that, in Browning's dramatic circle, comes very close to his own experience. The lyric turns on the question of time: its companion-piece is entitled *In a Year* and its theme is three days' absence from a beloved woman. The three days have a double effect on the speaker. The lovers are so intimately united that in one sense the parting is no parting at all ('how fresh the splinters keep and fine, – / Only a touch and we combine': the unusual image suggests the violence of each seemingly small rupture). But in another sense, three days is an enormous gap: the lover carefully counts out the hours of separation, as if they represented so much time to be spent in torment. The counting conveys more effectively than hyperbole how the absence appears nearly infinite; the lover must assure himself, by an obvious effort of mind, that an end to absence will come. Three days, besides, 'that change the world might change as well / Your fortune.' Here only one kind of change is feared, change which might occur in the three-day absence from the beloved, and which might make that three-day absence permanent. The alterations of the years ahead, which 'teem with change untried, / With chance not easily defied,' do not dismay the lover; he will then have his lady beside him.

Three days was an accustomed interval between Browning's later visits to Elizabeth, and the precise length of the interval was often noted by him. He wonders at her 'surprise that I shall feel these blanks between the days when I see you longer and longer' (*LRBEB*, I, 283; Nov. 21, 1845). A subsequent letter is dated 'Day before to-morrow!' (ibid., II, 709; May 17, 1846). During the summer of 1846, the intervals became increasingly difficult to bear. 'I will just write my joy at its being little more now than twenty-four hours before I shall see you, I trust' (ibid., II, 801; June 19, 1846). 'Do *you* know the days and the times and the long interval, – you, as *I* know? How strange that you should complain, and I become the happier!' (ibid., II, 805; June 22, 1846). 'May nothing overcast the perfect three hours on Tuesday, – those dear, dear spaces of dear brightness ... I most long to see you again, – always by far the most I long, the *next day* – the very day after I have seen you' (ibid., II, 869–70; July 12, 1846). 'Remember there are three days before our Saturday' (ibid., II, 898; July 23, 1846); 'having been used to ... calculate my time by the number of days since I saw you – whence, knowing to my cost that two days had gone by since such a event, I thought what I wrote' (ibid., II, 900; July 24, 1846). 'I am very well considering that there are three days to wait' (ibid., II, 983; Aug. 21, 1846). Browning's remarks on the intervals between visits closely resemble the speaker's in this lyric, both in their emphasis on the seeming length of the interval, and in their dating of his life according to the visits.

What fears Browning had during his conditional engagement, and especially during the summer of 1846, centred on what might happen to break the engagement or postpone the marriage. There is confidence, but also the touch of a man reassuring himself aloud, in such remarks as 'Thank God I shall see her to-morrow – my dearest, best, only Ba cannot change by to-morrow! – What nonsense!' (ibid., II, 639; Apr. 19, 1846). The end of each summer month, from June on, brought a despondent letter from him begging for a definite date for the marriage. The August letter is very pessimistic, and Browning's joyful notes following the wedding show how considerable had been his fear that it might never take place. Elizabeth's fears, however, concentrated not on the here and now, but on the future, especially on the possibility of her failing Browning in some way. This kind of apprehension Browning was ready to pooh-pooh. His reactions to these two types of fear are precisely those of the speaker of *In Three Days*.

One oddity in the time sequence of the poem is apparent on first reading. Although there are three days, there is only one night. This manipulation is part of the poem's play with time. Literally, the lover counts only one night because the nights are short: the alteration of a few words in the repeated opening and closing lines shows this ('And just one night, but nights are short'; 'And one night, now the nights are short'). But in another sense, the whole three-day interval constitutes a night; the lover's days are the hours spent with his mistress. This is what is implied in the figure of 'life's night' which 'gives my lady birth' in the second stanza. This explains, too, why only one morning seems to dawn in the repeated three lines; three days, one night, then 'two hours, and that is morn.' The phrasing of 'that is morn' again conveys, I think, a double sense. 'Then just two hours, and that is morn': the two hours sound like part of the curious sequence, an interval to wait after the three days and night; but the phrase 'then comes morn' would have conveyed this equally well. The two hours, I surmise, are the 'that' which makes up the morn; the lover's visit is his morning, as absence is his night. Night, however, has one compensation, the light of the moon. So the life's night in the poem brings the beloved before the speaker like a moon; the image of her (also the image of Elizabeth in *One Word More*) is his light through the dark interval. (This figure had been used by Browning of his visits to Elizabeth: 'So, till To-morrow, – my light through the dark week' [ibid., I, 104; June 24, 1845]. 'How kind to write to me and help me thro' the gloomy day with a light! I could certainly feel my way in the dark and reach to-morrow without very important stumbling, but now I go cheerfully on' [ibid., II, 709; May 17, 1846]).

In the last reference Elizabeth's letter is the light through Browning's gloom, the moon of his night. In the poem the beloved's lock of hair has this role. This is what explains its juxtaposition to the moon image at the end of stanza ii and gives point to its isolated appearance in stanza iii. Like the moon, the lock of hair reflects something of the complete being that makes the day. Like the moon, it has manifold lights and darks. It has more: it has the same warmth and scent as all the lady's hair, and its light is an embrowned gold. In colour and touch it is closer than any moon to its original. Browning, of course, possessed a lock of Elizabeth's hair, and it, as well as her letters, was cherished by him (*LRBEB*, 1, 425; Jan. 27, 1846).

In a recent illuminating article on Browning's style (*ELH*, 32 [1965], 62–84), Robert Preyer has repeated Donald Davie's reservation about some of the detail in *By the Fireside*:

> Of this passage [lines 54–65] Donald Davie remarked that it was not at all clear if the 'syntactical pattern acts out a train of feeling significant to the burden of the whole' [*Articulate Energy*, 74]. One feels that a habit of language and expression has got out of control, that a hypertrophy of style has set in. The passage has a sort of vitality – but it is the vitality of a weed or a fungus, not precisely spurious, but then not particularly useful either.

Some of Browning short intense descriptions of nature do tend to separate themselves from their poems. Their vitality strikes and sticks, while the part they should play in the whole is forgotten or unexamined. Such a judgment as the above, however, must be made with caution. Not that Browning is incapable of a hypertrophy of style; but because such a lapse is less than likely in a comparatively short poem (265 lines), written at the height of Browning's power, on a subject close to his heart, and in a form (the lyric) that is in *Men and Women* usually tightly structured.

Certainly *By the Fireside* offers memorable snippets of description. Besides the autumn leaf and toadstools referred to above, there are the hawks (which Geoffrey Tillotson remembers[1]), the chapel, the slim stream, the old man and the children, and more. What is the point of it all? To some extent Mr Preyer's answer of overflowing vitality seems suitable, but I think with this difference. The vitality seems to me a deliberate part of the dramatic viewpoint; it grows out

1 *Sewanee Review* 72 (1964), 389

of the speaker's past and present joy. One function of love, amorous
or other, in Browning is to stimulate the ability to see both literally
and figuratively, and to relax tension in such a way as to encourage
whimsy and fantasy. The speaker in *Waring* delights in sketching
likely settings for his friend. The speaker in *A Lovers' Quarrel* could
once exuberantly play games of fancy with his lady, and even now he
sees nature clearly and in detail; were his lady present, he says, he
could read the book of nature. But vitality does not seem a sufficient
cause of the *By the Fireside* detail, for the spacing and selection of
detailed description leave the impression of deliberateness. And
deliberate I think it is.

When we come to *By the Fireside*, we see, first and obviously, that
it is a poem that plays with time. The title points to two fireside
scenes, one present and one future. In the present scene, time passes
slowly; Leonor reads, then muses; between her reading and her
musing come her husband's reflections. The first stanza points forward
to an autumn that proves to be not annual but symbolic, 'life's
November.' The speaker pictures himself in the future remembering
the past; then in the present he remembers the past; then he comes
into the present to speak to Leonor of the past; briefly imagines a
future after death; returns to the past and its unique moment that
defines the present and gives meaning as well as occupation for the
future. At the end he comes full circle to make the same assertion as
at the beginning.

It is hardly surprising that the poem plays with time, for of course
it centres on the 'moment one and infinite,' a point in chronological
time when another kind of time impinged on it and altered its
significance. This break through time, the lover says, enables him to
do what others cannot – to defy time, to bless age rather than youth.
Thus a love poem that looks not only to the high point of love past
but also to the future: 'youth seems the waste instead.' Thus, too, the
November imagery throughout. This is not a conventional spring-
flower love, the 'obvious human bliss,' but one that can set the seasons
upside down. It has its high point in a literal autumn scene, its happy
future in life's November, and its image of the lover is a tree shedding
leaves.

We see time present and time future in detail, as we see time past.
We twice step out of time, once in the moment one and infinite, and

once in fancy after death. We see significant time break through clock-time. We see clock-time slowly ticking in Leonor's two fireside poses, and in stanza ii where repetition gives a sense of the slow time of old age: 'While the shutters flap as the cross-wind blows / And I turn the page, and I turn the page ...' I think, however, that the poem plays with space as well as with time, and that what it does with space may very well help explain the passages of enlarged detail mentioned above.

Again, some of the use of space is obvious. The title indicates a specific place into which past and future love is drawn by memory and imagination. There is contrast between the two hearthside scenes, each with its still figure, and the large outdoors scene, full of stir and colour and sound and action. In the first helf-dozen stanzas there is a playing with perspective in the image of the inner and outer archways. Greek prose will offer a path and cover for the speaker's musings. Book leads to outer trellis, which is firm and unalterable by the speaker's reflections, 'like your hazel-trees.' But the reading mind, though conducted first where the words lead, then where observation suggests, and though moving within the pattern words and observation make, walks independently. It constructs its own pattern within, though governed by, the outer frame. Inner and outer arches lead to another country in a phrase ('by green degrees') perhaps meant to recall Marvell. The mind begins to pursue its own path and finally leaves the frame behind altogether.

The mind's mental country deserves some attention, for its components and the way they are arranged are less casual than at first they appear. How much so is up to the reader to decide. The first item is the 'ruined chapel,' which is placed 'half-way up in the Alpine gorge.' The scene's first line of structure, a gorge, is established, and its possible dimensions, Alpine. Another far-off building, secular this time, is noted; its indefiniteness marks its distance. The next stanza begins with 'a turn,' and the turn focuses attention on the near scene. The observer does not now reach out, but feels the scene reach in, the woods 'heaped and dim' seeming to gather for some drama like the imagined peers at the end of *Childe Roland*. A small stream is heard, alive as the streams Browning put into *A Lovers' Quarrel* or the Thamuris fragment of *Aristophanes' Apology*. (Such threads of water often appear in natural scenes of more than natural meaning;

cf. the stream that is Shelley in *Pauline*, the intersecting streams in *Love Among the Ruins*, the snaking river in *Childe Roland*.[2]) The following stanza turns us again to the far scene, this time not to two halfway buildings marking human activities, but to the lake with its tiny city and the sky with the mountain-peak. The upper and lower limits of the distant scene are set. Again, with stanza x, back we come to the near scene, and we discover we are on a mountain-side. On the inner side is 'straight-up rock'; on the outer the gorge drops away. The edge is marked by boulder-stones with lichens and ferns that seem to attach themselves to the rock like something alive ('lichens mock ... small ferns fit / Their teeth'). Such aliveness is most obviously to bring the scene sharply before our eye, but it also conveys a sense of nature's more than ordinary significance.

This sense of animation behind which some meaning may lurk informs the whole Alpine scene. Consider the effect of woods that are 'heaped,' of a tower that 'breaks solitude.' Or the even more daring effect of lines 51–3: 'Oh the sense of the yellow mountain-flowers, / And thorny balls, each three in one, / The chestnuts throw ...' We are invited to infer more than one meaning of 'sense,' and the connotations of 'three in one' can hardly be missed. Yet all this is delicately done. The phrases attributing significance to the scene are not many, nor, except for the last cited, of a kind to give pause. Browning backs away, so to speak, after he inserts such hints; the 'three in one' phrase is followed by two stanzas in which the associations are Lilliputian or fairy (the leaf is a shield, the moss is 'fairy-cupped / Elf-needled,' a crew of toadstools peep out). Nor does the structure of the scene clearly impart significance. Yet the stream is to reappear during the moment one and infinite. Path and gorge will be used again figuratively. The chapel, the first item introduced, is the last noted before the great moment, and much attention is given it between. Further, the potentiality at least of a symbolic scene might be inferred from the fact that Browning has constructed a setting with the precise outline of Dante's *Purgatorio*: mountain with path encircling it, lake

---

2 Cf. also: 'The live little spring-source, from the mountain, is a very real and peculiar advantage: one would value *that* greatly in England: what a vein of life there is in such a streamlet!' (*Learned Lady*, 47; Aug. 30, 1877)

at the base of the mountain, heaven at its peak. (Browning had, of course, explicitly used the mountain of Purgatory before, in *Sordello*.) Again, such a suggestion must be treated with care. This is no allegorical country, if it is a mysterious one. Yet, the moment one and infinite pulls our eyes toward a star in a tender sky. And on the other hand, those who dance to the tune of conventional love drop off into a gorge. Between, the lovers pursue their due mountain-path, with due pilgrimage off the path to a chapel just before the moment of revelation.

In one sense, *By the Fireside* centres on a love-scene in which occurs a moment of extraordinary closeness. In another sense, just suggested and never pressed, the moment has transcendent reality. In one sense, the natural scene is memorable only because the lover invests it with his own emotion. In another sense, again just suggested and never pressed, the natural scene is given an active role in the drama ('how the world is made for each of us'). Or a halfway point between immanence and transcendence may be chosen, with the view that nature has given a little more than the lovers have bestowed ('the forests had done it').

The mushrooms that puzzle Mr Davie and Mr Preyer I would explain as follows. Clearly their sudden appearance is of a piece with the general animation of the scene, and they are the fruit of the day's cycle rather than the year's. I think they are meant to suggest the brief powerful passion that in stanza xxii is of 'youth, flowery.' The speaker chooses for his own love the image not of a flower but of a tree, a tree whose best moment comes with the shedding of its last leaf. Just before the mushroom stanza, we move in for a close examination of a fallen leaf (also part of the detail objected to above). The point of focusing on a literal fallen leaf, of again establishing 'November hours,' is clear. Later the speaker will put beside his own love less abiding emotions, as the leaf here is laid by the mushrooms. To juxtapose a fallen leaf and flowers twice would be too heavy an effect for this poem: I think the mushrooms here take over the symbolic role of the flowers. Leaf and mushrooms are contrasted suggestively. The leaf is brightly and sharply coloured; the mushrooms pastel and streaked. The leaf is aggressive, metallic and martial, a shield; the mushrooms are timid, soft and coddled. The leaf is alone, unique; the mushrooms protrude in a group, a 'flaky crew.' There is an echo in 'rose' and 'dew,' which are associated with the mushrooms, of early youthful passion. Except for the last point mentioned, the contrast of masculine and feminine might serve the two images equally well. But when the connection of the brilliant autumn leaf and the symbolic leaf of the lover's tree is recalled, it seems some such explanation as the above, some explanation connecting stanzas xii and xiii with the core of the poem, is more feasible.

The more common image in Browning for brief youthful passion is the conventional flower. But the mushroom will reappear in *Mr. Sludge* with a function much like the one I suggested above: 'a youth whose fancies sprout as rank / As toadstool-clump from melon-bed' (299–300). And note in the following passages how the flower's characteristics would also suit the ephemeral mushrooms, born of the sun for a day's life:

> What Youth deemed crystal, Age finds out was dew
> Morn set a-sparkle, but which noon quick dried
>
> While Youth bent gazing at its red and blue
> Supposed perennial, – never dreamed the sun
> Which kindled the display would quench it too.
> (*Jochanan Hakkadosh*, 302–6)

In the *Epilogue* to *Dramatic Idyls*, second series, flower and tree represent different kinds of poetry:

> Touch him ne'er so lightly, into song he broke:
> Soil so quick-receptive, – not one feather-seed,
> Not one flower-dust fell but straight its fall awoke
> Vitalizing virtue: song would song succeed
> Sudden as spontaneous – prove a poet-soul!
> >   Indeed?
> Rock's the song-soil rather, surface hard and bare:
> Sun and dew their mildness, storm and frost their rage
> Vainly both expend, – few flowers awaken there:
> Quiet in its cleft broods – what the after age
> Knows and names a pine, a nation's heritage.

In the second quotation the mushroom's dew is also present. In the third, the single tree and many flowers are like single leaf and many mushrooms. Further, the 'knows and names' (a favourite biblical phrase for Browning) of the enduring poetry above recalls the *By the Fireside* remark about enduring love: 'I am named and known by that moment's feat.' It is a deep-rooted tree that is fit image of such love; 'rose-flesh mushrooms, undivulged / Last evening' suggest quite another kind.[3]

After the scene has been set, and a close look taken at several autumn details, the focus moves to the middle distance, to the first item noted in the scene, the chapel. Now action begins: the chapel is re-located; we cross the bridge for a closer examination. Browning again in stanza xiv, as in stanza vii, uses the interregative mood, which gives the effect of distance, of the observer peering out at the scene. But the scene is in the memory all the while, and so the questions also imply an observer auxious to impose as little as possible from the outside upon his mental scene.[4]

In this way, the question of agency in nature is like the question of agency in love. The scene, like the moment of love, lives in the speaker's brain. Like his love it is natural, and meant to be so, but more than natural. Like his love, the line between who gives and takes, and between objective and subjective, is unclear. In the moment one and infinite, man and woman and forest exist in a great harmony where there are no longer two persons in the Alpine setting, but some kind of inexplicable fusion. Then the ordinary dispensation of affairs takes over; the three move apart and darkness falls. But who has caused precisely what is uncertain. The 'great Word' is mentioned.

---

3 The first poem Ford Madox Ford remembered learning runs as follow:

A mushroom springs up in a night.
Take warning little folk.
An oak it takes a hundred years to grow ...
But then it is an oak!

(Ford Madox Ford, *Provence: From Minstrels to Machine* [Philadelphia, 1935], 139)

4 Cf. the similar care in the late *Dubiety*, where the speaker feels after an old memory:

What is it like that has happened before?
A dream? No dream, more real by much.
A vision? But fanciful days of yore
Brought many: mere musing seems not such.
Perhaps but a memory, after all!

'The forests had done it' too. Leonor is also a cause, and the lover himself is a cause for he must respond at the right time – 'when a soul declares itself – to wit, / By its fruit, the thing it does!' The word fruit brings us back to the 'drop of the woodland fruit,' and recalls the image of the last surrender of love, the falling leaf. The leaf is said to 'unfasten itself,' and the words again mark how various and interdependent is the agency, for a host of causes converge to bring about this seemingly independent action.

Browning gives seven stanzas to the chapel, stanza xiv pulling in toward it, and stanza xx away. The components of the chapel scene he will use again in other decisive scenes:

> ... we faced the church
>   With spire and sad slate roof, aloof
> From human fellowship so far,
>   Where a few graveyard crosses are,
> And garlands for the swallows' perch, –
> ...
>   You judged the porch
> We left by, Norman; took our look
> At sea and sky; wondered so few
>   Find out the place for air and view;
> Remarked the sun began to scorch;
> ...
> What was the sea for? What, the grey
>   Sad church, that solitary day,
> Crosses and graves and swallows' call?
>
> Was there naught better than to enjoy?
>   No feat which, done, would make time break ...?

The woman of *Dîs Aliter Visum* is a trifle querulous; she has no one to claim he is 'named and known by that moment's feat.' Hers may be seen as a failed *By the Fireside* setting of church, water, birds, silence. Similarly in *Fifine at the Fair* (lxii), a church at sunset near the sea, with birds prattling in the graveyard, evokes from Don Juan the remark that 'this is just the time, / The place, the mood in you and me,' as he responds in his way to his moment.

Browning inscribes a date on his chapel – 'good thought of our architect's.' He has a predilection for specific dates and events, and the dating of the chapel serves to stress its particularity, as, for instance, the dating of the Franceschini affair will stress its uniqueness. Time moves cyclically in *By the Fireside* – in the revolution of the seasons, in the aging of the lovers and the arrival of the next generations. But the cycle is broken by something unique, the strange moment. Further, the speaker claims that he and Leonor will step out of the cycle after death. The most important part of their lives is linear, with a beginning and an end; if repetition occurs, so also does the unrepeatable, what belongs to particular date and place.

In stanzas xvi and xvii, Browning remarks on the smallness of the chapel flock and how ordinary its occupations. Its simplicity is of a piece with the simplicity of the whole poem. Browning has scaled down the scenes informed by the great moment, not so much for contrast I think, as to demonstrate how the extraordinary moment may illuminate prosaic moments. Beside other love poems, this one may appear placid in its tranquillity and domesticity. Reading and musing by the fire, walking in the woods – these are not scenes that at first glance suggest themselves as material for a great love poem. Similarly with the amused forward look at the old man or the kindly outward look at the little flock. But ordinary scenes and people may be visited by extraordinary favours. For all that the chapel and its surroundings are insignificant, they are also silent and aware. Place as well as time in this poem can be at once casual and infinitely meaningful.

And the little flock has, after all, a certain appropriateness. Like illustrations from some book of the hours, the labourers act as daily shepherds of the various parts of the scene, each of the four being associated with one of the four elements. The woodman who stores nuts is in a November poem where literal and figurative fruits of the trees are important. The hemp-dresser's soaking hemp and the fowler's victims appear in the momentous scene, and the charcoal burner cannot but make us recall the poem's two firesides.

Browning spends some fifteen stanzas on the setting before he turns to the chief figure in it. The pertinence of the play with time now begins to be apparent, for the speaker's tribute to Leonor is not for her beauty or charm but for what she enables him to do with time. Because of her, he can 'dare' (the word is twice used) look backward and forward. (In line 103 there is the suggestion of an Orpheus who can keep his Eurydice.) She must 'see and make me see.'[5] The pertinence of the detailed description also begins to be apparent. From now on, Browning will pick up various details and invoke the scene by shorthand, so to speak, as he moves into interior drama and symbolic landscape. 'Grey heads abhor' the path toward age and death, but we remember the old man at the poem's beginning whose serenity is unmarred by his dumb colourless existence. The path 'leads to a crag's sheer edge with them; / Youth, flowery all the way, there stops – / Not they ...' The conciseness is deadly and reminds us of Browning's mastery in showing the irresistible force of time, as in the slow edging of the guillotine toward Guido in his second speech. But the path in stanza xxii also reminds us of the earlier Alpine path, which safely skirts a gorge, leads off to the chapel, and then to something more.

There are a great many unobtrusive repetitions with variety in *By the Fireside*. Along with the play on time and place, and the variety of agency suggested, they give the poem its strong sense of layers of significance. Various paths appear: the Alpine path, the flowery path, the path back to the past. Firesides re-occur, and also Novembers, forests, hazel-trees,[6] and leaves. One could easily multiply this list of particulars that are turned to symbolic use. Less noticeable are abstract qualities, verbs, and so on. One kind of pride appears in stanza xxv, another in stanza xxxiii. One kind of mixing is in stanza xxvi, another in stanza xlvii. Two meanings of 'prompt' are associated with Leonor in stanzas xxiv and xxviii. The lovers twice stoop (xxv and xxxvi). Different kinds of greyness are suggested by the grey heads of stanza xxi and the grey evening of stanza xxxvii. (Here the grey evening with one star is a miniature image of Leonor's illumination of the greyness of all time, including a colourless old age's. Perhaps her eyes are deliberately made grey in this connection. In stanza xxxviii sights and sounds, lights and shades make up a spell, as if all the colours and sounds of life were so concentrated in the great moment that old age will not regret the vanishing of the

5 Is this version of Leonor as a Maker-See also a defiance of the conventional Cupid? His motto, says Panofsky, was 'I am blind and I make blind' (*Studies in Iconology*, 105).

6 The hazelnut tree is associated with fertility and erotic fulfilment; cf. Peter Dronke in *The Medieval Lyric* (London, 1968), 194

pleasant hues and the 'music of all thy voices.'[7]) The poem centres
on the moment one and infinite, but there are other moments too, in
stanzas xlvii, xlviii, and li. And if we are tempted to suppose these
repetitions are not deliberate, we have only to look back at the 1855
By the Fireside to see that Browning later altered the original 'for a
second' (237) to 'for a moment' and the original 'that hour's feat'
(251) to 'that moment's feat.'

The tale breaks off when the speaker addresses Leonor. (He seems
not to speak literally, though he may, for her pose in stanza xxiii is
the same as at the end, except that she reads here and muses there –
following the same sequence, incidentally, as will the old man with
his wise Greek book.) He now places himself on the path to the past.
Another item from the Alpine scene is put to symbolic use, the stream
that goes over rocks. And again, though the symbolism is not pressed,
we may recall that this is a watery poem with its streams, pond, lake,
mists, and pearly rain, and that its water is used with a certain
appropriateness. It is perhaps possible to read time as an ever-rolling
stream: something for children playfully and idly to sail ships on;
something that is remembered by breaking a chain of recollections
into pearly drops; something that may be caught in history, as in the
chapel's stagnant pond, for the chapel commemorates time past in
more ways than one, as we see by its engraved date, its past 'joys and
crimes,' and its John the Baptist, forerunner of the moment that
is its reason for being. And ever-rolling time may also be fed by
meaningful time, by a far-off stream, as moments may be by a
moment.

7 Note how the *Prologue* to *Asolando* ('The Poet's age is sad') is here
anticipated; age may be less sensory but is more perceptive. And, cf. the
powerful description of a similar experience in *Aeschylus' Soliloquy*
(from *New Poems*):

> All sounds of life I held so thunderous sweet
> Shade off to silence – all the perfect shapes
> Born of perception and men's imagery
> Which thronged against the outer rim of earth
> And hung with floating faces over it
> Grow dim and dimmer – all the motions drawn
> From Beauty in action which spun audibly
> My brain round in a rapture, have grown still.

As in *By the Fireside*, where a hue becomes 'dumb,' sensory effects mingle:
sounds shade to silence.

It is interesting to note that the speaker stresses how little such joy as his was to be expected: 'how little I dreamed ...'; 'who could have expected this ...?' The speaker in *Two in the Campagna* yearns for something extraordinary, to 'drink my fill / At your soul's springs.' This man expects only the 'obvious human bliss, / To satisfy life's daily thirst.' He experiences nothing of the Campagna lover's pain; in fact, by his own admission his 'heart, convulsed to really speak, / Lay choking in its pride.' The Campagna lover was prepared to be 'unashamed of soul.' In *By the Fireside* it is Leonor who makes the decisive move, and when she does so the last leaf is said to 'unfasten itself.' It is a trifle curious (in stanza li) to call the lover's action a 'feat.' The only way to make some sense of the word, and of his pride in what appears his mere acceptance of a gift, is to see the descent of love here as an analogy of the descent of grace. There as here the recipient adopts a double attitude: he is held responsible for his action, yet claims it is of God. When it is noted how close to a Beatrice role is Leonor's, and how Browning makes it possible to infer divinity behind the act of love, the analogy is persuasive.[8]

The great moment comes at sunset, a time of day that is significant elsewhere in Browning. More often than not, however, it is a time possessed by thoughts of mortality, and its use here is like the use of autumn and old age – a reversal of conventional symbolism. In *Aeschylus' Soliloquy*, Aeschylus sits down 'at set of sun' and feels himself 'dying down into impersonal dusk.' Bishop Blougram selects a 'sunset-touch' as upsetting to an unbeliever's unbelief. Sunset is the time of death for Sordello, and of engagement for Childe Roland.

---

8 Browning, incidentally, used to emphasize how unlikely were the chances of his finding an Elizabeth Barrett (he uses the unicorn image in this connection); how, having found her, he did not win – she granted – the gift of love. 'In sober earnest, it is not because I renounced once for all oxen and the owning and having to do with them, that I will obstinately turn away from any unicorn when such an apparition blesses me .. but meantime I shall walk at peace on our hills here nor go looking in all corners for the bright curved horn!' (*LRBEB*, I, 199; Sept. 16, 1845); 'so far from catching an unicorn, he [Browning at a party] saw not even a respectable prize-heifer, worth the oil-cake and rape-seed it had doubtless cost to rear her' (ibid., I, 486; Feb. 21, 1846); '*that* too is no more a merit than any other thing I do' (ibid., I, 295; Nov. 28, 1845); 'I think of the great, dear *gift* that it was, – how I "*won*" NOTHING (the hateful word, and *French* thought)' (ibid., I, 335; Dec. 21, 1845).

When Browning takes us back into the scene, he juxtaposes as before the ordinary (the hawks[9]) with the portentous (the silence). But now, as tension builds, he concentrates on the portentous. It follows the visit to the chapel, a visit marked by slightly condescending comment and a string of unsurprising sentiments (marked by the 'and's' in stanza xxxiv). Once again, notice is taken of the moss. The word 'stoop' is twice used, once with 'kneel.' No undue emphasis is given it, yet the repetion faintly suggests that the act may be significant. It is as if the two lovers perform a rite before a pilgrimage. To be sure, they go to the chapel in a mood of casual curiosity and inspect it like the usual tourists. Yet it is a focal point of change. Similar treatment is accorded the rosary.

At the climax there is, in the well-known phrase, a double sense of time. All the while, chronological time, marked by moving water, twilight, and grey evening, moves gently on. It says much for the strength of Browning's poem that time does seem both to stop and to move steadily on. The stream, for instance, has its sound cut nearly to silence as it slips down the rocks, and with such subduing it appears to become almost entirely visual and still like a stream in a painting. But we know it moves all the time. After two stanzas the experience is over and we are out of it, before we are hardly aware of what has happened. Reflections upon it begin. (As Mr Preyer remarks of *Saul*, this is an excellent way to convey a sense of the great moment.[10])

The first reflection is one familiar in Browning's poetry at this time, the pathos of the vision denied: 'Oh, the little more, and how much it is! / And the little less, and what worlds away!' To be sure, the speaker says that 'each of us' has his moment. But his drama is a rare enough phenomenon in Browning's poetry for all that, and not to be commanded at will. The speaker's experience makes him conceive of nature's forces moving in to bring a decisive moment first to one person, then to another. The third speaker of the *Dramatis Personae Epilogue* conceives of the world in a similar way. For the former it is

9 Though see Mario Praz: 'For ... the falcon which returns to the falconer ... I can find no precedents ... but the comparison of the lover to a hawk, which could still appear somewhat novel to the anonymous poet of the thirteenth century ... had become a commonplace later on' (*Studies in Seventeenth-Century Imagery* [Rome, 1964, 2nd ed.], 95)

10 Robert Preyer, 'Two Styles in the Verse of Robert Browning,' *ELH*, 32 (1965), 72

the forests that so converge; for the latter, the sea. Then, for both, 'they relapsed to their ancient mood.' The natural scene is released, as it were, relaxes and separates out again into its components. The careful naming and describing of the components is part of the speaker's endeavour to pull them together in imagination as they once were in the moment.

One curious sentiment appears in lines 246–7: 'Be hate that fruit or love that fruit, / It forwards the general deed of man ...' Should not hate retard the general deed of man? Not if it is hatred of what ought to be hated, but this is not what the speaker says. Has his experience made him the least bit complaisant about all being right with the world? Or is he simply saying that the decisive shaping of individuals is what moves the world on?

The last two stanzas bring us back to the present – to Leonor and the fireside and the man who means to muse again on his great moment, 'as I said before.' They bring us full circle to the beginning and to the circles within circles of reflection that follow. They are of a piece with the casualness of the whole poem. The inimitable experience is such that it can properly be narrated beside a chimney-corner: 'How well I know what I mean to do ... One day, as I said before.' Time and place and manner have all known the experience of complete harmony. Their casualness is born not of Browning's carelessness but of his vision of that harmony.

14 MAGE AND PROPHET

Heaven's gift takes earth's abatement!
He who smites the rock and spreads the water,
Bidding drink and live a crowd beneath him,
Even he, the minute makes immortal,
Proves, perchance, but mortal in the minute,
Desecrates, belike, the deed in doing.
While he smites, how can he but remember,
So he smote before, in such a peril,
When they stood and mocked – 'Shall smiting help us?'
When they drank and sneered – 'A stroke is easy!'
When they wiped their mouths and went their journey,
Throwing him for thanks – 'But drought was pleasant.'
Thus old memories mar the actual triumph;
Thus the doing savours of disrelish;
Thus achievement lacks a gracious somewhat;
O'er-importuned brows becloud the mandate,
Carelessness or consciousness – the gesture.
For he bears an ancient wrong about him,
Sees and knows again those phalanxed faces,
Hears, yet one more time, the 'customed prelude –
'How shouldst thou, of all men, smite, and save us?'
Guesses what is like to prove the sequel –
'Egypt's flesh-pots – nay, the drought was better.'

Oh, the crowd must have emphatic warrant!
Theirs, the Sinai-forehead's cloven brilliance,
Right-arm's rod-sweep, tongue's imperial fiat.
Never dares the man put off the prophet.

Fifteen years after *Sordello,* Browning again puts on the robes of

Moses. In the interval he had tried the colourful priestly garment of *Bells and Pomegranates* and been dissatisfied. But when he returns to the Moses role in *Men and Women*, the mood is different from *Sordello*'s. The exuberance and defiance are gone, as is the relish in isolation and uniqueness. Now the awareness of the human flaw even in the miracle (is 'carelessness or consciousness' an astute criticism of his own poetic faults?) causes a certain disenchantment with display. To retire to a private bliss, like the earlier retirement to a garden full of rose-trees, is now all the sweeter. Yet the miracle, in the perverse style of miracles, comes when the prophet is weary. Browning had been confident and resilient and ready for success in *Sordello*. With this, his best collection, he seems more diffident and detached.

Browning uses the Moses figure in *One Word More* chiefly to contrast public and private personae, the prophet and the man. But the figure is interesting in other ways. First, Browning speaks at some length of the Israelites, Moses' audience, whose derision mars not the miracle itself but the prophet's pleasure in it. It is interesting to note how many of the poems which treat poetry and the other arts emphasize a tension between artist and audience, or between artist and imitator. In *Memorabilia* one man's reverence for Shelley stirs another to laughter. In *Popularity* the Spasmodic poets seize on the Keatsean style, once it is popular, and serve it up for their own profit. In both *Andrea* and *Fra Lippo Lippi* there is dissension between the artist and some part of his audience. In *'Transcendentalism'* a young artist tries to please his audience but is reminded of his true calling by a fellow-poet. In *How It Strikes a Contemporary* a contemporary observes a poet's activities, and the monologue demonstrates the distance between the two; we sense throughout what a strange being the poet appears to his observer, and the sense of strangeness is corroborated by the sudden break in tone and interest in the last two lines. It may be, too, that Browning in several poems reminds himself how time alters the attitudes toward artists, how a Galuppi can outlive his impatient listeners, how a Keats will eventually find appreciation, how even a Master Hugues can find a reproachful performer of his fugues, how the Florentine artists of the early Renaissance may be vindicated, how Giotto may yet triumph as his admirer would have him triumph. In all these poems, there exists, stronger or weaker, a tension between performer and recipient

231 MAGE AND PROPHET

that recalls the old tension in *Sordello* and Browning's efforts to resolve it there.

In *Sordello*, when Browning assumes the guise of Moses, he does so to perform the miracle of producing water from rock, and it is the same miracle he uses in *One Word More* as a metaphor for his poetry. I have noted how, in *Sordello*, he is at pains to emphasize the miraculous in creative achievement. In the *Men and Women* poems on poetry, too, the mystery of creativity is strongly emphasized. Here the poems on poetry part company somewhat with those on the other arts, for though inspiration is no doubt important for Andrea or Fra Lippo Lippi (and alas was not for Master Hugues), it is somewhat taken for granted. Perhaps this is because these are historical characters, two of whom express their own thoughts; an artist is unlikely to waste a great deal of time contemplating the artistry that is in him, and there is a limit to how much he can say about it. But again, it is interesting that no poet is given a dramatic monologue except the anonymous poet of '*Transcendentalism*' who reads a lesson to his younger contemporary. Shelley and Keats are given lyrics, but not dramatic tongues. The poet of *How It Strikes a Contemporary* is observed by an outsider. What Browning has to say about poetry he will say indirectly.

All the poems about poetry have as a common theme the mystery of creation. In '*Transcendentalism*,' living poetry is like a miraculous rose that a mage can cause to appear in a barren room. (In the late lyric *Natural Magic* love creates a similar miracle, bringing flowers, fruit, and birds into an empty room. And Christopher Smart's poetry could 'pour heaven / Into this shut house of life.') In *How It Strikes a Contemporary* poetry is the written correspondence between the poet and God, and it remains closed to the observer. Perhaps, incidentally, we may fancy the two kinds of poet in the 'Essay on Shelley,' objective and subjective, pictured here. The '*Transcendentalism*' poet should create the rose to restore youth to his audience; he has misread their needs. ('Boys seek for images and melody, / Men must have reason – so, you aim at men. / Quite otherwise!') He writes with reference to his audience, and will produce an object, the rose, as he himself is an object of contemplation. But the second poet, the subjective kind, writes with reference to God only; his letters are specifically directed to the Deity, and so private are they that we do not see them.

The finest metaphor for the mystery of creativity is the producing of Phoenician dye in *Popularity*. Keats works from a natural source and creates a produce potential with wonder ('one drop worked miracles'). There is reference to another miracle, that of Cana of Galilee. Many an onlooker is ready to talk about the dye ('criticize, and quote tradition'); so, in *'Transcendentalism,'* books on the meaning of the rose are readily produced; so, in *Master Hugues*, ingenious fugues take the place of inspired music. But Keats is the originator, the man who like Moses extracts from an unlikely and impenetrable source an essential liquid. (The shells 'enclosed the blue'; similarly in *The Ring and the Book*, the artist's gold is enclosed and must be extracted.) From the life of the sea Keats can reproduce the glory that was Solomon's (Solomon is seen as king and lover, but he also wrote songs) and the glory that is nature's; the colour that entranced the ancients, and the sustenance that will feed the moderns. The stress in *Popularity* is on the bitter knowledge that it is the imitator and popularizer who profits from the true poet's work.

The use of Solomon's contrived glories and the flower's natural ones, Keats' conscious work ('cunning come to pound and squeeze / and clarify') and his material fresh from nature ('Live whelks, each lip's beard dripping fresh, / As if they still the water's lisp heard'), combines craftsmanship and material, what is done and what is given. The same combination is achieved by the use of craftsman and metal in *The Ring and the Book*. Ancient tradition (Old Testament or pagan, Solomon or Astarte) and contemporary flower (Solomon 'took' the throne, but the gold 'burns' in the bluebell) imply the bearing of tradition on present artistic performance. So Castellani's is a craft 'imitative' of old Etruscan art.

The inimitable dye's sceret had been forgotten, and the aura of ancient mystery hung about it. It is blue, one of several Mediterranean blues in *Men and Women* – in *Karshish* and *Saul*, for instance – blues associated with the area about that sea, and with the sea's coolness and relief. Blue is also the colour of the one heavenly gem selected for *One Word More*'s Mosaic vision: 'Proves she [the hidden side of the moon] as the paved work of a sapphire / Seen by Moses ...? ... the paved work of a sapphire. / Like the bodied heaven in his clearness shone the stone, the sapphire of that paved work.' It is a wondrous colour, and Keats can produce

Enough to furnish Solomon
   Such hangings for his cedar-house,
That, when gold-robed he took the throne
   In that abyss of blue, the Spouse
Might swear his presence shone

Most like the centre-spike of gold
   Which burns deep in the blue-bell's womb,
What time, with ardours manifold,
   The bee goes singing to her groom,
Drunken and overbold.

The rapture is not Keatsean precisely; it is a Keats lover who speaks.
There is too much and too quick movement for Keats, and a sound
too close to speech. This is more like a Christina Rossetti lyric in
clarity of diction, clean rich colour, and ardent biblical imagery. The
quintessence of blueness is suggested not by adjectives or by a list of
metaphors but by contrast and by a sensuous combination of Old
Testament and nature imagery. Though the gold shines and burns,
it is not seen as clearly as the blue; or rather, the blue is sensed by the
peripheral vision while the eye focuses on the golden centre. To sense
the blueness of a summer sky, it is more effective to follow some one
object moving through it than to scan the heavens.

Browning, as he likes to do (in *By the Fireside*, for instance), plays
with perspective in looking at Keats himself in the second stanza.
Keats is 'my star, God's glow-worm,' and the speed of the eye in these
four words is dizzying. It goes out to the star, then on to the eye of
God, then back to the other side of the star. The proportion is nicely
correct. The star may be as tiny as a glow-worm to the eye of God,
but it is accessible; glow-worms are not seen beyond a certain distance.
The effect is of an Almighty who walks the universe like a private
estate, where all is within reach. Browning reinforces the effect with
his next words: 'Why extend / That loving hand of his which leads
you ...?' To establish various views of Keats at the beginning of the
poem is appropriate; it is these and other views with which Browning
is concerned. The reader is encouraged to consider Keats from the
standpoint of the speaker, of God, of Keats' future admirers, his past
detractors, his present imitators; or the reader may test his own

reaction in the rapturous central stanzas. The quick contrast of views is also appropriate in a poem that moves rapidly from metaphor to metaphor, and that deflates so rapidly in tone from stanza x to the final stanza xiii. Such rapid movement and shifting tone help give prominence to the sustained high intensity of the stanzas quoted above.

In *Memorabilia* the tribute to the force of Shelley's poetry is indirect and very simple. The dropped eagle feather that shines on the barren moor is an image intended to shine in this brief poem: no other is attempted. Nor is any more expression of the speaker's feeling for Shelley allowed than this one metaphor. Such feeling, like the feather, is enclosed within, and not for public viewing. Shelley is not even given the several ardent stanzas Browning grants to Keats. To be sure, he had already explicitly praised Shelley more than once. This tribute to Shelley does not make of him and his poetry something miraculous. But it does make of them something mysterious, something descended on the routine miles of heather from another atmosphere; from a creature moving faster and higher than earth-bound men; something that shines out in contrast with the blankness surrounding it. Yet for the laughing contemporary of Shelley's, there was no more wonder to his presence than the laughing Israelites found in Moses' water. Both take their wonders for granted.

In *By the Fireside* the lover says he was 'named and known by that moment's feat'; in the late poem quoted on page 219 Dante is named and known; and Browning would use the pair of verbs also in *Development*, *Asolando*'s *Prologue*, and *Ponte dell' Angelo*. In *Popularity* 'one man saw you, / Knew you, and named a star!' The phrase probably derives from its only biblical usage, the twice repeated words of God to Moses, when Moses is allowed as far as man may into the divine presence. When Browning selected his revised *Men and Women* of 1863, he opened it with '*Transcendentalism*,' where the poet is portrayed as mage. He closed it with *One Word More*, where the poet is Moses. It was the same progression of the poet, from mage to phophet, from would-be Faust to Elisha, that he was to use in Book i of *The Ring and the Book*. But the progression is implicit in the figure of Moses alone, for Moses (like Paracelsus, or like Karshish's Christ – and Moses is an Old Testament type of Christ) was said by some to be a mage and to work his miracles by magic:

'the father of lies suggested a calumny, and ascribed them [Moses' miracles] to magic.'[1]

Browning chooses as analogy for the poet's song the miracle at Meribah, the striking of water from rock. The likeness of this miracle to Browning's other metaphors for the creation of poetry, I have noted above. But the miracle, like Moses himself, has its own traditions. Browning drew on one in *Sordello*, the tradition that Moses, by his manner of performing the Meribah miracle, forfeited his entrance to the Promised Land:

> ... awkwardly enough your Moses smites
> The rock, tho' he forego his Promised Land
> Thereby, have Satan claim his carcass, and
> Figure as Metaphysic Poet ... ah,
> Mark ye the dim first oozings? Meribah!

But in *One Word More*, Browning does not draw upon this tradition, even with tongue in cheek. (Or is *Sordello* entirely tongue in cheek? Browning, after all, wrote two *Pisgah-Sights* late in life.) The Meribah miracle has also an iconographical tradition. It is usually made to represent in particular the flow of water from Christ's side during the crucifixion, and in general the refreshing power of grace.[2] Thus iconographically it can save life, in one form or another, and Browning implies something about the function of poetry in his repeated choice of this miracle as analogy for poetry.

Moses as a type for the poet must, then, have pleased Browning: his relations with the Israelites, his role as mage or prophet, his

---

1 Calvin, *Institutes of the Christian Religion*, I, viii, 6

2 ' "Cleaving the strong rock" is far more than a mere allusion to Moses the chosen leader. No cleric of the seventeenth century, as liturgically literate as George Herbert, and brought up on typology, could mention this act of Moses' without thinking both of the water from the side of Christ, the living rock ... and of the mystical regenerative power of water, so stressed, for example, in the services for Easter Even' (Rosemond Tuve, *A Reading of George Herbert*, 27–8).

Or see Louis Réau, *Iconographie de l'Art Chrétien*, vol. II, *Iconographie de la Bible* (Paris, 1956), 200–2. M. Réau notes the popularity of the miracle; it appears in the windows of Bourges, Mans, and Tours, and it is treated seven times by Poussin.

Meribah miracle. And Moses was a traditional biblical type for the poet. Not as familiar a type as David, but then Browning preferred less familiar characters, Paracelsus and not Faust, Sordello and not Dante. Even so, Moses had been given prominence of place by Milton in the first lines of *Paradise Lost,* and Sidney in the *Defence of Poetry* named him as one of those 'that did imitate the inconceivable excellencies of GOD' in his hymn. Calvin also refers to Moses' 'Song,' which is Deuteronomy 32 (*Institutes,* I, viii, 7). And one Thomas Churchyard, in his *Musicall Consort of Heavenly Harmonie* (1595) suggests Moses as the father of poetry: 'Moises by some is thought the first deviser of verse, and his sister Marie devised the exameter.'[3]

But the Moses of *One Word More* is Wordsworth's, surely, more than anyone else's. 'Heaven's gift takes earth's abatement,' says Browning, and 'Heaven's gift' is Wordsworth's phrase in the *Prelude* for the poet's inspiration.[4] The *Prelude* was published in 1850, after *Sordello* and before *One Word More,* and it was seen by Browning.[5] In Book I, 14–18, Wordsworth sees the poet both as a new Adam and as a Moses being led toward the Promised Land. And Wordsworth, like Browning and like Browning's Moses, knows 'in our existence spots of time, / That with distinct pre-eminence retain / A renovating virtue, whence ... our minds / Are nourished and invisibly repaired.' Browning's spots of time, and those of his Moses, are rather spots out of time that illuminate time. Browning's Nature is closer to Blake's and Shelley's than to Wordsworth's so that validation for what is in Nature and in time, for what lies this side of the moon, comes from outside the natural and the temporal.

In *One Word More,* Browning must have been especially happy with his old poetic prototype because he, like Browning, had

---

3 Cited in Lily B. Campbell, *Divine Poetry and Drama in Sixteenth-Century England* (Cambridge, 1959), 55. I am indebted to Allan Pritchard for this reference.

4 'If thou partake the animating faith / That Poets, even as Prophets, each with each / Connected in a mighty scheme of truth, / Have each his own peculiar faculty, / Heaven's gift ...' (*The Prelude,* XIII, 300–4).

5 'Yet let us hope that your gift of the "Prelude" is of excellent omen' (to Charles E. Norton, from Florence, Dec. 9, 1850). Holograph letter in the Houghton Library, Harvard University; by permission of the Harvard College Library

experienced a private, incommunicable, and sustaining experience.
Jethro's daughter is mentioned after the lines about 'Heaven's gift'
quoted at the beginning of this chapter. But Browning comes later
to another experience of Moses:

> Moses, Aaron, Nadab and Abihu
> Climbed and saw the very God, the Highest,
> Stand upon the paved work of a sapphire.
> Like the bodied heaven in his clearness
> Shone the stone, the sapphire of that paved work,
> When they ate and drank and saw God also.

> What were seen? None knows, none ever shall know.

This is what the dark side of the moon is like, the private side of a
man, of a Browning or an Elizabeth. Unless it proves more sinister,
in the menacing alternative suddenly and oddly inserted here:

> Proves she like some portent of an iceberg
> Swimming full upon the ship it founders,
> Hungry with huge teeth of splintered crystals?

The magic of love, like other magics, might be baleful. Browning
is insistent about the moon's magic in this poem where moon like
Moses seems capable of being seen as either mage or prophet. He
altered the word *grace* to *charm*, and *pleasure* to *magic* in lines
159 and 160 when revising his proofs.[6] Still, whether the magic is
black or white, devouring or illuminating, pulling downward or
drawing up, of sea or mountain-top, its mark is privacy. It is not
simply that it is not shared, but that it cannot be shared. It is by
nature incommunicable, and so Heaven's gift cannot take earth's
abatement. It belongs to the world of silence, and the likeness of
the lunar paradise to heaven is finely caught by Browning in the
word silence. 'Where I hush and bless myself with silence ...' The
first version had been 'Where I hush and bless myself with beauty,'[7]

---

6 MS copy of *One Word More*, entitled 'A Last Word,' Pierpont Morgan
   Library, New York; quoted by permission of the Library
7 Line 197, MS copy of *One Word More*, entitled 'A Last Word,' Pierpont
   Morgan Library, New York; quoted by permission of the Library

but the substitution is superior in all ways. For the world of silence, so appropriate after the 'hush,' is the world beyond words, 'these filthy rags of speech,' as the Pope will call them; beyond the 'artist's sorrow'; untouched and untouchable; 'silence 't is awe decrees,' Moses will say in the presence of God in *Asolando*'s *Prologue*. In *One Word More*, Moses' sight of God is Browning's analogy for his love. It is a demanding analogy for any earthbound love, but it is an analogy in keeping with the vision of bliss that runs through *Men and Women*.

IV DRAMATIS PERSONAE:

EXPANSION

15 TIME AND CHANGE:

JAMES LEE'S WIFE

A certain fear of the changes worked by time runs through many of the *Dramatis Personae* poems; such changes now have a new reality. In *James Lee's Wife* change in love occurs while the lover remains present, a theme Browning has hardly touched before. Light irony attended his treatment of the subject in *Earth's Immortalities: Love* and some melodrama in *In a Year.* But once highest love is attained in *Men and Women*, all is safe; until then, one strives. It is clear that in the 1855 volume Browning knows how rare a *By the Fireside* union is, but there is little consideration of how less idyllic unions survive in any very satisfactory way. In *Dramatis Personae* the love lyrics centre on more commonplace problems: in *James Lee's Wife*, a married couple separates, the man leaving the woman; in *The Worst of It*, the woman deserts the man; in *Dîs Aliter Visum* and *Youth and Art*, the crucial moment is missed once and for all (a rarity in *Men and Women*: even the *Statue and Bust* lovers have more than one chance), and potentially joyful unions never take place; in *Too Late*, the rejected suitor alternately mourns and scolds the woman who is now someone else's dead wife. The difference may also be seen in the two long poems, one from each volume, that centre on the incarnation. In the *Epistle of Karshish*, the drama is strong, the focus on wonder, not on the implications of the decision for the rest of Karshish's life. In *A Death in the Desert*, the decision has been taken long before, the focus is on the effects of time and especially on the threats it brings.

On the other hand, assertions of invincibility against the menaces of time are more pronounced than ever before. In *Saul* religious exaltation and in *By the Fireside* a profound love offer such invincibility: the conviction is shown growing out of experience. In *Dramatis Personae*, conviction grows from experience in *Abt Vogler*. But in *Rabbi ben Ezra* and *Prospice* the conviction must carry its own weight; it is asserted with a bare firmness that none of the fifty *Men and Women* speakers shows. A surprising number of the latter express themselves obliquely or only partially; even the redoubtable Bishop Blougram comes at his situation sideways. In 1864 the assertiveness of Rabbi ben Ezra and the *Prospice* speaker is as far on one side of neutrality as the quiet prolonged unhappiness of those affected by change is on the other. It is as if Browning's new interest in time's corrosion produced two opposite reactions, both strong. *James Lee's Wife* is the only poem on the theme of change pervasive in *Dramatis Personae* in which the speaker descends to despair and then regains hope. Perhaps for this reason as well as intrinsic merit, it is given the prominence of opening the collection.

In many *Dramatis Personae* poems, when the door closes finally against the past, the speakers are left to reconcile themselves with an unsatisfactory present. In *Men and Women*, even in near-hopeless poems, a certain vitality often precludes weary hopelessness. A sense persists that time may be redeemed. Perhaps many of the situations (as in, for instance, *A Serenade*, *A Woman's Last Word*, or *Women and Roses*) are still close enough to the moment of crisis to retain at least the impression of the possibility of choice. In *Dramatis Personae* even that impression has often gone.

Each of the love poems that follows *James Lee's Wife* and *Gold Hair* shows a speaker protesting against the irrevocable. In *The Worst of It*, the man whose wife has left him tries out different attitudes ('And, Dear, truth is not as good as it seems! / Commend me to conscience! Idle stuff! / Much help is in mine, as I mope and pine'). He turns to sardonic use some of Abt Vogler's imagery as he contemplates his wife's future behaviour: 'And a place in the other world ensure, / All glass and gold, with God for its sun.' Nothing alleviates the pain. What is constant in the poem, however, is less present pain than two unchangeable reactions within him whose conflict produces the pain. One is his concern for his wife. The other is his inability to forgive her. 'I knew you once: but in Paradise, / If we meet, I will pass nor turn my face.' He is presented as a Dido rather than a James Lee's wife. The reaction of the *Dîs Aliter Visum* speaker is simpler. She is indignant that her clever, scholarly suitor rejected her gifts and propelled them both into miserable marriages. The description of the other two spouses at the end does something to retrieve the sermonizing of 'what's complete here is finished,' but the over-all effect is very heavy. As with *Abt Vogler*, the moment itself has great strength, but the comment upon it is anticlimax. *Too Late* is a more feverish poem. The woman who rejected the speaker and married another has just died. Protest and despair, anger and pleading, possess him in turn. The ferocity of his contemplated action and the fervency of his toast at the end give poignancy even to much posturing. This is too civilized a speaker for a Heathcliff, at least in public; but this anguish is private and the likeness tells.

In *Dramatis Personae, Abt Vogler* follows the above poems, and here, as in a few *Men and Women* poems, there is a miraculous minute by which the speaker afterwards governs his life. But his reflections on it are more direct than anything Browning permitted the speakers of, say, *By the Fireside* and *Saul*. It is as if Abt Vogler must reassure himself, more than these speakers, that the moment has happened, and guide himself firmly by its implications. The moment is scarcely over before he reflects, 'Never to be again.' (I am observing the reaction in him, but note, especially in *Fifine*, Browning's remarks on the effects of music.) Browning is always fascinated by the return into this world of the man who has seen a vision. *Saul* touches on this. *By the Fireside* demonstrates it. Karshish was intrigued by it, and Browning's favourite Moses figure is a man who has spoken with God. In *Two Poets of Croisic*, lix, Browning says specifically:

> Well, I care – intimately care to have
>   Experience how a human creature felt
> In after-life, who bore the burden grave
>   Of certainly believing God had dealt
> For once directly with him: did not rave
>   – A maniac, did not find his reason melt
> – An idiot, but went on, in peace or strife,
> The world's way, lived an ordinary life.

Abt Vogler picks up several familiar Browning images. Solomon appears, as he did in *Popularity*, in connection with the miracle of artistic creation. But his role in *Abt Vogler* links him rather with the mage figure, for he 'named the ineffable Name,' and angels, demons, and all created things flew to do his bidding. An old Sordello verb for the growing of the work of art, 'dispart,' appears in line 11. The 'dared and done' of the second last line strikes a familiar chord, for Browning repeatedly uses this pair, and sometimes all, of Smart's trio – 'determin'd, dar'd, and done' – at the end of the *Song to David*. To Elizabeth he writes: 'How you have dared and done all this, under my very eyes, for my only sake' (*LRBEB*, II, 1067; Sept. 13, 1846). But in *The Ring and the Book*, Guido also claims twice to have dared and done (V, 454, 2051), and Tertium Quid applies Smart's three verbs to Pompilia's slaughter ('Why, murder was determined, dared, and done' [IV, 1106]). When the phrase recurs, it invites us to consider the quality of will and action that produces the verbs. Note, for example, how Browning uses the word 'done' in the following passage: 'I ... gave you my life, so much of it as you would take, – and all that is *done*, not to be altered now' (*LRBEB*, I, 176; Aug. 30, 1845). The 'doing' is an act of mental allegiance, but the commitment is made once and for all. So with Abt Vogler, who does not live in the anticipation of new and various moments but in the commitment to the one that has been (cf. ll. 63–4).

Rabbi ben Ezra also focuses on change, and its views coincide with those of *By the Fireside*. The poem, however, is straightforward exhortation, and such exhortation, especially when it speaks in abstracts like Power and Love, may irritate. Many Browning poems may imply what the Rabbi baldly advises. (On various kinds of power and love, note, for instance, *A Woman's Last Word, Andrea del Sarto, By the Fireside, Saul, Two in the Campagna, Love in a Life*.) But the particular situations of the above poems elicit a Browning who is eminently human. *Rabbi ben Ezra*, though it appears in a collection of 'men and women' (*The Worst of It, Dîs Aliter Visum*, and *Too Late* show vulnerable and wrong-headed enough human beings), may evoke another Browning, the moralizing one, who sometimes overshadows all the others. *Rabbi ben Ezra* might be a *By the Fireside* shorn of the particular experience that is the reason for the latter poem. But the conclusions are hardly a substitute for what happened.

The poem repeatedly picks up familiar Browning images. The flower imagery has a function like that in *By the Fireside*. The rose in stanzas ii and xi takes on the usual connotations of youthful rapture, and is again paired with the star. But the star is not here an image of the transcendent. It is a personal star, like that in *My Star*. When

the Rabbi wishes to speak of the transcendent, he names it in the
Old Testament figure of the Potter. The Old Testament image
of the spark is used in stanzas iii and v; the disturbing effect of fire
is stressed in both examples. Body and soul find corresponding
patterns of imagery; 'to feed / On joy, to solely seek and find and
feast' recalls the *Two in the Campagna* beetles, but in stanza xii (as
in the later *Ferishtah's Fancies* lyrics) due place is allotted to body
and to soul. In stanza xi, the desire for something permanent is
strongly evoked, as in *James Lee's Wife*. In stanza xv, gold is tried
by fire; a sunset, with glory fading into grey, is used metaphorically.
The most prolonged image is the Potter's wheel, to which Browning
specifically calls the reader's attention. The old spinning of time becomes the wheel, 'this dance / Of plastic circumstance.' 'I – to the
wheel of life / With shapes and colours rife, / Bound dizzily' anticipates the different wheel of the later *Ixion*. But it also recalls the
whirling life in the *Epilogue* to *Dramatis Personae, James Lee's Wife,
Easter-Day,* and especially (because of the 'shapes and colours')
Women and Roses, Aeschylus' Soliloquy, and Aprile's and the
Pauline poet's imagery. Against the whirl, 'thy soul and God stand
sure,' Browning here positing the two points of reality he will later
return to in *La Saisiaz.*

In stanza xiv, Browning makes use of military imagery, long a
favourite type of metaphor for him. During his *Bells and Pomegranates* years, he had a prolonged interest, never so consistently
pursued later, in patriotism, politics, statecraft, national characteristics, and military valour. How strong this interest was may be gauged
from the fact that all his plays except *A Blot in the 'Scutcheon* have
an important political theme. In projected works, too, Browning's
mind hovered over national and military leaders. He is said to
have considered writing a play on Justinian's general Narses,[1] and
when he cast about for a way of making money during his courtship
writing a novel on Napoleon did not seem impossible.[2] But except
for one, Browning's heroes up to 1846 do not ever gain power and

---

1 In 1836; cf. *The Diaries of William Charles Macready, 1833–1851,* ed.
William Toynbee (London, 1912), I, 277; cited in Joseph W. Reed, Jr.,
'Browning and Macready: The Final Quarrel,' *PMLA* 75 (1960), 597, n.2
2 '... Mr Colburn saying confidentially that he wanted more than his dinner
"a novel on the subject of *Napoleon*"!!! So may one make money ...'
(*LRBEB,* I, 194; Sept. 13, 1845)

use it wisely. It is as if he is convinced that all power must corrupt and is unwilling to touch it. Paracelsus uses power wrongly; Sordello dies from the struggle of deciding how to exercise it. Charles does succeed, but by simply existing; all his decisions are magically right. Djabal dies; Valence retires; Berthold is allowed to rule, but what his rule is like we have no idea; Luria dies; Chiappino is false. The *Cavalier Tunes* are tunes of a lost cause and a lost king; the 'lost leader' is false. The Italian in England is a banished patriot. Subsequently the study of power moves away from the political arena. It is best seen in 1855 in *Bishop Blougram's Apology*, and later in the Pope's speech in *The Ring and the Book*, where Browning does not simply show a man theorizing about power but attempting to exercise it as justly as he can.

With this shift, the imagery associated with political power, war, and military valour becomes more figurative. It modulates more and more to imagery of chivalry and adventure, races and games. Figures like the 'soldier-saint' Caponsacchi or the soldier-saints of *The Statue and the Bust* or the knight-to-be Childe Roland become much more common than conventional military figures. The image of life as a war or contest or game, with or without a goal, and with certain rules (as in *Easter-Day* and *Two Poets of Croisic*) replaces that of military strategy. The focus moves from the political cause to the individual motivation that makes the political cause. When Elizabeth, always more active politically than Browning, wrote *Aurora Leigh*, she made the poem's central conflict that between Romney's and Aurora's views. Romney is the practical social re-former, impatient of mere talk, and Aurora the poet who tries to influence men's souls and thence their social outlook. Both views finally find place, but Aurora's is given the edge. It is a preference Browning would have approved.

Browning was, of course, always interested in the use of power in the widest sense of the word, including kinds of religious and personal power. 'I have been all my life asking what connection there is between the satisfaction at the display of power, and the sympathy with – ever-increasing sympathy with – all imaginary weakness' (*LRBEB*, 1, 270; Nov. 16, 1845). The relevance of this interest to *Paracelsus* and *Sordello* is obvious, and the relation of power and love provides the underlying theme of Browning's plays. The power-versus-love conflict is, of course, also relevant to the love lyrics. And its possible theological development – perhaps basis – is also obvious.

If *Rabbi ben Ezra* is an exhortation, there are in *Dramatis Personae* other poems with no shadow of a sermon: the melancholy little lyric *May and Death*; *A Likeness*, which plays off colloquial patter against the delicacy of a small, fervent, private passion; the occasional piece, *A Face*. In *Confessions*, in fact, the dying man withstands a "reverend sir's" disapproving eye and relives an old bliss, an illicit love affair. In the short poems, even in *May and Death*, the passage of time does not bring anguish. In one, *Prospice*, it brings joy. Here the speaker takes for himself Rabbi ben Ezra's military imagery and marches out to meet death. So sharply imagined is the encounter, and so intense the tone throughout, that the poem carries the reader past the aggressive challenge at the beginning and into its own conviction.

James Lee's Wife includes some fine and neglected lyric verse. The imagery, when strong and restrained, is often like Hardy's and James Lee's wife might be a Hardy character. She has a series of nine lyrics, each marking a stage in her separation from her husband. At the beginning, the couple is united in name but the wife is apprehensive; at the end, they are parted. The technique is a shorter version of Tennyson's in *Maud*, for *James Lee's Wife* is a monodrama, the only one Browning wrote.

What prevents many readers from getting into the poem is, I think, the first lyric. It must be stressed again and again, even in such an obvious case as this, that Browning writes dramatically. The first lyric is meant to strike by its naivetes – naivetes of sentiment, imagery, and rhyme. Once we have glanced at later parts of the monodrama, we return to the first lyric not with impatience but with curiosity. Browning altered the lyric's title from *At the Window* (which is like the other lyrics' titles) to *James Lee's Wife Speaks at the Window* in order to make the situation quite clear. The woman is in her house, looking out; the two areas of house and outside nature, here at once established, form the two chief areas of symbolism in the poem. What the women sees out her window alarms her. The opening of the poem is in sound not unlike that of *A Lovers' Quarrel* ('Ah, Love, but a day'; 'Oh, what a dawn of day'), but the mood is opposite. Here autumn threatens, while there spring bores. Here a serious quarrel and the possibility of separation are suppressed; there a temporary quarrel and actual separation are gaily expostulated against. Windows are frequently a dramatic site in Browning (cf. his exchange with Elizabeth, p. 145 above) : in the *Love Among the Ruins* comparison of 'when the king looked, where she looks now'; in the 'windows fast and obdurate' of *A Serenade*; in the window of *The Statue and the Bust* where, like a blessed damozel, 'leaning out of a bright blue space, / As a ghost might lean from a chink of sky, / The passionate pale lady's face' is seen – room and outside being inverted in fancy; in Andrea's 'should you let me sit / Here by the window with your hand in mine,' which alters to 'Come from the window, love, – come in, at last, / Inside the melancholy little house.' In later work, a window may become explicitly, sometimes solely symbolic, like Don Juan's tower window :

> I had flung both frames o' the window wide ...
> ... kept open house, – to fancies manifold
> From this four-cornered world, the memories new and old,
> The antenatal prime experience – what know I? –
> The initiatory love preparing us to die;

the householder's 'fuss and trouble of street-sounds, window-sights' in *Fifine*'s *Epilogue*; the display window in *Shop*, or, in *House*, the window through which a peep is allowed. There are significantly windowless crypts in *A Lovers' Quarrel* and *Any Wife to Any Husband*, and a windowless wall in the *Prologue* to *Pacchiarotto*, 'the body, – the house, no eye can probe.'

As with the house image, the window's use depends on the viewer. What James Lee's wife sees is the symbolic threat of cyclical nature: 'Wilt thou change too ... With the changing year?' In a few short lines she sets up the seasonal context that so often implies human change, change which may threaten or be accepted or be welcomed. For her, change means threat: 'Should I fear surprise?' The 'old' is also the dear, the good and true; the 'new' something other. (In *By the Fireside* the fearless lover anticipates seeing with his beloved 'new depths of the divine.' In 1868, however, Browning was to ask his dead wife, 'Can thy soul know change?' and to rejoin rapidly, 'Hail then ...' Even in this rhapsody, though, the 'distance and the dark' threaten.)

The wife's dilemma is seen in the third stanza. After the three questions of the second verse comes the assertion with which she tries to reassure herself, assertion that sharpens into imperative. The first stanza looks out the window; the last flees its view, the woman urgently demanding an embrace that will block out other sights ('Me, to bend above, / Me, to hold embraced'). The frantic need recalls 'Pauline, mine own, bend o'er me' and 'Be a man and fold me / With thine arm,' where both speakers desperately want shelter, from themselves and what they know rather than from any outside threat. In the first stanza, nature threatened outside the window; in the last, the woman makes her own nature: 'For the lake, its swan; / For the dell, its dove.' The bird outside is 'estranged' by a harsh nature, but in her imagination bird and nature belong idyllically together, as unquestionably and patly as 'dell' and 'dove.' The cause of her anxiety is shown in one word, 'but': 'Thou art a man, / But I am thy love.' She prefers to attribute the unnamed difficulty to her husband's masculinity, and she concedes him the right to some difficulty on this account alone, only provided she retains a sure if small place. The same clause and conjunction had been used by Elizabeth in her efforts to assure Browning that he was not to be encumbered by their provisional engagement: 'I trust you wholly – but you are a man, & free to care less' (*LRBEB*, I, 298; Nov. 28, 1845).

Browning had previously used similar short lines in two lyrics like this one, *In a Year* and *A Woman's Last Word*. *In a Year* also uses a two-beat line, but the two stresses are not emphasized and almost become three; a pattering rhythm runs under the slow beat and the patter effect is reinforced by the clinch of the eight-line stanza (though the four rhymes occur *abcadbcd*). In *At the Window* the two stresses are heavy and dramatic; the seven lines have three rhymes (*ababcbc*) and the rhyme is prominent. Rhyme like image is bent to one simple dominant purpose. The first stanza maintains a certain strength even in its obvious rhyme, the second rhymes tritely, the third approaches doggerel. Deterioration in rhyme is made to mark the woman's inner deterioration of spirit. Of course, rhyme and image lend themselves to parody, and Swinburne amused himself with the obvious phallic variation on the last stanza;[3] he published a more polite version in *Heptalogia*. It hardly needs repeating that Browning's mastery of rhythmic effect means this near-doggerel is here for a purpose. But if the 1864 reader doubted this, he had only to read on in the volume:

3 *Letters*, ed. Cecil Y. Lang (New Haven, 1958), II, 106

... this young beauty, round and sound
    As a mountain-apple, youth and truth
With loves and doves, at all events
    With money in the Three per Cents.
(*Dîs Aliter Visum*, 61–4)

'He rhymed you his rubbish nobody read, / Loved you and doved you – did not I laugh!' (*Too Late*, 89–90). James Lee's wife's rhymes for the last stanza are 'love' and 'dove' and 'above,' and her language indicates how facile is the sentiment she allows herself to indulge in.

James Lee and his wife live on a farm on the coast of France. Browning can therefore make play with the imagery of earth and harvest and seasonal change; of sea and ships; of wind and of sun. The cycle begins with a notice of the changing season, but the first lyric moves to a fairy-tale country of lake and dell (not actual sea and bare field), of swans and doves (not actual swallows and magpies). In a sense, the first poem is out of the cycle, so wilfully blinkered is the speaker. The last lyric is called *On Deck*; it shows husband and wife separating by the husband's wish and the wife's consent. What this last lyric's imagery returns to, however, is not the first poem's, but the second's, which plays on real and figurative ship's journeys. James Lee's wife never comes full circle, for the beginning of her self-exploration and ordeal is an unreal world incapable of redemption.

Browning gives to the second lyric a title meant to startle: *By the Fireside*. And what he writes is, in effect, an ironic inversion of the original poem. Not a union, but a separation. Not a touching of earth and heaven with mountain-peak and star in Dante fashion, but a touching of earth and hell with abyss and infernal flame. Nature, in such an inversion, would not bear small signs of her once and potential harmony. She would be mere nature, obeying seasonal changes, bringing in death along with life impartially and impersonally. So she is in *James Lee's Wife*. Her elements would not be in harmony, as fire, air, earth, and water blend in the moment one and infinite; instead there would be conflict, not only between man and nature but also within nature. So in *James Lee's Wife*. And the natural imagery exemplifying love would not be of something generously given, of grace. It would be of something earned, of works, of cultivation and weeding. So in *James Lee's Wife*. Time would not be a series of moments made significant by a unique moment. It would be solely horizontal time, Chronos pursuing his appointed path as surely as in a Renaissance painting. Behind him, frozen infernal time would threaten. So in *James Lee's Wife*. Space would not be a melting of walls, but a sense of constriction with the stress on enclosure. The shape of the poem would not be circling, a play with past, present, and future, but linear, governed by the ever-painful present. And if the first *By the Fireside* may be fancifully seen as a Purgatory journey around a mountain whose culmination is hope and a star, *James Lee's Wife* may be fancifully seen as a journey up from the frozen centre of the Inferno, its nine poems like so many circles of hell. In the first poem, James Lee's wife is frozen. As the series progresses, she begins to feel and to come to terms with reality. Her lyrics end with *On the Deck*; it is as if she embarks on Charon's return trip, back to a place where hope is possible once more.

But if, in the second poem, she begins to acknowledge the failure of her marriage, it is just a beginning. The shock of admitting the truth is seen in the lyric's rhythm (the dramatic pauses and stresses), its imagery (again, dramatic contrasts, images of extremity), and its diction, which is highly coloured.[4] The woman thinks in the exclamatory mood ('God help you ...! Spare the curse! ... now, gnash your teeth!'). The lyric is built on ironic contrast, which the changes in perspective reinforce. First is the contrast between this *By the Fireside* and the earlier one, where man, woman, and hearthfire constituted a far different home. This hearthfire burns shipwreck wood, and we are invited to consider the 'dim dead woe / Long ago / Befallen this bitter coast of France!' ('Bitter' can be a strong word for Browning: 'My love, this is the bitterest ...'[5]) But in line 8, we come, with the contrasting tense, suddenly into the present ('poor sailors took their chance; / I take mine').

The second stanza like the first lyric looks (at least in fancy) out the window, considers firelight across the sea, goes out to present sailors and follows their envious eye back to the supposedly happy

---

4 Cf., for an excellent analysis of the lyric's style, Robert Preyer, 'Two Styles in the Verse of Robert Browning,' *ELH* 32 (1965), 69–71
5 Cf. Elizabeth's use of it in the two following examples: 'of one class of griefs, (which has been called too the bitterest) I know as little as you ... the unworthiness of the dearest' (*LRBEB*, I, 35; Mar. 5, 1845); 'the bitterest "fact" of all is, that I had believed Papa to have loved me more than he obviously does – : but I never regret knowledge' (ibid., I, 233; Oct. 13, 1845). Or Browning: 'Nor think "bitterly" of my kindness, that word!' (ibid., I, 296; Nov. 28, 1845)

home. The woman seeks contrast or precedent (stanza iii) for her torment, and she seeks them in the dim past (stanzas i and iii) or in a far-off stylized present. The second poem is moving in toward the core of the misery. It is the only one with an indoor setting (unless *Beside the Drawing-Board* has, but it takes no account of its setting). It is the only one with an explicit night-time setting. It gazes into the hearthfire at the beginning, and by the end what we see is not the shipwreck wood, but planks that open; not heartfire, but hell-flames. For there is contrast, too, in the repeated phrase 'gnash their teeth.' The first use is sharp but not startling. In the second, biblical echoes of torment are heard, and the change in person (like the change in tense above) brings the anguish home: '(now, gnash your teeth!) / When planks start, open hell beneath / Unawares?' Yet as she reaches in, the woman also reaches out, as if to steady herself with the thought of like misery or stiffen herself with the irony of misplaced envy.

The inner and outer domains of the first poem reappear, but now Browning's enclosure imagery is much stronger. Storm-drenched sailors envy 'the warm safe house and happy freight.' The reader recalls the later house:

> Or narrow if needs the house must be,
> Outside are the storms and strangers: we –
> Oh, close, safe, warm sleep I and she,
> – I and she!

But here the ship of love has rotted from within, 'all through the worms i' the wood, which crept, / Gnawed our hearts out while we slept.' Betrayal from within is especially menacing, and the enclosed serpent or worm, eating or growing or laying eggs, is a common Browning image for such a threat: 'Sirs, that first simile serves still, – / That falsehood of a scorpion hatched, I say, / Nowhere i' the world but in Madonna's mouth' (*The Ring and the Book*, VI, 909–11); 'a worm inside which bores at the brain for food ... the bite / Of a worm inside is worse to bear' (*Martin Relph*, 14, 19–20); 'the inch-long worm, / Free of our heel, would grow to vomit fire, / And one day plague the world in dragon form' (*Parleying with Mandeville*, 85–7). Most like this *By the Fireside* in lyric line and charged emotion is lyric VII from *Ferishtah's Fancies* (9–12):

253 TIME AND CHANGE: *James Lee's Wife*

But faults you ne'er suspected,
    Nay, praised, no faults at all, –
Those would you had detected –
    Crushed eggs whence snakes could crawl![6]

Lyric III, *In the Doorway*, plays with the imagery of warmth and cold like lyric II, now not the warmth and cold of indoor and outdoor worlds but of seasonal change and of figurative warmth and coolness in personal relations. James Lee's wife now returns, as it were, to lyric I. That is, she again looks out at the autumn landscape and comments on the changing season. But the difference from the first poem marks her increasing equilibrium. The poem opens with two stanzas of fine verse:

The swallow has set her six young on the rail,
    And looks sea-ward:
The water's in stripes like a snake, olive-pale
    To the leeward, –
On the weather-side, black, spotted white with the wind.[7]
"Good fortune departs, and disaster's behind," –
Hark, the wind with its wants and its infinite wail!

Our fig-tree, that leaned for the saltness, has furled
    Her five fingers,
Each leaf like a hand opened wide to the world
    Where there lingers
No glint of the gold, Summer sent for her sake:
How the vines writhe in rows, each impaled on its stake!
My heart shrivels up and my spirit shrinks curled.

---

6 Something that eats away from within may readily be inspired by a hearthfire, such as *Two Poets of Croisic*'s, which is also of oak and also shipwreck wood: 'Fire in his pandemonium, heart of oak / Palatial, where he wrought his works concealed / Beneath the solid-seeming roof I broke ... fire's slow tunnelling of vaults and arcs!' (ii). The hell here is magnificent rather than demonic.
7 Browning likes the combination of colour in 'black, spotted white with the wind.' Cf. 'churning the blackness hoary' (*The Ring and the Book*, x, 1109) and 'churned the black water white' (*Balaustion's Adventure*, 82)

The misery is evident, but it is recognized (unlike lyric I) and stated simply (unlike lyric II). The parallels between withered vine and shrivelling heart are presented without undue flair, in a straightforward way very like Hardy's. Moreover, the woman now sees with her eyes. There are no more swans and doves; the description is precise, and also unadorned. The sparseness and selectiveness mark a new sharpness of mind; the assertive mood and simple syntax a new strength. It is not surprising that the next lyric can open the first discussion between the couple ('I will be quiet and talk with you' – though what follows is 'And reason why you are wrong'). Perhaps *In a Doorway*, lyric III, is meant to remind us that *At the Window* saw the world through glass; this view is unimpeded.

Line 13 above, with its writhing and impaling, recalls a *Childe Roland* landscape. But line 14 recognizes the tormented spirit that makes such a landscape. The woman moves through this parallel to bare simple assessment in stanza iii (again unlike the romanticized first lyric). Man and woman possess little; like their farm and small house, and like the barren late autumn, they themselves are impoverished. The last stanza is a plea to make of this world a *By the Fireside* world, to imitate the 'power to put life in the darkness and cold.' The plea is a recollection that there can be exceptions to the change that seems as inevitable as the seasons. *A Lovers' Quarrel*, in its crypt imagery, demonstrated the defeat of darkness and cold. It, like *By the Fireside*, was a November poem, but a November poem with hope.

In the Doorway introduces images that will reappear as the monodrama progresses. The swallow is departing with summer; she, like the magpie and unlike the swan and dove, is observed; she is also a flying creature, and wings are important in lyric IV ('how the light, light love, he has wings to fly') and in lyric V. Lyric VI is a lengthy expansion of what the 'infinite wail' of the wind may mean; the sea also figures there. The woman here likens herself to the vines, but in the last poem's last stanza, she adopts a tree as her image ('your skin, this bark of a gnarled tree'[8]), again recalling ironically the original *By the Fireside*. Biblical olive and vine will appear in the next poem. The

8 Mrs Orr deserves a perennial foot-note to this stanza: 'We learn from the two last monologues, especially the last, that James Lee's wife was a plain woman. This may throw some light on the situation' (*Handbook*, 236).

fig-tree furls[9] 'her five fingers, / Each leaf like a hand opened wide ...,' and it is surely not over-ingenuity to see here the forecast of the significant hand in *Beside the Drawing-Board.*

When James Lee's wife can say, 'Whom Summer made friends of, let Winter estrange,' she is ready to talk with her husband. (The shrinking spirit may have shrunk not only from lost love, but also from such a confrontation.) *Along the Beach*, lyric IV, has notable strengths (especially in the last two stanzas), but it is less memorable in itself than as a picture of the speaker. This is the only poem in which she speaks directly to her husband or of him, and it is the only poem in which we feel a deliberate dramatic distance. Here, if anywhere, we might find evidence for Browning's appraisal of her: 'I was always very fond of her, but I fancy she had not much tact, and did not quite know how to treat her husband. I think she worried him a little. But if you want to know any more, you had better ask the Browning Society, – you have heard of it, perhaps?'[10] It is like Browning to provide an *Along the Beach*, to insist on the particular rather than the general wrong, to imply the possible difficulties of James Lee, to make clear the nature if not the details of the impasse. The last stanza is ballad-like, and said to be so ('fit subject for some new song'). Stanza vii, which leads into it, and the last stanza itself bring the monodrama back to its previous focus. James Lee and his wife as disputants are left behind. It is the suffering woman we return to – not too sombrely, for we have been granted a glimpse of her peculiarities – but with the right touch of bittersweet irony, of objectivity and involvement (the song is sung, but the subject sings it). We return inside her viewpoint and to an ordeal that has changed: from now on, there is no hope of reconciliation.

The fifth lyric, like the third, chooses certain details of the natural scene to tell a symbolic love-tale. Or rather, to speak of love's effect, for this central lyric says least about the woman's plight, and most of what love can do. Turf and rock recall Browning's play elsewhere with these images, notably in *Red Cotton Night-Cap Country or Turf and Towers*, and the turf is related to the imagery of earth and

9 A repeated Browning verb and image; cf. especially its use in *Fifine*. It is connected with Browning's enclosure imagery.
10 A reported conversation in Lilian Whiting, *The Brownings: Their Life and Art* (Boston, 1911), 251–2

harvest in the monodrama, especially in the preceding lyric with its biblical imagery of the fertile promised land. As in *Along the Beach*, where James Lee is as barren as his farm, this turf is 'dead to the roots,' sun-scorched. In the former poem, the woman tended her unlikely soil, and not only harvested no crop but was faulted for her faithfulness. Here the emphasis shifts from the unproductive soil to what may adorn it 'with such a blue and red grace.' Love becomes less a cherishing with a view to eventual reward than a gift without reckoning. It settles down 'unawares,' just as in lyric II hell could open 'unawares.' If the unknown can contain seeds of misery, it once brought something else that was as real; James Lee's wife is working her way toward the moral of Ferishtah's second parable.

Rock is the other substance graced by a colourful visitor, rock that is 'baked dry; of a weed, of a shell, no trace: / Sunshine outside, but ice at the core, / Death's altar ...' The image of something dead or dying at the centre haunts James Lee's wife: the ship eaten away by wormwood; this rock; 'our heart's core,' which cannot, in lyric VI, preserve one beauty changeless. What fights such sinister images are similar ones, with a difference; these are images of something that preserves life in its roots. Fig-tree and vine do so; in lyric III the woman notes only so much of them as seems dying, but at the end she chooses for herself the image of a tree. Deep-rooted, long-lived – the image was to please Browning and imply steadfastness from *By the Fireside* through *James Lee's Wife* to *La Saisiaz*.

Love settles with 'a blue and red grace,' and the two colours, as I have noted, are favourites with Browning. There is some danger in reading other usages into this poem, but a case can be made, I think, for associating the red with human passion and the blue with whatever extraordinary greatness of spirit love may inspire. The red is an obvious association; Elizabeth, for instance, is 'human at the red-ripe of the heart.'[11] Here the red butterfly wings 'scorch / Like a drop of fire / From a brandished torch.'[12] Blue is sometimes a heavenly colour in Browning. Elizabeth is red-ripe at the heart but lives 'within the holier blue'; the sapphire's blue is memorable in the

11 Cf. H.N. Fairchild, 'Browning's Pomegranate Heart,' *Modern Language Notes* 66 (1951), 265–6
12 Cf. *Aurora Leigh* (1058–60): 'butterflies, that bear / Upon their blue wings such red embers round, / They seem to scorch the blue air into holes / Each flight they take.'

heaven of *One Word More*.[13] But intense blue may be associated
with creative achievement, as in *Popularity*. Similarly, the associations here are not with what may be divine in erotic love, but with
what is extraordinary for a 'level and low' mankind. Thus the blue
imagery is of chivalry and of fairyland:

> No cricket, I'll say
> But a warhorse, barded and chanfroned too,
> The gift of a quixote-mage to his knight,
> Real fairy, with wings all right.

In artistic creation, the mage is used to stress the inexplicable. There
is no such stress here, but there is a touch. Love, like creation, cannot
be explained by a sum of the parts of man. It seams less to grow like
a plant than to alight from some airy region. In lyric IV, this seemed
to indicate that love is volatile ('the light, light love, he has wings to
fly'); here the connotations are quite different.

Under the Cliff, lyric VI, draws Browning himself into *James Lee's
Wife*. The speaker reads six stanzas of an early Browning poem on
the wind. Like the wind of *In the Doorway*, this is a sighing or moaning voice, which may wail of some woe. (The *By the Fireside* word is
used in the poem within a poem, and also in the comment on it:
'why this is the old woe o' the world.') What strikes the speaker is
that Browning's poem is very youthful; it sees the world as a show-
place for the young man who will be the exception to human frailty.
The comment (in stanzas vii–xi) is especially interesting as a footnote
to the development of Paracelsus and Sordello. Yet the effect of the
insertion is to turn us back to these poems or outward to Browning,
and to distract us from the speaker. (Did Browning assume the reader
would not know the poem's source? Or did he wish to indicate James
Lee's wife's problem is part of a larger universal problem? That, as she
thought her love sure, so he thought himself sure of his triumph?)
But the distraction, if it interferes with the dramatic viewpoint,
strengthens the theme. Stanza x is surely a Wordsworthian echo
('kind / Calm years, exacting their accompt / Of pain, mature the

---

13 Cf.: 'It is the rock of summer, the extreme, / A mountain luminous half
way in bloom / And then half way in the extremest light / Of sapphires
flashing from the central sky, / As if twelve princes sat before the king'
(Wallace Stevens, *Credences of Summer*, vi)

mind'), and stanza xii if not an echo of Keats' words is of a Keats' theme ('"Here is the change beginning, here the lines / Circumscribe beauty, set to bliss / The limit time assigns"'). The initiation into what time does comes at the appropriate season of midsummer; the young man looks out over 'a sparkling foreign country' as if he surveys some promised land. But the young man's country 'next minute must annul.'

Stanzas xii–xvi are among Browning's most powerful treatments of change. What is most interesting is the double attitude as James Lee's wife attempts but cannot maintain robust acceptance of change: 'Rejoice that man is hurled / From change to change unceasingly, / His soul's wings never furled!' The tone of these lines is also that of other Browning poems, and is sometimes taken as the only tone Browning knew. Here man is a plaything of the wind, and we recall the *Two in the Campagna* pain over this. It is as a thing of the air he is to think of himself, something that does not furl its wings, unlike the rooted fig-tree that 'furled / Her five fingers'; something like cricket or butterfly, or even more like 'light, light love,' for cricket and butterfly settled on earth. Once commit oneself to a particular time and place, however, and change can bring pain: 'Nothing can be as it has been before; / Better, so call it, only not the same.' (Abt Vogler also asserts this: 'many more of the kind / As good, nay, better perchance: is this your comfort to me?' So did Luria: 'Is it with life as with the body's change? / – Where, e'en tho' better follow, good must pass ...?' [II, 271–2].) The woman returns to her early, unhappy word, 'bitter.' She returns, too, to another part of the soul's anatomy, the hands (a more human part than wings); we are back to the fig-tree and away from airborne creatures. Or rather we are back to the drowning man of *By the Fireside* (the lyric where 'bitter' appears), but this time the drowning is not because one ship of love founders:

> Only, for man, how bitter not to grave
>   On his soul's hands' palms one fair good wise thing
> Just as he grasped it! For himself, death's wave;
>   While time first washes – ah, the sting! –
> O'er all he'd sink to save.

Sting in conjunction with death has an echo of Paul, while the air imagery strongly resembles *Fifine*'s. This is a poem with the rhyme

scheme of *Two in the Campagna* and the original *By the Fireside*. It
ends with the pain of the former.

James Lee's Wife can be divided into three trios: the first ends
with the courage to face the problem; the second with grief over
inevitable change; the third with freedom and imagined joy. Lyric vii,
Among the Rocks, is the first in which nature is not sinister or
melancholy. Even with such a title, the poem sees the earth as
genial; it is personified as smiling and benign. The sun does not
shrivel, but may be basked in; the sea has ripples that run in mirth;
the sound is not of wind, but of an auspicious lark. James Lee's wife
is shown working her way toward new strength. 'Give earth yourself,
go up for gain above!' James Lee was, in lyric iv, an earth without
harvest; the greater earth, 'old earth,' is pictured as knowing where
harvest must be sought. The moralizing of this stanza, and of the
whole ensuing lyric, may irritate. But it is hardly surprising that at this
stage the woman should collect her strength by moralizing on her
ordeal in some way. It is a method of leaving pain behind without
suppressing it. The woman of lyric iv, moreover, would express
herself in this way. She will not, however, end her monodrama with
moralizing.

The original *Beside the Drawing-Board*, lyric viii, was twenty-eight
lines, and, I think, stronger in impact and more consistent with the
other lyrics than in its final eighty-three-line version. The original
tells us enough: that James Lee's wife is sketching a hand (a recuper-
ating exercise, probably), and while doing so, stumbles on her first
impulse to love again, to give herself again if only in a small way.
The original makes the process quite clear: the action of drawing, the
first mention of happiness and of time flying by without consciousness
of pain, the kiss. The use of the hands and finger-tips, the reappear-
ance of 'grace,' the kiss given, which is so unlike the embrace received
in lyric i – all tie this poem to the rest of the monodrama. It marks
the last stage in the woman's recuperation, and it is interesting in two
ways. First, throughout the series until now, the focus has been on
nature, and until lyric vii on man against nature. But what completes
the cure is something human, a girl's coarse hand.[14] Second, the

14 Cf. *Aurora Leigh* (161–71): 'Humanity is great; / And, if I would not
   rather pour upon / An ounce of common, ugly, human dust, / An artisan's
   palm or a peasant's brow, / Unsmooth, ignoble, save to me and God, /
   Than track old Nilus ... set it down as weakness'

act that finally releases James Lee's wife is an artistic one. She makes an amateur sketch, and the act of giving herself, of seeking beauty (she also fancies how she might seek skill or power), though expressing it awkwardly, is salutary.[15] She is momentarily overcome by the human form: 'the beauty in this, – how free, how fine / To fear, almost, – of the limit-line!' (Browning repeated these lines in the revised version.) The awe is unexpected in her; so is the kiss. So is what comes of them in the last lyric.

Browning's altering of the moment of truth shows he was dissatisfied with it,[16] and certainly it is difficult to work out. It is not some inexplicable breakthrough, but a change in view gradually effected. The poem falters here, for it is hard to handle this middle ground that shows no ecstasy or gaiety, and it is too early to show serenity. The couplet ending the original and revised versions is the same ('Go little girl with the poor coarse hand! / I have my lesson, shall understand'), but the lesson is more explicit in the latter. In the first version, the parallel between the coarse hand and James Lee's unrewarding nature may be ascertained but is not clearly implied as in the second version. The woman had before given herself to James Lee, but the difference in this giving of herself is evident. It is what explains the difference in tone between the hurt self-righteousness of *Along the Beach* and the generosity here. ' "I must live beloved or die," ' has been her view, she implies. But now she approaches a view of love as unreserved giving, a view offered elsewhere by Browning. 'Nearer we hold of God / Who gives, than of His tribes that take, I must believe,' says Rabbi ben Ezra. 'Should he play / The helpless weakling, or the helpful strength / That captures prey and saves the perishing?' Ferishtah is asked by God (1, 27–9). Auden's well-known line is a revision of James Lee's wife's old view of things that would have pleased Browning.

With the last lyric, James Lee is released, and generously so; his wife does not even demand a place in his memory. 'There is nothing

15 Cf. *Fifine at the Fair*, where Don Juan's drawing provides an example of pivotal importance; but he draws with a shipman's broken pipe and on the sand. His wreckage imagery, like his earth, air, sea, and flame images, have different implications than James Lee's wife's.

16 He was, in fact, dissatisfied with the series as a whole: 'But I have expressed it all insufficiently, and will break the chain up, one day, and leave so many little round rings to roll each its way, if it can' (*RBJW*, 123).

to remember in me' is an astonishing contrast to lyric I; again 'grace'
is used of what might have been memorable. The woman asks only
that her husband acknowledge that their past love had validity:
'in turn, concede to me, / Such things have been as a mutual flame.'
This poem is titled *On Deck*, but its maritime imagery is not
menacing nor its fire like the ironic hearthfire or the hell-fire of the
second poem. Yet the woman is not off for new adventure. She is
possessed by her love. (Browning gives her a phrase close to a *Men
and Women* pair of lyrics: 'Well, you may, you must, set down to
me / Love that was life, life that was love.' If my reading of the two
lyrics – one as quest, the other as hunt – is correct, then James Lee's
wife may here be conceding that her past devotion was possessive
as well as entire – a view supported by Browning's remarks on her
quoted above.) The image she uses of James Lee's words and looks
is that which shapes *Women and Roses*, and which Aprile and the
Pauline poet and Aeschylus use of their imagined images: '... whose
words and looks will, circling, flee / Round me and round while life
endures.' In one sense, then, the woman does return to the beginning
of her monodrama, for she again yearns and imagines James Lee
loves her. The difference is that she now knows she is indulging in a
reverie. There are no more swans and dells or pat rhymes; the rhyme
is that of *Two in the Campagna* and the first *By the Fireside*, and of
Under the Cliff; the metre is closer to the former two than the latter.
The woman now thinks precisely, knows her own devotion and her
husband's lack of it. If she prefers to end in a rapture of hope, she
also ends with a question-mark.

James Lee's Wife is worth attention in its own right. It is also inter-
esting because its play on various images calls attention to these
images elsewhere in Browning. Wind is one such, the wind of lyrics
II and VII, for instance, recalling the unpredictable wind of *Two in the
Campagna*. But there are other winds in Browning; some, like
Paracelsus', seem to mock the possibility of any kind of permanence:

> While we read,
> The sharp salt wind, impatient for the last
> Of even this record, wistfully comes and goes,
> Or sings what we recover, mocking it.
> This is the record; and my voice, the wind's.   (IV, 445–9)

Paracelsus had earlier found the wind less purposeful if as sad: "T
is the melancholy wind astir / Within the trees' (III, 997–8). The
wind's message was of change: 'Gone, gone, / Those pleasant times!
Does not the moaning wind / Seem to bewail that we have gained
such gains / And bartered sleep for them?' (III, 1006–9). Paracelsus'
views on change are important, and it is appropriate the wind should
speak thus to him. And a later Browning would himself also associate
the wind with melancholy: '... such a wind as now howls – what a
sound! The most melancholy in the whole world I think' (*LRBEB*, II,
580; Apr. 1, 1846). But the wind in Browning is fairly consistently
a wind of change. Even when change is for the better, the wind may
announce it.

> Out there came
> A moon made like a face with certain spots
> Multiform, manifold and menacing:
> Then a wind rose behind me. So we met.
> (*Epistle of Karshish*, 292–5)

> For what purpose the wind knows best,
> Who changes his mind continually.
> (*Christmas-Eve*, 191–2)

> Eddying down till it find your face
> At some slight wind – best chance of all!
> (*By the Fireside*, 212–13)

> Chance, the wind, change, the rain ...
> (*Fifine at the Fair*, 474)

> ... outside, rain and wind combine ...
> With a malice ...
> (*Never the Time and the Place*, 8–11)

> Only, at heart's utmost joy and triumph, terror
>   Sudden turns the blood to ice: a chill wind disencharms
> All the late enchantment!
> (*Ferishtah's Fancies, Epilogue* 25–7)

Browning prefers to associate wind with earthbound imagery, and it often plays something of the mixed role of clouds, mist, or water in his poetry. Thus with the ambiguous words and wind association: '"Words are but words and wind. Why let the wind / Sing in your ear, bite, sounding to your brain?"' (*Red Cotton Night-Cap Country*, 2329–30) ; 'words, mere wind, / Would cheat me of some minutes' (*The Ring and the Book*, xi, 1493–4) ; 'our human speech is naught, / Our human testimony false, our fame / And human estimation words and wind' (ibid., xii, 838–40; here the repeated 'human stresses the conditions under which these statements are valid). Wind, like word, has its necessary uses on this earth, Browning would say.

Fire imagery also plays through *James Lee's Wife*: the sun's fire, which may be genial or may scorch or may depart; the flame of mutual love, and the hearthfire that should grow from it but may deteriorate to hell-fire. The imagery of fire appears in much of Browning's verse, and its connotations are consistently those of vitality, notably of the spark of life that makes man's spirit. Browning's light imagery is frequently noted; fire might be called the tangible form of it. He once proposed translating *Prometheus Bound*, and the Prometheus legend is used in *Parleying with Mandeville*. In the latter, the connection with Browning's favourite sun image is clear. 'Prometheus ... offered an artifice whereby he drew / Sun's rays into focus ... made fire burn.' The Pope in *The Ring and the Book* and Rabbi ben Ezra make a religious rather than legendary connection between fire (here man's soul) and its origin. 'My poor spark had for its source the sun'; 'untroubled by a spark ... A spark disturbs our clod.' (The image is useful as analogy, not as a definition of substance, as Fra Lippo Lippi's audience demonstrates: 'Man's soul, and it's a fire, smoke ... It's vapour.' Karshish opts for the latter – 'that puff of vapour from his mouth, man's soul' – but unlike the above disputants incorporates into his metaphor the 'wily' vapour's 'source.') 'Any wife' also notes the source ('thanks to Him / Who never is dishonoured in the spark / He gave us from his fire of fires, and bade / Remember whence it sprang').

But the usage may be entirely secular, as in Aristophanes' variation on Job ('I know the soul, how the spark ascends') or the *Two Poets of Croisic* hearthfire sparks, each of which symbolizes some man's career ('Son / O' the coal, – as Job and Hebrew name a spark, – /

What bard, in thy red soaring, scares the dark?' [46–8]). Or, by extension to general flame, the common metaphorical association of fire with vitality may be made (as in, for example, *Love Among the Ruins*). In the two *By the Firesides* and in *A Lovers' Quarrel* hearthfires figure, and may be readily associated with the spirit and life of the home.

Sometimes the usage suggests variations on Michelangelo's image of creation, the touch of God's finger. In *Mesmerism* the purpose is demonic ('the hands give vent / To my ardour and my aim / And break into very flame'; 'do my fingers dip / In a flame which again they throw ...?'). Don Juan has his usual ingenious variation:

> ... some girl by fate reserved
> To give me once again the electric snap and spark
> Which prove, when finger finds out finger in the dark
> O' the world, there's fire and life and truth there,
> > link but hands
> And pass the secret on.   (xci)

However Abt Vogler's use is serious: 'But here is the finger of God, a flash of the will that can.' So is Cleon, in his subjectivism: 'all this joy in natural life is put / Like fire from off thy finger into each ... But 't is pure fire, and they mere matter are; / It has them, not they it' (203–4, 206–7).

The spark, as man's spirit, is encased, and enclosed fire is an image that intrigued Browning. 'Thus shall he go on, greatening, till he ends – / The man of men, the spirit of all flesh, / The fiery centre of an earthly world' (*Colombe's Birthday*, IV, 249–51). In the *Paracelsus* quotation, page 270 below, fire is buried light, which melts gold; in the molten metal, the images of light and fire coalesce. Enclosed fire (as volcanic or lighthouse gleam) is Browning's metaphor for his own creativity (*LRBEB*, I, 17, 74). Gold is mined, but fire may be struck from the unlikely source of rock (the image recalls Moses' miracle with rock and water). ''T is the sparks' long succession one by one / Shall show you, in the end, what fire was crammed / In that mere stone you struck' (*In a Balcony*, 644–6). 'Fancy the fabric ... ere steel strike fire from quartz' (*The Grammarian's Funeral*, 70–1). This is the image that makes up the *Ferishtah's Fancies* fifth lyric:

> Fire is in the flint:[17] true, once a spark escapes,
> Fire forgets the kinship, soars till fancy shapes
> Some befitting cradle where the babe had birth –
> Wholly heaven's the product, unallied to earth.
> Splendours recognized as perfect in the star! –
> In our flint their home was, housed as now they are.

It may also affect the resuscitation imagery of *The Ring and the Book*. Browning says the life in him abolished the death of things; life as fire in him calls to buried life (the gold when enclosed in the dark is not living fire) and brings it to light so it may burn (thanks to the sun) with a life of its own.

But fire has various uses. Like gold, the image is double-edged. Fire is useful and often necessary, but it may also be dangerous. In this it resembles the sun (a vertical sun, or naked belief, 'would wither up at once,' says Blougram, who also says that 'belief's fire, once in us, / Makes of all else mere stuff to show itself'). If a Guido is typified as fiery, his is an infernal conflagration; images of burning, branding, ash, and smoke run through his second monologue; Pompilia testified that he

> changed
> Into a fury of fire, if once he was
> Merely a man: his face threw fire at mine,
> He laid a hand on me that burned all peace,
> All joy, all hope, and last all fear away,
> Dipping the bough of life, so pleasant once,
> In fire which shrivelled leaf and bud alike.   (VI, 773–9)

But fire, even when destructive, may be purifying. In his double use of purifying and demonic fire, Browning again draws on biblical usage. 'For he is like a refiner's fire'; one of Browning's favourite images is the refining of gold or the trying of gems by fire. The Pope thinks that Guido may be saved 'so as by fire' (X, 714); if Paul's meta-

---

17 Cf. *Timon of Athens*, I, i, 23–4: 'The fire i' the flint / Shows not till it be struck.' Mario Praz notes, in his *Studies in Seventeenth-Century Imagery*, that this pairing is common in emblem literature.

phor sounds severe, consider Browning's application of it in a letter
to Elizabeth: 'If you could save my soul, "so as by fire," would your
dear love shrink from that?' (*LRBEB*, II, 612; Apr. 10, 1846). In
Childe Roland, much tension is generated by our ignorance whether
the fire imagery is infernal and permanent, or purifying and life-
giving. Childe Roland seems given over to passivity, his purpose cold:
'neither pride / Nor hope rekindling.' He had previously suffered a
like deprivation: 'Out went my heart's fire and left it cold.' His landscape may witness to 'the fiend's glowing hoof,' 'wild cats in a red-hot
iron cage.' ''T is the Last Judgment's fire must cure this place.' But
at the end, the sun's red no longer leers; it is 'kindled through a cleft,'
like the sun through the grating when Sordello dies. 'Burningly it
came on me ... in a sheet of flame / I saw them and I knew them all' –
and Childe Roland acts, now appropriating fire imagery for his own
use. It is as purifying fire, too, that Aristophanes sees satire ('Satire
– to burn and purify the world ... / Finds out in knaves', fools',
cowards' armoury / The tricky tinselled place fire flashes through, /
No damage else, / Sagacious of true ore' [*Aristophanes' Apology*,
787–927]).

Fire lends itself readily to contrast – with darkness, with cold, with
other elements and especially water. Browning likes working by contrast, and fire and water (or ice) make up one of his favourites.
Evelyn Hope was made of 'spirit, fire and dew.' The use of fire and
water I have noted in *Women and Roses* and in *James Lee's Wife*.
Fire and ice imagery, associated with southern and northern climates
and temperaments, is prominent in *Luria* and *Fifine*. With Caponsacchi, fire and light are associated with order and meaning, water
with chaos:

> After all, I shall give no glare – at best
> Only display you certain scattered lights
> Lamping the rush and roll of the abyss:
> Nothing but here and there a fire-point pricks
> Wavelet from wavelet ...   (VI, 1171–5)

Guido's second monologue develops the contrast of himself as fire
(the volcano from the earth, he says, not the gold) and of Pompilia
as water ('my heart ... grows the stonier for your saving dew! / You
steep the substance, you would lubricate, / In waters that but touch

to petrify' [XI, 2224–7]). Water, like fire, may come in sinister or
benign form.

Fire and water are the ordeals by which Miranda seeks to expiate
fancied sin. *Two Poets of Croisic*, like *James Lee's Wife: By the
Fireside*, begins with a fire of shipwood, then moves to float in fancy
near the Croisic shore. Browning estimates his own temperament is
many parts ice and water to a few fire: 'To be grand in a simile, for
every poor spark of a Vesuvius or a Stromboli in my microcosm there
are huge layers of ice and pits of black cold water – and I make the
most of my two or three fire-eyes, because I know by experience, alas,
how these tend to extinction – and the ice grows & grows' (*LRBEB*,
I, 74; May 24, 1845).

M.H. Abrams has demonstrated how prevalent among Romantic
poets was the image of the wind to symbolize life;[18] he mentions the
biblical and classical traditions that make the image an appropriate
one. Browning prefers another image for life that also has both
biblical and classical tradition behind it, that of fire. His wind tends
to be random, whimsical, and sportive, or to appear so. It may be
like or of the Spirit of God, but what Browning stresses is how it
blows where it lists.

18 M.H. Abrams, 'The Correspondent Breeze: A Romantic Metaphor,' in
English Romantic Poets: Modern Essays in Criticism, ed. M.H. Abrams
(New York, Oxford, 1960), 37–54

16 GOLD

Browning's use of gold imagery is associated chiefly and properly with *The Ring and the Book*. Before 1868, gold is a frequent enough image, sometimes skilfully developed in the context of one poem (such as *Love Among the Ruins* or *Andrea del Sarto*) and with various kinds of implication. It does not, I think, bear the kind of special significance that, for example, Browning's light imagery usually does, or suggest the kind of interpoetical echo of certain favourite Browning phrases (see and hear, stoop, yearn, for example). But after *The Ring and the Book*, gold begins to figure consistently in a usage connected with Browning's light and enclosure imagery. I think Browning's interest in gold imagery at about the time of the composition of *The Ring and the Book* was stimulated by the tale in, and explains much about, that curious little poem *Gold Hair*.[1]

Gold, of course, has the great advantage of a long traditional usage. The search for gold (ancient and contemporary: the California gold rush began in 1848), or for a transformer of other metals to gold, as well as the many functions of its properties, real or imagined, provide the poet with numerous associations. But Browning at first rejects the assistance of such tradition, as he did with the rose image, which only becomes prominent after it attains a personal

---

1 *Gold Hair: A Legend of Pornic* was published in the *Atlantic Monthly* for May 1864, then in *Dramatis Personae* on May 28, 1864. W.O. Raymond (in *The Infinite Moment*, chapters IV and V) has shown how Browning first mentioned the source of *The Ring and the Book* in September 1862 and began to work diligently at it after the publication of *Dramatis Personae*. DeVane (*Handbook*, 286–7) suggests *Gold Hair* was written in the summer of 1862. The evidence is not conclusive, but then the point of the date is not vital. Whether in 1862 or later, and whether connected with *The Ring and the Book* or not, Browning found certain gold images coalesce in a bizarre tale and made a poem of it.

significance. A certain logic, too, attends the prominence of any image: its concrete and symbolic qualities both fit some kind of metaphysical and/or psychological coherence, as with light and enclosure imagery. If anything, Browning is apt to be iconoclastic or ambivalent about the traditions of imagery – which is also a way of acknowledging them.

If the use of gold imagery before the sixties is more or less random or individual, there is one use in *Paracelsus* that anticipates much to come:

> For some one truth would dimly beacon me
> From mountains rough with pines, and flit and wink
> O'er dazzling wastes of frozen snow, and tremble
> Into assured light in some branching mine
> Where ripens, swathed in fire, the liquid gold –
> And all the beauty, all the wonder fell
> On either side the truth, as its mere robe;
> I see the robe now – then I saw the form.   (II, 161–8)

I quoted earlier the *Paracelsus* passage where truth is spoken of as buried light in the form of fire, and it will be noted that when light as truth transmutes itself into gold here, it is a fiery gold. It is fire-clothed (truth, the light, in the robe of beauty and wonder, the flame) ; and it is liquid, the liquidity marking the proximity of fire, which, melting the gold, transforms it into a stream, thus making it more like light; and the liquidity marking, too, the depth of penetration into the earth's core, where fire and liquid ore mix as buried light. Part of the fascination of gold is the place where it is found – in the enclosure of earth. Here, as often in Browning, the enclosure and the emer-gence of gold are prominent (cf. *Gold Hair, The Ring and the Book, Two Poets of Croisic*). Yet another association is anticipated in the curious use of the word 'ripens' to describe what is happening to underground gold. The gold seems something organic; I suspect that 'ripen' is used here mainly to emphasize the gold's vitality (like 'liquid,' which suggests movement). But later, Browning would more than once parallel gold with honey; of similar colour, and similarly enclosed, honey enriches the suggestiveness of gold imagery. 'Virgin as oval tawny pendent tear / At beehive-edge when *ripened* combs o'erflow ... the artificer melts up wax / With honey, so to speak'

(*The Ring and the Book*, I, 12–13, 18–19, italics mine). Honey adds
to gold the specific suggestion of a depositor, as well as an animal
vitality, qualities of sweetness and nourishment, and a long tradition
of usage.

But if gold is here connected with truth and light, it also has other
uses. Minted, it may become the instrument of temptation. A few lines
after the quotation above, Paracelsus admits he could console himself if he could learn to 'breed / Gold' (193–4). Light is light, whether
of sun, moon, or star; and dark is dark; cloud, mist, or colour mediate.
The contrast and the mediation please Browning and suit his habits
of mind. Light is hardly ever ambivalent. But gold may be baneful
as well as precious, and in the 1842, 1845, 1855, and 1864 collections
it is as likely to be the one as the other.

I have already touched on the use of pure gold in the song 'Nay
but you, who do not love her' and in the Barrett-Browning letters.
The purity of gold, which Browning expands on in *The Ring and
the Book*, is hardly touched on elsewhere in *Bells and Pomegranates*,
except insofar as pure gold will come unscathed through fire.
(The lady of *The Glove* decides to try 'in a crucible, / To what
"speeches like gold" were reducible.') But other substances besides
gold may be extracted from the earth, tested by fire, and found to
radiate light. Jewels, obviously, share these functions, and Browning
makes use of the properties of various jewels, especially in his later
poetry. In *Bells and Pomegranates*, people, as well as their speeches,
may be tried like gold or jewels. The fleeing duchess will endure like a
true gem the 'jewel-finder's fierce assay / Of the prize he dug from
its mountain-tomb – / let once the vindicating ray / Leap out amid
the anxious gloom, / And steel and fire have done their part' (the
'mountain-tomb' recalls variations on Browning's enclosure imagery,
and of course the gold from 'old tombs at Chiusi').

Gems, like gold, radiate the sun's light – or, in Donne's usage,
produce their own, like stars (Browning quotes inaccurately, but not
so as to affect the image) : ' "I take my jewels from their boxes; call /
My Diamonds, Pearls, and Emeralds, and make / Myself a constellation of them all!" ' (*LRBEB*, I, 405; Jan. 19, 1846; the source is
Donne's *Epithalamion on the Lady Elizabeth and Count Palatine*).
So, in *Shop*, the poet 'throws / You choice of jewels, everyone, /
Good, better, best, star, moon, and sun !' (73–5). The Druid sphere
of crystal with enclosed bubble intrigued Browning in 1846 ('Our

Druids used to make balls for divining out of such all-but-solid gems with the central weakness – I have had them in my hand' [*LRBEB*, II, 933; Aug. 5, 1846]) and he used it later in *Fifine at the Fair* (cii), the combination of light, circle, and gem imagery no doubt pleasing him. Clara in *Red Cotton Night-Cap Country,* 'like a diamond in the dark, / Should extract shining from what else were shade, / And multiply chance rays a million-fold' (2138–40). For the diamond, like the prism, can break pure white light into the spectrum, if it is not 'cut awry / Or left opaque, – no brilliant named and known. / Whate'er my inner stuff, my outside's blank' (*Inn Album,* 417–19). The Fisc prefers a different stone for woman, and his ingenious imagery draws together the fire and water that may be fancied to compose jewels:

> First, infancy, pellucid as a pearl;
> Then childhood – stone which, dew-drop at the first,
> (An old conjecture) sucks, by dint of gaze,
> Blue from the sky and turns to sapphire so:
> Yet both these gems eclipsed by, last and best,
> Womanliness and wifehood opaline,
> Its milk-white pallor, – chastity, – suffused
> With here and there a tint and hint of flame, –
> Desire, – the lapidary loves to find.   (IX, 199–207)

(The passage is peculiarly the Fisc's own, the rhetorical Latinate flourishes – 'pellucid as a pearl' – and alliterative abstractions – 'womanliness and wifehood' – and straight-faced concessions to human frailty – 'a tint and hint of flame, – / Desire.') A broadly ironic variation on this is in *Parleying with Bartoli* where the woman would be a pearl if she were not low-born; she is white, but cheap.

The digger, tester, or manipulator of gold and gems appears briefly in the *Bells and Pomegranates* poems, and he is usually surrounded by an aura of mystery. In *In a Gondola* the lady bids her lover be a mage and suck out her soul from her body as the mage loosens their spirit from gems. In *The Englishman in Italy* the gypsy plies his tinker's trade, as in *The Flight of the Duchess* gypsies do mysterious things with the mineral riches of the dukedom. The old man of *The Laboratory* is a sinister obscure figure, like the *Romeo and Juliet* alchemist, and if Artemis is benign, she nonetheless practises magic. Paracelsus was an alchemist and a magician of sorts; I have already noted the mage imagery touched on in *Pauline* and important in *Sordello*. Whether mage, gypsy, chemist, or goddess, the handler of the earth's secret substances retains the air of mystery. (The Mosaic miracle used in *Sordello* and *One Word More*, the extraction of water from rock, may be considered a prophetic form of mining.) The *In a Gondola* lady who wishes her soul sucked from her body anticipates the subversive, literal soul-sucking of a demonic mage, the mesmerizer of *Mesmerism*. The assayer or craftsman of gold or gems is of constant interest to Browning. Castellani's name and art find place in *The Ring and the Book*, and in *Red Cotton Night-Cap Country* is 'a jeweller – no unsuggestive craft! Jules in *Pippa Passes* implies that the sculptor's may also be a suggestive craft, working as it does with

> marble! – 'neath my tools
> More pliable than jelly – as it were
> Some clear primordial creature dug from depths
> In the earth's heart, where itself breeds itself,
> And whence all baser substance may be worked.   (II, 100–4)

Sculpture also engages in its appropriate form of resuscitation if it can 'lay bare those bluish veins of blood asleep,' as Jules has it (II, 109).

In *Andrea*, gold is the colour of the aspiring man, whose reach toward the sun exceeds his grasp. But the golden-haired Lucrezia is interested in graspable gold ('And shut the money into this small hand'). Andrea is useful to her because he has converted his golden aspirations into coin; when he wishes to communicate his meaning to her best, he must translate it into monetary terms. To Andrea, the placid uxorious spouse and 'faultless painter,'[2] his life is grey and

---

2 Cf. two remarks by Elizabeth Barrett: 'Our "event" just now is a new purchase of a "Holy Family," supposed to be by Andrea del Sarto ... It is probably a fine picture, and I seem to see my way through the dark of my ignorance, to admire the grouping and colouring, whatever doubt as to the expression and divinity may occur otherwise' (to Mrs Martin, *LEB*, I, 121; Jan. 30 1843). And, concerning Browning: 'The truth is ... it is easier to find a more faultless writer than a poet of equal genius' (to Cornelius Mathews, ibid., I, 133; April 28, 1843)

silver.[3] 'All is silver-grey / Placid and perfect with my art: the worse!
... Too live the life grew, golden and not grey, / And I'm the
weak-eyed bat no sun should tempt.' But reject the intangible gold
as he may try, part of Andrea remembers it, and what haunts him
in memory and in symbol is his transmutation of this gold into
something base: 'I surely then could ... / Put on glory, Rafael's
daily wear, / In that humane great monarch's golden look ...
The jingle of his gold chain in my ear ... When I look up from
painting, eyes tired out, / The walls become illumined, brick from
brick / Distinct, instead of mortar, fierce bright gold, / That gold
of his I did cement them with!' Other, lesser artists are like flames
blazing toward the sun, in the fashion of the soldier-saints of *The
Statue and the Bust*. But Lucrezia is interested in buried gold, gold
shut into her little grasp, and cold hard cash, not gold aspirations
that are warmed and softened by the sun. Her image is the moon
('my face, my moon, my everybody's moon'). Her jewel is the moon-
like pearl, cool and white, unlike King Francis' jingling gold chain.
She is self-contained and perfect ('those perfect ears ... the same
perfect brow, / And perfect eyes, and more than perfect mouth, /
And the low voice my soul hears, as a bird / The fowler's pipe, and
follows to the snare'). Lucrezia with her moon-imagery, and Andrea
who sometimes aspires toward the sun, are dramatic embodiments
of what in *Numpholeptos* are the types of fatal woman and victim.

   Andrea del Sarto's is the most extended development of gold
imagery in *Men and Women*, the only other considerable use, an
ambivalent one, being in *Love Among the Ruins*. In *Master Hugues*,
it is truth that is associated with gold, an association more frequent
in Browning's later poetry. Gold here is not, as in *Paracelsus, The
Ring and the Book*, and *Two Poets of Croisic*, buried treasure,
although it may be obscured. In *Old Pictures in Florence*, there is a
hint of buried gold and fire that will re-emerge triumphantly: 'the
Campanile ... shall soar up in gold ... Shall I be alive that morning
the scaffold / Is broken away, and the long-pent fire, / Like the
golden hope of the world, unbaffled / Springs from its sleep ...?' (cf.

---

3 On the two contrasting patterns of imagery, see Mario L. D'Avanzo,
   'King Francis, Lucrezia, and the Figurative Language of "Andrea del
   Sarto," ' *Texas Studies in Literature and Language* 9 (1968), 523–36;
   Elizabeth Bieman, 'An Eros *Manqué*: Browning's "Andrea del Sarto," '
   Studies in English Literature 10 (1970), 651–68; and especially Roma A.
   King, Jr., *The Bow and the Lyre* (Ann Arbor, 1957), 11–31.

the gold and fire imagery of the buried city in *Love Among the Ruins*). The poem ends with a morning-vision, as it began with one ('white and wide / And washed by the morning-water-gold, / Florence lay out on the mountain-side'). The opening image is sensuous, appropriately so in a poem about Renaissance painting. (This Florence seems something of a woman, like the Edith of *Too Late*: 'There you stand, / Warm too, and white too: would this wine / Had washed all over that body of yours, / Ere I drank it, and you down with it, thus!') But it also faintly anticipates *The Ring and the Book* resuscitation imagery, with morning freshness and gold on the mountain-side. The associations here, however, are rather with the birth of the New Jerusalem, the water-gold suggesting Browning's image (used several times in *Dramatis Personae*) of that city's sea of glass and gold. Gold in *The Ring and the Book* is, of course, a special case, appearing not only in Book I but also throughout the poem and in numerous forms.[4] The curious legend of *Gold Hair* gathers in literally many of Browning's figurative uses of gold imagery. This gold awaits the resurrection, but when prematurely brought to light divulges what it had concealed – the golden-haired girl's hoarded gold pieces:

> With Heaven's gold gates about to ope,
> > With friends' praise, gold-like, lingering still,
> An instinct had bidden the girl's hand grope
> > For gold, the true sort – 'Gold in Heaven, if you will;
> But I keep earth's too, I hope.'

If pure gold is the image of something perfect, it is rarely found in this state. Nor is it surprising to find that Browning does not think it should be.[5] Pictor Ignotus, seeking to preserve his artistic purity ('Blown harshly, keeps the trump its golden cry? / Tastes sweet the water with such specks of earth?') paints himself into useless nullity;

---

4 For a summary of many of Browning's gold images, see Barbara Melchiori, *Browning's Poetry of Reticence* (Edinburgh and London, 1968), chapters III and IV.

5 Cf. Francis Bacon: 'Mixture of falsehood is like alloy in coin of gold and silver; which may make the metal work the better, but it embaseth it.' This is from the essay 'Of Truth,' and it is, of course, truth with which *The Ring and the Book* gold is associated. Browning inverts Bacon's emphasis.

his imagery is virginal; he is nonetheless violated. Gold in *Two Poets of Croisic* comes up 'rude / And rayless from the mine'; like Keats' whelks, it needs work. Even Thamuris' inspired walk is not a path of pure gold: 'ore with earth enwound / Glittered[6] beneath his footstep' (*Aristophanes' Apology*, 5194-5). Sun on water presents the eye with a foresight of the pure gold that belongs in the New Jerusalem – 'God's sea, glassed in gold' (*The Ring and the Book*, VI, 1161). But on earth, gold must be mined, assayed, and put to use:

> all the good
> I find in fancy is, it serves to set
> Gold's inmost glint free, gold which comes up rude
> And rayless from the mine. All fume and fret
> Of artistry beyond this point pursued
> Brings out another sort of burnish.
> (*Two Poets of Croisic*, clii)

To be useful, gold has need of alloy; this simple fact is important in Book I of *The Ring and the Book*. But Browning uses a variation of it in the cognate image of honey:

> As some greedy hind
> Persuades a honeycomb, beyond the due,
> To yield its hoarding, – heedless what alloy
> Of the poor bee's own substance taints the gold
> Which, unforced, yields few drops, but purity, –
> So would you fain relieve of load this brain,
> Though the hived thoughts must bring away, with strength,
> What words and weakness, strength's receptacle –
> Wax from the store! Yet, – aching soothed away, –
> Accept the compound! No suspected scent
> But proves some rose was rifled, though its ghost
> Scarce lingers with what promised musk and myrrh.
> No need of farther squeezing.   (*Aristophanes' Apology*, 2719-31)

---

6 Note the frequency of the word in Browning. And cf.: 'And now there will remain of this excellence – sermons, these few lines of "glittering gold." That true "gold" will be discovered there by the worthy assayer I do not doubt; that it glittered once I seem bound to gratefully say' (Browning, Introduction to Thomas Jones, *The Divine Order* [London, 1884]).

The last reference is startling. For *Sordello* ends with the dismissal of ghosts who leave the pungent odour of musk, not the sweetness of roses. There Browning chose for himself the musk scent; musk, we recall, is the base that makes the fugitive rose fragrance of perfume last. He would also choose for himself the alloy that makes pure soft gold take form and last; 'the artificer melts up wax / With honey, so to speak; he mingles gold / With gold's alloy' (*The Ring and the Book*, I, 18–20).

> The baser stuff
> Was but the nobler spirit's vehicle.
> Who would imprison, unvolatilize
> A violet's perfume, blends with fatty oils
> Essence too fugitive in flower alone.[7]
> (*Aristophanes' Apology*, 3412–16)

To be of use to men, gold or fragrance or honey must be re-imprisoned in ring or perfume or comb. (We recall Keats' dye, which became a cheap extract, bottled and retailed by imitators.) During a significant moment, the precious substance may exist pure and free ('what was born in a great white light,' Browning says of works of art). And Browning once used the image of gold hair (as originally painted and as now seen) for poetic inspiration and performance: 'these "too muches" for the everybody's picture are so many helps to the making out the real painter's picture as he had it in his brain. And all of the Titian's Naples Magdalen must have once been golden in its degree to justify that heap of hair in her hands – the *only* gold effected now!' (*LRBEB*, I, 7; Jan. 13, 1845). But as spirit must abide in body and in time, so inspiration and love must find their incarnations, goodly enough, in something earthbound.

The images of gold and honey and the rose's fragrance are hardly surprising choices for images of inspiration and love. As so often with Browning, his images are familiar Renaissance ones, and the

---

7 Note, in comparison, Shakespeare's sonnet 5, lines 9–14:
> Then were not summers distillation left
> A liquid prisoner pent in walls of glasse,
> Beauties effect with beauty were bereft,
> Nor it nor noe remembrance what it was.
>> But flowers distil'd though they with winter meete,
>> Leese but their show, their substance still lives sweet.

Renaissance knew these three as symbols for incarnation, especially for the incarnation of Christ:

> Thou [Mary] art the holy mine, whence came the gold,
> The great restorative for all decay
>   In young and old;
> Thou art the cabinet where the jewell lay:
> Chiefly to thee would I my soul unfold.
> (George Herbert, *To All Angels and Saints*)

'Give it me back!' says Browning of his Old Yellow Book where he mined gold. 'The thing's restorative / I' the touch and sight.'[8] Christ as the rose of God is similarly familiar, and Rosemond Tuve reminds us that 'Christ is traditionally honey and the honey-like manna' (*A Reading of George Herbert*, 51). I have also noted how Browning uses Moses' act of striking water from rock as a metaphor for his own writing of poetry, and how, in traditional iconography, this symbolizes the wounding of Christ during the crucifixion. And 'that great and famous hymn by Prudentius, *Inventor rutili dux bone luminis* ..., plays upon the double idea of Christ as Light and Christ as the Rock; out of the rock's heart, struck by flint, generate new seeds of light' (ibid., 67–8).

The great yearning of the alchemist was to find the secret that would transform base metals into gold. His search may provide an image of the conquering of time by art. It may also provide an image for man's salvation, immediate or eventual, and it is to this the Pope refers when he asks: 'Where is the gloriously-decisive change, / Metamorphosis the immeasurable / Of human clay to divine gold, we looked / Should, in some poor sort, justify its price?' (*The Ring and the Book*, x, 1615–18). But Browning sees use for other metals. The image he prefers to the transforming of base metal is the finding, extracting, and shaping of gold.

This is an image of resuscitation and at first reading, resuscitation, at the end of Book I of *The Ring and the Book*, seems simply a convenient and interesting figure for man's type of creation. The

---

8 J.C. Maxwell remarks on a Donne use of 'restorative' gold in 'A Donne Echo in "The Ring and the Book," ' *Notes and Queries* 16 (1969), 208. Cf. also 'Lemnius commends gold inwardly and outwardly used, as in Rings, excellent good in medicines' (Burton, *Anatomy of Melancholy*, II, iv, 1, 4)

usual prototype is, of course, the creation of the world by God; early
sources, as well as various implications of the concept, are given
by M.H. Abrams in the section 'The Poem as Heterocosm' in *The
Mirror and the Lamp*. But when Browning in Book I cites the
example of God as creator, he cites it only to reject it as a satisfactory
image ('Inalienable, the arch-prerogative / Which turns thought,
act – conceives, expresses too!). Man is a made thing, and he
'repeats God's process in man's due degree ... / Creates, no, but
resuscitates, perhaps ... Mimic creation, galvanism for life' (716–40).
What interests me is not the familiar parallel of God and poet as
creators, with due difference allowed – a difference that Browning
emphasizes more than the likeness.[9] What interests me is the unusual
word to describe man's imitative creation ('resuscitates') and the
two examples of resuscitators (a would-be Faust and Elisha).
The word and the examples and such phrases as 'something dead
may get to live again' suggest to me that Browning is proposing
another prototype than the creation of the world for the poet's
activity; that 'mimic creation' is close to resurrection, a word similar
to 'resuscitation' in sound and meaning.

Resurrection imagery is faintly, but I think unmistakably, evoked
at the beginning of *The Ring and the Book*. The ring held up to the
reader's view is fashioned by' Castellani's imitative craft,' Castellani
providing the figure of yet another creator, perhaps in the relation
to the poet that the poet is to God (is his craft, compared with the
poet's, 'mimic creation?'), but at any rate a craftsman who imitates
something in matter as the poet may imitate something in words.
What Castellani imitates are

Etrurian circlets found, some happy morn,
After a dropping April; found alive
Spark-like 'mid unearthed slope-side figtree-roots
That roof old tombs at Chiusi.

9 Compare Panofsky's observation that the words *creare, creator, creatio,*
and their vernacular equivalents are not applied to artists until the
sixteenth century, and in Italy not before about 1540–50. 'While
Dürer speaks of the "new creature which the artist creates (*schöpft*) in
his heart" as early as about 1525 ... Leonardo da Vinci ... studiously avoids
the terms *creare* and *creazione* in favor of *generare* and *generazione*,
a fact unfortunately neglected in all available translations and paraphrases'
(*Renaissance and Renascences in Western Art* [London, 1970], 188n.)

Something found alive on an old tomb some April morning carries
strong suggestions of resurrection – for some purpose or other, if only
to emphasize the liveness Browning hopes his poem (the ring) may
have or the vividness of his original inspiration from the book.[10]
But I think the imagery more significant than this. I have noted the
echo in 'something dead may get to live again'; other echoing phrases
are 'I fused my live soul and that inert stuff' (469); 'the life in me
abolished the death of things, / Deep calling unto deep' (520–1).

The implications of this figure are quite different from those that
may be drawn from the traditional prototype for the poet, the
creating God. One possible implication of the latter is that the poet
creates his enclosed, consistent world, the poem, and reigns over it
aloofly. But the image of the autonomous enclosed world that obeys
nothing but its own laws is a sinister one in *Pauline*. A Prometheus
figure is how Paracelsus originally sees himself, a helper of mankind
but aloof from them: 'I seemed to long / At once to trample on,
yet save mankind, ... to wring some wondrous good / From heaven
or earth for them, to perish ... as who should dare / Pluck out the
angry thunder from its cloud, / That, all its gathered flame dis-
charged on him, / No storm might threaten' (1, 460–8). Goethe
and others had used Prometheus to indicate the poet's necessary
isolation from the world in order to create (cf. Abrams, *The Mirror
and the Lamp*, 383). But Paracelsus' change of heart at the end
brings with it patience for the slow struggle of mankind. Sordello's
Goito-world is perfect, enclosed, and self-sufficient. The break outward is necessary, and when half of Sordello becomes Mankind, 'all's
changed.' Sordello's change recalls Aprile's phrase: 'God is the perfect poet, / Who in his person acts his own creation.'

Many writers who used the poet/God-creation analogy considered
that in his invention of fantasy the poet showed his power most
forcefully. Sidney, Puttenham, and later Dryden (in Caliban,
Shakespeare seemed 'to have created a person who was not in
Nature'), and especially Addison extol 'the fairy way of writing';
Addison, like Dryden and like Warton later, praises Shakespeare for

---

10 'The happy morn' is a Christmas rather than an Easter morn, familiar
   either through 'Christians, awake, salute the ...' (1750) or 'This is the
   month, and this the happy morn' (*On the Morning of Christ's Nativity*,
   1). But of course the first morn leads to the second.

his creation of Caliban: 'It shows a greater genius in Shakespeare to have drawn his Caliban, than his Hotspur, or Julius Caesar: the one was supplied out of his own imagination, whereas the other might have been formed upon tradition, history, or observation' (cited in Abrams, ibid., 275). This is logical enough if one takes as the prime type for the creating artist the God who creates *ex nihilo*; the closer the poet comes to creating *ex nihilo*, the greater he is. But if the prime type is rather the resurrecting God, the artist is seen less as maker than as resuscitator, less as inventor than as actor, less as ruler than as informing spirit. The creation myth has the disadvantage that man cannot invent out of pure nothingness or even completely formless chaos; the resurrection parallel is closer to what the poet actually does. There are places in Browning (for instance, in *Women and Roses*) where the artist's material seems to have a volition of its own, and so is less like matter waiting to receive form than form waiting to be re-embodied. The poet would best be seen, then, not so much in an exhibition of power (the creating and maintaining of a universe) as of love (long before *The Ring and the Book*, Browning had used the incarnation as the prime example of this) ; not of the marvellous but of the human. When Browning does depict the creature so admired as an example of Shakespeare's inventiveness, he measures him in human terms, as a primitive, an example of 'natural religion,' and finds him wanting. 'Making and marring clay at will? So He ... Loving not, hating not, just choosing so.' A God merely of power and arbitrary will seems to Browning no fit image for the worthy artist.

Much of Browning's concept and imagery in Book I of *The Ring and the Book* he might have found in Jacob Boehme, whose work he knew, and whom he mentions in '*Transcendentalism*':

The gold disappeared in Saturn, so that nothing is seen but a contemptible matter, till the right artist sets upon it, and again awakens the Mercury in the inclosed gold, and then the dead inclosed body of the gold does again revive in Saturn ...

Thus likewise it is with man; he lies now shut up after his fall in a gross, deformed, bestial dead image; he is not like an angel, much less like unto paradise; he is as the gross ore in Saturn, wherein the gold is couched and shut up ... He is a bad thorny bush, from whence notwithstanding fair rose-buds may bloom forth, and grow out of the thorns ... the artist who has made him takes him in hand, and brings the living Mercury into his gold or paradisical image disappeared and shut up in death

Hereby it is clearly signified to the artist chosen of God how he shall seek; no otherwise than as he has sought and found himself in the property of pure gold ... for man and the earth with its secrets lie shut up in the like curse and death, and need one and the same restitution. (*De Signatura Rerum*, xlvi, xlvii, xlviii)

My reading of the gold imagery in *The Ring and the Book*, then, ties together the opening lines of Book I, the crafting of the ring, and the Faust-Elisha examples. It gathers up Browning's many references to the poet as mage, but, as in *Pauline* the mage of black arts is rejected, so here even the worthy mage gropes for truth and rests upon a lie. The best prototype for the poet is the prophet,[11] the Elisha who raises the dead and thereby anticipates Christ's raising of Lazarus; anticipates, too, the other resurrection not to be repeated.

---

11 Again, note other references to poet as prophet, notably as Moses. In 1888, Browning revised *Pauline*, line 1019, originally 'I shall be priest and lover as of old,' to 'I shall be priest and prophet as of old.'

V PACCHIAROTTO,

ASOLANDO:

VARIATIONS

In 1876 Browning published his first collection of short poems in twelve years, the prickly *Pacchiarotto*. Between it and the 1864 *Dramatis Personae* had appeared some of his most remarkable long poems: *The Ring and the Book, Fifine at the Fair, Aristophanes' Apology*, and *Red Cotton Night-Cap Country*, for example. Performance and assertion from 1868 on had shown increasing independence from the demands of an audience, and Browning's audience after 1868 (the year of the start of *The Ring and the Book*) was considerable. He had published the difficult *Fifine* in 1871, and had declared the poet's independence in *Aristophanes' Apology* in 1875. The title-poem of the 1876 collection reads in full *Of Pacchiarotto, and how he worked in Distemper*, and in distemper most of the collection is executed. The exceptions are the four narrative poems, each of which has its own mood. But the lyrics, which centre on poetry, on love, and on religion, are nearly all marked by impatience and protest, and especially a reluctance to suffer unjustified aggression – whether from the reader in the lyrics on poetry, or the loved one in the love poems, or from God himself in the little allegory *Fears and Scruples*. The collection's *Prologue* and *Epilogue* read as if they have reference to Elizabeth Barrett, and in these references Browning is gentle and quiet. The *Prologue* seems entirely hers, and the mood one of rest tempered only by the yearning to rejoin her. But when Browning turns to what is on his, the earthly, side of the *Prologue's* 'wall,' it proves as troublesome as the householder's cares in *Fifine*, and he is not disposed to suffer it patiently.

In 1864, in *Prospice*, separation from his dead wife was for Browning a matter of the endurance of death, feeling 'the fog in my throat,' before the reunion. *Prospice* means 'seeing ahead,' and there appear no serious obstacles to sight, except for the great final one. In 1868, in 'O Lyric Love,' the speaker does not march forward to meet death, but prays for present grace through the distance and the dark. It is not that the fog of death may not be met valiantly enough, but that current needs are not satisfied in any simple way by the courage that faces death or the anticipated bliss of reunion. In 1871, in *Fifine*, an unhappy widower, a 'householder,' endures his state with very little patience. (Before reunion with his wife, he takes the opportunity to point out to her ghost what a miserable time he has had of it.[1]) The obstacles between the two are neither fog nor dark and distance but an enclosing house. Now the limits seem concrete and impenetrable, whether the enclosure is the mortal one of the body or more generally of the earthly environment. Death is here so welcome a release that the focus is not, as in *Prospice*, on the courage of the man dying, but on his morose relief at deliverance. In 1876 Browning allows himself to express his irritation, and to attack the causes of it; perhaps this is why he feels no need to complain to his beloved, like the householder. From the memory and unseen presence comes only comfort, and if the image of the enclosing house and wall is again used in *Pacchiarotto*'s *Prologue*, it is not entirely impenetrable. There is a certain pleasure, too, in lying in the sun on the grass near the wall, while waiting for hope to be fulfilled. It was fifteen years since Elizabeth had died, and would be thirteen more before Browning did. There was need not to batter himself against the walls of the cage he saw around him.

Most of *Pacchiarotto*'s lyrics make some use of house or wall or similar imagery; several are shaped by such imagery. *House* and *Shop* are obvious examples. *Fears and Scruples* shows God hidden in an impenetrable house. *Appearances* makes use of nothing but two rooms. *Natural Magic* uses one, and shows what love can do to it (the heart as a room that may be transformed by love also appears in a

1   'What i' the way of final flourish? Prose, verse? Try!
        Affliction sore long time he bore, or, what is it to be?
        Till God did please to grant him ease. Do end!' quoth I ...
    Cf.:
        Instruction sore long time I bore,
          And cramming was in vain;
        Till heaven did please my woes to ease
          With water on the brain.
    (Charles Kingsley, *The Water-Babies,* chap. VIII)
    I am indebted to Jay Macpherson for this reference.

Ferishtah's Fancies lyric). *St. Martin's Summer* contrasts the speaker who wants to build only a bower with the woman who wants a house. In *Pacchiarotto*, Browning's life and poetry make a house, which has a high private room for himself, and is besieged by saucy chimney-sweeps (the critics). For such a collection, it is appropriate that the *Prologue* begins 'O the old wall here' and develops through house and wall imagery.

Browning had, of course, for many years put to personal use the imagery of house, room, and wall. When he left Casa Guidi in 1861 after Elizabeth's death, he had a painting made of the drawing-room, 'just as she disposed it and left it ... the room has not an inch in it without a memory for me.'[2] And he repeated to his friends during that trying summer that he would not again keep house; the wording is interesting especially for *Fifine* but also for *Pacchiarotto*. 'I shall never again "keep house." ' 'No more "housekeeping" for me, even with my family. I shall grow, still, I hope – by my root is taken, remains.' 'London may suit me better than a brighter place for some time to come – but I shall have no ties, no housekeeping.'[3] His friends in Italy live in a house of his imagination, like the garden-full of rose-trees and soul-full of comforts that provided refreshment long before. 'They are all like portraits in the one habitable room of a house. I go in among them many a time in the course of the day & night.' 'I do seem to know that you understand my first satisfying people outside – & then sitting down quietly with the inmates of my soul's little house.'[4]

The *Prologue*'s tone is at first relaxed: 'How I could pass / Life in a long Midsummer day.' But the next line introduces features that Browning will later turn to another use ('my feet confined to a plot of grass'), and the next a certain tension ('my eyes from a wall not once away!'). Creepers clothe the old brick wall, but these are not devouring images of the change that alters man's work. The bricks are 'nothing loth' to be so covered, for the vines are like the pleasant curtains that nature hangs over the world's bare walls in *Easter-Day*

2 To Sarianna Browning, *New Letters*, 140; July 22, 1861
3 To Sarianna Browning, *New Letters*, 133; July 5 [1861]. To E.F. Haworth, *Letters*, ed. Hood, 65; July 20, 1861. To the Storys, *Browning to His American Friends*, 76; Aug. 20, 1861
4 To the Storys, ibid., 96, 116; Jan. 21, 1862, and Mar. 5, 1863

and *A Lovers' Quarrel*. They similarly represent a layer of reality. When someone passes, and perhaps sings, behind the wall, life emanates outward and makes the vine tremble and pulsate. The house is the body 'no eye can probe' but life is 'divined as, beneath a robe, the limbs.' (Browning likes variations on this image. Paracelsus used it of beauty and truth. The *Bells and Pomegranates* series are as the ornaments on the Hebrew priestly garment. Christ's robe sweeps up the narrator in *Christmas-Eve* [there is biblical precedent for this, of course]. Christopher Smart donned the 'singing-dress.') When the wall throbs, 'my heart may guess / Who tripped behind' ('if the wind can't get through houses and walls, Ba can and does, as my heart knows' [*LRBEB*, II, 737; May 28, 1846]). But after the rapture comes reflection: 'Wall upon wall are between us,' one being 'this ring / Of the rueful neighbours.' The surrounding ring, like the ring of peers and giants around Childe Roland, gathers with no friendly purpose; they enclose and overlook the speaker. ('The place is even prettier than I thought, but I feel somehow walled-about and over-looked, as one says of London suburban houses.'[5]) The speaker is now a 'prison-bird,' his plot now a jail's exercise-yard. Yet a bird can make noises, 'storm-notes,' if not now songs like those behind the wall.[6] He also has wings; can 'though cloistered fast, soar free.' The feet of stanza i are forgotten: 'forth to thee!'

Enclosure in the *Pacchiarotto* volume is not that built by a man's psychological or metaphysical self, nor is it the enclosure of love. It is the enclosure of man the social animal, and its walls closest in function to literal house walls. Privacy is what they try to maintain; communication what they try to regulate. When Henry James wanted to describe the older Browning he knew, he picked up this image: 'the image I began by using ... completed itself: the wall that built out the idyll (as we call it for convenience) of which memory and imagination were virtually composed for him stood there behind him

---

5 To Julia Wedgwood, *RBJW*, 73; Sept. 2, 1864
6 Cf.:

> My soul was singing at a work apart
> Behind the wall of sense, as safe from harm
> As sings the lark when sucked up out of sight
> In vortices of glory and blue air.
> (*Aurora Leigh*, 1053–6)

And cf. with this, of course, 'O Lyric Love'

solidly enough, but subject to his privilege of living almost equally on both sides of it. It contained an invisible door through which, working the lock at will, he could softly pass and of which he kept the golden key ... showing it, happy man, to none.'[7] But the poet in *Pacchiarotto* is a man besieged. Chimney-sweep critics in *Of Pacchiarotto*, dauntless in ignorance, tell him to do something about his smoke; he can laugh at them, but only from a high private room and after some spleen. In *At the Mermaid* he is advised what kind of poetry would make him popular. In *House* he is told to bare his private life for public consumption. In the *Epilogue* he is told to produce poetry of the quality of the classics. 'All the neighbour-talk with man and maid – such men!' is the householder's complaint in the *Epilogue* to *Fifine,* but in *Pacchiarotto* Browning scarcely talks with the rueful neighbours. He attacks.

> Here's my work outside: opine
> What's inside me mean and mortal!
>   Take your pleasure, leave me mine!
> ...
>   'Ah, but so I shall not enter,
>   Scroll in hand, the common heart –
> Stopped at surface: since at centre
>   Song should reach *Welt-schmerz,* world-smart!'
>   'Enter in the heart?' Its shelly
>   Cuirass guard mine, fore and aft!
> Such song 'enters in the belly
>   And is cast out in the draught.'
> (*At the Mermaid,* 54–6, 129–36)

>   'For, oh the common heart![8]
>   And, ah the irremissible sin
> Of poets who please themselves, not us!'
> ...

---

7 *William Wetmore Story and His Friends* (Boston, 1903), 2 vols., II, 89

8 Note the repeated phrase, and how it recalls Naddo on 'common sense' and the 'human heart.' The Browning of *Pacchiarotto* resembles the Browning of *Sordello* in many ways.

'Thoughts? "What is a man beside a mount!"
Loves? "Absent – poor lovers minutes count!"
Hates? "Fie – Pope's letters to Martha Blount!" '
...
Don't nettles make a broth
   Wholesome for blood grown lazy and thick?
Maws out of sorts make mouths out of taste.
My Thirty-four Port – no need to waste
On a tongue that's fur and a palate – paste!
   A magnum for friends who are sound! The sick –
I'll posset and cosset them, nothing loth,
   Henceforward with nettle-broth!
(*Epilogue*, 57–9, 179–81, 217–24)

Pacchiarotto ends with 'We'll up and work! won't we, Euripides?'
The reference is interesting, for five years earlier in *Aristophanes'*
Apology Browning put into Aristophanes' mouth an apologia for the
independence of the artist. The artist's strength is renewed only

    in some closet where strength shuts out – first
The friendly faces, sympathetic cheer:
'More of the old provision, none supplies
So bounteously as thou, – our love, our pride,
Our author of the many a perfect piece!
Stick to that standard, change mere decadence!'
...
Let strength propose itself, – behind the world, –
Sole price worth winning, work that satisfies
Strength it has dared and done strength's uttermost!
...
... 'you teach men, are not taught!'

Aristophanes is here describing Euripides, for whom independence
is necessary, even from his friends (their requests sound like pleas
for more *Men and Women*). It is to a solitary sea-cave that Euripides
must retire regularly in order to write. Browning had used the sea-
cave in *Pauline* as an image of self-inflicted sinister isolation for the
young poet; he must look without for any light. Paracelsus and

Sordello finally conceive of isolation chiefly as inimical to their
responsibility toward society. By 1875 the danger for Browning was
not the kind of self-sufficient isolation of a Sordello, but the diffusion
of his gifts before the sermon-hungry Victorians. In *Pacchiarotto* he
insists on not only the poet's but specifically his own right and need
for privacy. His insistence on this is often seen (not incorrectly) as
part of his own fierce personal aversion to exposing himself. It is
useful to fancy, however, what might have happened to Browning
had he acceded to the demands of his audience. Given his interests
and his sense of responsibility, it is perhaps surprising that there is not
more moralizing in his later poetry.

The poet as creator must work alone. So does his prototype, God.
The poet's house at least has windows ('a peep through my window, if
folk prefer'), but God's house is, like the *Prologue*'s, a house impenetrable by mortal eye. The poet says of his house in the poem
House: 'Outside should suffice for evidence: / And whoso desires
to penetrate / Deeper, must dive by the spirit-sense ...'[9] In the
Prologue, where walls of mortality are, as in *Fears and Scruples*, of
'solid brick,' the spirit can only 'hold on, hope hard in the subtle thing
/ That's spirit.' These dwellings have no windows, and penetration
from inside or out is by some other means, some trembling of a vine
that proves only a veil. Such penetration the God of *Fears and
Scruples* does not seem to grant. Such penetration, for himself,
Browning is not averse to. It is the exposing earthquake or the
publisher's tour he dislikes. Throughout his poetry he stresses, for
reader and writer alike, the necessity of diving or digging or working
to extract something difficult. Keats works at his whelks, which first
had to come from the sea-depths. *The Ring and the Book* gold is
mined, and Browning's imagination working on it is 'deep calling
unto deep' (I, 521). 'Thence bit by bit I dug / The lingot truth, that
memorable day' (I, 457–8). Later, any fact is like a stone fallen into
a pool; by its waves, onlookers try to judge the 'depth of deed already

9 Browning always reserves a place for the 'fit and few' readers. (The
Miltonic phrase Elizabeth Barrett used of Browning's audience in 1845
[*LRBEB*, I, 15; Feb. 3, 1845]). Cf.: 'Write as conscientiously for the few
– your idealised "Double" (it comes to that) – and you may soon suit him
with the extremely little that suits yourself' (Anne Thackeray, *Records of
Tennyson, Ruskin, and Browning*, 221–2; Feb. 24, 1886).

out of reach' (1, 845[10]). In the *Pacchiarotto Epilogue* the mining image reappears, contrasted, as above, with easy delving.

> A mine's beneath a moor:
>> Acres of moor roof fathoms of mine
> Which diamonds dot where you please to dig;
> Yet who plies spade for the bright and big?
> Your product is – truffles, you hunt with a pig!
>> Since bright-and-big, when a man would dine,
> Suits badly: and therefore the Koh-i-noor
>> May sleep in mine 'neath moor!

The moor is insistent, and it recalls another moor, that of *Memorabilia*. There the eagle-feather, shining like any diamond, inverts the image. The treasure comes from above, not below (and, dropping from heaven, is gift rather than reward). But it is no less rare and remote, if improperly valued by most.

Besides house and wall imagery, there is another familiar image group in the poetry of this time. The mage of *Pauline* and the ghosts of *Sordello* and their successors had merged in the mage-prophet figure that is the type of the poet in *The Ring and the Book*. But less earthly remnants of the ghost image begin to appear in Browning's later poetry. These ghosts are not connected with the making of poetry. They may be ghosts from the past (as in the *Fifine Epilogue* or *St. Martin's Summer*), and beneficent or haunting depending chiefly on their visitant. These ghosts resemble the walking painters of *Old Pictures in Florence* or the *De Gustibus* pair, except that the *Men and Women* ones are playfully conjured – a young man's ghosts. Or they may be strange unearthly beings, like the inhabitants of the unearthly fairy realm in *Pauline, belles dames sans merci*, for Browning's late ghosts are almost invariably women. The supreme example is the white goddess of *Numpholeptos*. The most developed example is in *Fifine*, where Don Juan plays with phantom women (the two Helens, his Helen-Cleopatra-Saint trio) and repeatedly

---

10 The figure is common and may derive from Heraclitus (cf. *Pantagruel*, xviii). Elizabeth also uses it: 'See how far you are from the truth-well' (*LRBEB*, II, 952; Aug. 10, 1846); '... if you have found truth or not in the water-well' (ibid., I, 513; Mar. 3, 1846).

converts Elvire into a phantom. Yet the fairy world need not be
threatening. *Pacchiarotto* contains a short lyric, *Natural Magic*, in
which love brings flowers, fruit, birds into a bare room (making it
like Browning's 'mystic country'). The metaphor is said to be 'a fairy-
tale! Only[11] – I feel it!' But *Numpholeptos* involves another kind of
woman and hence another kind of fairy-land: 'What fairy track do
I explore? / What magic hall return to ...?'

Ghost plays against actual woman in *Fifine*: the actual Elvire is a
ghost to Don Juan, but a ghost is reality to the *Epilogue*'s householder.
The *Numpholeptos* petitioner yearns for his pallid ghost to transform
herself into a human woman. In *St. Martin's Summer* a ghost
conquers and routs a present rival – or hardly rival; her lover wants
only a fleeting affair. He will not tempt his absent goddess; merely,
like Caliban, sneak a brief amusement ('as safe we chuckle, – under
breath, / Yet all the slyer, the jocoser'). Here the queen is like the
Numpholeptos lady, or like one of Don Juan's Elvires, imperious and
deserving some fickleness. The situation is low comedy. But a sudden
crisis changes all. ('Terror' is used of it, as of the actual presence of
Christ in *Christmas-Eve*; his anticipated presence had produced, as
here the flirtation produced, modified self-approval.) The present
woman becomes 'the ghostly flesh-disguised! / Nay, all the ghosts in
one!' The man has betrayed his reality by playing at his comedy:
'Undone me – / Ghost-bereft!' It is, of course, impossible to escape
the memory of Elizabeth Barrett in all this, and the episode of Lady
Ashburton. What is important, I think, is not to read hasty identifica-
tions into these poems. Browning's dramatis personae are by no
means simple masks.

Numpholeptos is striking in its use of many favourite Browning
images. The moon-female association is here turned to sinister use.
Whiteness ('pallid' had been used in *Women and Roses* and *Fifine*),
cold, remoteness play through the poem. The lover, like the *Women
and Roses* speaker, tries to draw his queen toward sun-imagery –
toward gold not whiteness ('blood-streaked, sun-warmth, action-time,
/ By heart-pulse ripened to a ruddy glow / Of gold above my clay').

11 'Only' is often a pivotal word in Browning: 'The old trick! Only I discern
 – / Infinite passion ...'; 'endure his act! / Only, for man, how bitter ...';
 'Only, at heart's utmost joy and triumph, terror / Sudden turns the blood
 to ice'; 'Only they see not God, I know.'

294 BROWNING'S LYRICS: AN EXPLORATION

Twice, a sunrise is an image of bliss. The rays of colour, streaming from white light, are earthly paths. Unhappily they derive not from the sun, but from 'your blank pure soul, alike the source / And tomb of that prismatic glow' (note the similar function of Sordello's font-tomb maidens). Gem imagery parallels the prismatic ('like the gem, / Centuply-angled'; 'the topaz tint'; 'your pilgrim jewelled'). The menace of endless quest hangs over the poem ('Well, the quest shall be renewed,' 'No fresh adventure!,' 'Forth at your behest / I fare'), a menace like that in *Women and Roses, Love in a Life, Childe Roland*, and here shown slowly becoming a reality. Enclosure imagery prevails, as the woman is allowed supreme judgment over the man's actions (she annihilates them, thus making a complete contrast with Leonor, in whose poem every small circumstance is given due significance). Garb and flesh make up the man; the woman has a 'shrouding robe.' When his experience is laid at her feet, 'the blade is shut in sheath, / Fire quenched in flint.' Even 'O you' is the turning to reproachful usage of an old Barrett-Browning pleasantry. The rhyme is the unobtrusive couplet which Browning used to much effect in *My Last Duchess*. The poem haunts Browning readers for more than one reason.

'Asolando,' Browning tells us in his dedicatory preface, is a manu-factured word, derived from the sixteenth-century Cardinal Bembo, who had his own Asolo book. It means ' "to disport in the open air, amuse oneself at random." ' The collection, then, is the disporting of Browning's late years, his play with old themes and images. The book was to have been another series of *Jocoseria*; the new title, while retaining the suggestion of playfulness from the old, also links the poems with Asolo, scene of Browning's early *Pippa Passes*. But Asolo is much more than an Italian setting. Here, if we read literally Browning's *Prologue* to *Asolando*, came an early dramatic confronta-tion with Italy, Browning's first love-affair:

> How many a year, my Asolo,
>   Since – one step just from sea to land –
> I found you, loved yet feared you so –
>   For natural objects seemed to stand
> Palpably fire-clothed!

Asolo was the scene of one of Browning's beginnings, and his *Prologue* does not exaggerate the special place it held in his memory. 'I used to dream of seeing Asolo in the distance and making vain attempts to reach it – repeatedly dreamed this for many a year,' he wrote in June 1889.[12] The random disportings, then, are written with an eye on Browning's youth, and the past looms large in the collection. In the *Prologue* and *Epilogue* we are particularly conscious of a man looking behind and ahead, measuring his journey and judging it, and in these two poems Browning does not disport.

Asolando was published in 1889. The Browning who does not begin his poetic career with lyrics (though he associates them with youth) ends it with a collection that includes some remarkable lyrics. He states in the *Prologue* that he has lost the faculty of seeing pictures and hearing music. Thus it is another kind of lyric he writes now. It may be the generalizing kind, which Irving Babbitt dislikes, and which, apart from the rest of Browning's work, are slight (*Truth, Now, A Pearl, A Girl, Poetics*). Or he may write short fables like *Which?* Perhaps the most powerful lyric in the collection is *Dubiety*, where Browning speaks simply, in a dramatic voice close to his own, and feels after an old experience.

Asolando is sub-titled *Fancies and Facts*. The alliterative pair is common in Browning but it deserves a title-place in a collection much concerned with appearance and reality. The book was published on the day of Browning's death, when he was seventy-seven. Appearance and reality, fancy and fact and fiction and truth – what constitutes these, and how each relates to the other had interested him all his life, but especially from *The Ring and the Book* on. In this book, the evidence is peculiarly that of age, with emphasis on memories. But the perception is not a thing of the past.

The *Prologue* sets the stage. Such heightened senses as the young Sordello's are said to show a world subjectively coloured; with age, comes real perception. Browning draws on colour imagery, lens imagery, gem imagery (*Numpholeptos* uses the same conjunction) to demonstrate his thesis. The old association of Moses with the poet is made by the use of the burning bush. As in the *Prologue* to *Pacchiarotto*, the natural world is clothed (Browning's favourite

12 Lilian Whiting, *The Brownings*, 282; June 10, 1889

'palpably' is again given place). Fire imagery is associated with life and vitality, now youth's vitality. This is what transfigures the bush, burning but unconsumed ('terror' again appears, here with beauty). But fire imagery is left behind, 'for the purged ear apprehends / Earth's import, not the eye late dazed.' The biblical emphasis on the ear and the word is recalled, for even the sight of 'the naked very thing' does not bring knowledge. '"Call my works thy friends! / At Nature dost thou shrink amazed? / God is it who transcends."' Both the amicable relation with nature and the transcendence of her creator had long been present in Browning's poetry.

The *Prologue* inevitably recalls two earlier anticipations of old age, those in *By the Fireside* and *Aeschylus' Soliloquy*. *By the Fireside* looks to a rather more genial old age than that in *Asolando*'s *Prologue* and *Epilogue*. Yet *Asolando*'s tone is not that of Aeschylus either. Its detachment has a different quality. At the same time that it separates itself from youthful enthusiasm, claims its own superior perception, feels for its own memories, it also re-immerses itself in old passions and produces some surprising if not great lyrics.

> I myself
> Grow to silence, fasten to the calm
> Of inorganic nature ... sky and rocks –
> I shall pass on into their unity
> When dying down into impersonal dusk.

This is how Browning's Aeschylus anticipates his death. Earlier Aeschylus noted the diminishing of artistic sights and sounds, and for him the Poet's age is sad. (He sees himself as a tragic mask.) But Browning in *Parleying with Mandeville* had preferred Euripides to Aeschylus: 'A myth may teach: / Only, who better would expound it thus / Must be Euripides, not Aeschylus' (204–6). In *Balaustion's Adventure,* he quotes Elizabeth Barrett's lines on Euripides, 'the human with his droppings of warm tears.' In *Asolando,* if there is detachment, it is not impersonal.

It is appropriate that a volume sub-titled *Fancies and Facts* should contain four varieties of *Bad Dreams*, and should try to pin down a fleeting impression in *Dubiety*. Yet a careful reading of the volume does not, I think, support DeVane's conclusion that 'the major theme of *Asolando* [is] that facts are superior to fancies, however lovely'

(*Handbook*, 530). Or rather, does not support it in any simple way. In *Pauline* there had been two different kinds of fancy, and the word's meaning throughout Browning's verse has a wide range. Similarly with 'fact' and 'dream.' 'As is your sort of mind, / So is your sort of search: you'll find/What you desire' (*Easter-Day*, 173–5). 'I cannot understand it – we [Elizabeth and himself] differ in our appreciation of facts, too – things that admit of proof.'[13] Fact to the speaker of *Asolando*'s *Prologue* is what the voice of God says to him. Fact to the Pope's imaginary multitude is 'the lust and pride of life' (*The Ring and the Book*, x, 1892). And thus the reported sermon at the end of *The Ring and the Book* (xii, 598–603):

> I demand assent
> To the annunciation of my text
> In face of one proof more that 'God is true
> And every man a liar' – that who trusts
> To human testimony for a fact
> Gets this sole fact – himself is proved a fool.[14]

'Is not outside seeming / Real as substance inside? / Both are facts, so leave me dreaming': this is the request of the male speaker in *Asolando*'s *Flute-Music*. In *Development* there proves

> no warrant for the fiction I, as fact,
> Had treasured in my heart and soul so long –
> Ay, mark you! and as fact held still, still hold,
> Spite of new knowledge, in my heart of hearts
> And soul of souls, fact's essence freed and fixed
> From accidental fancy's guardian sheath.

13 Browning to George Barrett, in *Letters of the Brownings to George Barrett*, 165; Feb. 4, 1852
14 Cf. with these lines the following entry in Coleridge's notebooks: '*Facts*! never be weary of discussing and exposing the hollowness of these – every man an *accomplice* on one side or other / & then human *Testimony*!' Or: 'Facts – & I had it from a man on the Spot, who *saw it*, – &c and never have I been with 3, 4, or 5 *Men of the Spot* who did not quarrel & dispute & contradict' (*The Notebooks of Samuel Taylor Coleridge*, ed. K.H. Coburn [New York, 1957–], vol. ii, text volume, notebook entries 2122 and 2043).

298 BROWNING'S LYRICS: AN EXPLORATION

The poem aims to dissociate the worth of Homer's poetry from its
basis in fact, since it can be 'proved there was never any Troy at all.'
(The biblical equivalents of Homer's higher critics are obvious.) The
aim is achieved, but there is a double-twist not mentioned in the
poem. Wolf's fact is not, after all, a fact, as Schliemann had demonstrated over a decade before this poem. 'I was reading the wonderful
letter of Schliemann, this morning. It strikes me that you ... might
fancy something of this kind – Bring out an edition of ... the
"Agamemnon" of Aeschylus – which, in default of a better translator,
I would try my hand & heart at – and illustrate it by photographs of
all the "find" at Mycenae.'[15]

'"No dream's worth waking," Browning says.' Thus Browning,
quoting his supposed self in *Development*. But of course all depends
on the dream, and as with 'fact' there are dreams and dreams from
Pauline to *Asolando*. 'We shall start up, at last awake / From life,
that insane dream we take for waking now': thus (for one example)
the *Easter-Day* speaker, in whose poem is a dream-vision. Dreams are
not infrequent in Browning. *Women and Roses* was said to have been
inspired by a dream. *Childe Roland* was said to have come upon
Browning like a dream (DeVane, *Handbook*, 229), and it has echoes
of *Pilgrim's Progress* and the *Inferno*,[16] both dream-visions. Browning
has his own dream-visions, of course (those in *Christmas-Eve* and
Easter-Day, and Don Juan's Venice-vision), or simply poems that

15 Browning to George Smith, in Lachlan Phil Kelley, 'Robert Browning
    and George Smith: Selections from an Unpublished Correspondence,'
    Quarterly Review 299 (1961), 323–35; Dec. 22, 1876
16 Besides the path and the test, cf. with *Pilgrim's Progress* 'Apollyon's
    bosom-friends.' With the *Inferno*, cf. the imagery of canto xxxi. Dante and
    Virgil are in a pit, surrounded by giants, whom Dante takes for towers
    ('che non son torri, ma giganti' [31]; 'the hills, like giants at a hunting,
    lay, / Chin upon hand, to see the game at bay' [190–1]). Light is uncertain
    ('Quiv'era men che notte e men che giorno' [10]; 'Not see? because of
    night perhaps? – why, day / Came back again for that! before it left, /
    The dying sunset kindled through a cleft' [187–9]). Noise is stunning
    ('quando / Carlo Magno perde la santa gesta, / *non sono si terribilmente
    Orlando*' [16–18, italics mine]; 'not hear? when noise was everywhere ...'
    [193]). For a more general comparison, see Ruth Sullivan, 'Browning's
    "Childe Roland" and Dante's "Inferno,"' *Victorian Poetry* 5 (1967),
    296–302.

are or relate dreams (*Women and Roses, Bad Dreams*). Some poems
have a dream-like atmosphere, though they are not specifically said
to be dreams (*Childe Roland, Love in a Life*). There are also
numerous remarks about dreams.

Dreams are often mentioned in the Barrett-Browning correspondence, the chief one being the dream of living together. For Browning
it could be a powerful plea: 'Now while I *dream*, let me once dream!
I would marry you now and thus ... And it will continue but a dream'
(*LRBEB*, I, 214; Sept. 25, 1845). The effect of the last sentence,
after what has gone before, is like the reversal at the end of *Any Wife
to Any Husband*: '... And I wake saved. – And yet it will not be!'
Browning's most poignant use of such contrast comes at the end of
Caponsacchi's monologue. It is, however, Elizabeth who makes the
chief use of the dream figure in the letters, her double life naturally
encouraging such imagery. Often the dream is accompanied by fear –
of her betraying it, of its reality. Ivory and horn gates appear several
times. Her new commitment may 'all be *mirage* ... the recurring
dream-fear!' (ibid., I, 323; Dec. 15, 1845). 'I must live in a dream ...
time goes .. seeming to go round rather than to go forward' (ibid.,
I, 299; Nov. 29, 1845; the figure is interesting in view of the menacing
motion in several dream-like poems by Browning). In a five-week
period not long after the conditional engagement occur a half-dozen
reflections on dreams.[17] It is only when marriage is close, then over,
that the references recur.[18] Browning then also catches up the usage,
but not as a figure for unreality: 'What a glorious dream ... without
a single interval of blankness, – much less, bitter waking!' (ibid., II,
1059; Sept. 10, 1846). Dreams, like facts, need human commitment
to take on reality. Yet the impossible dream, like the mistaken fact,
will break the man who commits himself to it.

Asolando is a coming full circle, for Asolo, as Browning says in the
Prologue, was an early paradise for him. The volume is a coming
home, yet more than this. The homecoming is that of a much-
changed person to a much-changed place. And *Asolando* ends with

17 Besides the examples cited, cf. *LRBEB*, I, 275, 292, 305, 340; Nov. 17,
Nov. 24, Dec. 4, Dec. 21, 1845
18 *LRBEB*, II, 847, 958, 966, 1061, 1063, 1065; July 5, Aug. 12, Aug. 15,
Sept. 10, Sept. 12, Sept. 13, 1846

quite another kind of movement, for the *Epilogue* shows a man marching toward a goal rather than coming back to a beloved if altered refuge. If the tone is now strident, the movement is one Browning long before chose for himself. In the *Prologue* he links two earthly points. In the *Epilogue* he reaches out and can only hope the clouds break to reveal a star.

CONCLUSION

The best source of enlightenment for Browning poetry is more
Browning poetry. At least this has been my experience in working
out this essay. I began considerably puzzled by many lyrics, but
convinced that each lyric should be read not only as an integral whole
in itself, but also as part of Browning's entire poetic production.
When reading the non-lyric poetry, I took care to consider each poem
on its own terms. That is, I did not skim about, looking for likenesses
to various lyrics, nor, above all, did I go image-hunting. (I thought at
first, in fact, that Browning made little consistent use of most
images.) As I proceeded, the poems gradually became more and more
difficult to read as self-contained units. By the time I came to grips
with *Fifine*, the inter-poetical echoes were unmistakable. When I
came to *Asolando*, the lyrics no longer seemed impossible of penetration; some of their images were like familiar friends. On a solitary
reading of *Pauline*, for example, I observed that it clearly centres on
kinds of freedom and security. The concepts of nature, of poetry, of
fancy, and of music are all interesting because varying and sometimes
ill-defined. But they gain new interest when Browning later smoothes
and strengthens what he here fumbles with; when he works out the
implications of these concepts, and makes them do ordered battle
rather than letting them jostle confusedly. Similarly with the imagery.
Images of light and dark, and of liberty and constraint, are obvious
on first reading. They take on new significance when Browning later
elaborates them, and connects them with other image-groups.
     One common image in Browning's poetry is that of house and wall.
It is an image prominent in *Pacchiarotto*, and is used also in *The
Ring and the Book*, *Two Poets of Croisic*, and *Easter-Day*, to take
only three examples. In *The Ring and the Book*, a cave has similar
functions – social, metaphysical, and psychological functions. Such
imagery cannot but draw the reader back to *Pauline* and forward to

Fifine, and to invite investigation of its various uses. Similarly with the rose image, so memorably rejected in *Sordello* and so suddenly prominent in *Men and Women*. Similarly with the imagery of gold, central in *The Ring and the Book* and insistent elsewhere – and frequent in Browning's beloved Donne, and in Boehme whom he also knew. Further, when the reader of Browning returns to his letters, especially to the Barrett-Browning correspondence, he finds the above images again and again.

He also finds throughout Browning's poetry, to take another kind of image, the persistent conjunction of mage and prophet as types for the poet. He observes Browning assume the role of Moses in two of his rare direct poetic appearances (in *Sordello* and in *One Word More*). Again, the image invites us to consider its functions, that is, to consider how Browning conceived of poetry. It also invites us to consider its traditions – of Moses as a type for the poet in Renaissance literature, or of prophet and poet in Romantic literature.

It is often easy to document and difficult to read a good poet's images. With Browning, even the documentation is not a matter of course. It is twenty years since Lionel Stevenson called for such work on the Victorian poets.[1] At the least, then, I think that I have indicated most and focused new attention on some of Browning's chief images, and that this exercise itself has a certain limited value. But I have also sometimes had the sense of approaching the centre of Browning's imagination, of perceiving something of its structure, of watching it work from the inside out. Insofar as this happened, it happened in the probing of an interesting image-group or poem. Whether it is valid or not, the reader of this essay must decide for himself.

In some ways, the various close readings of Browning's lyrics have pleased me most, for it is in returning to the particular poem that the general theory is tested. Further, it seemed to me that many lyrics easily bore – rather, wanted – the very close reading to which they were subjected. Browning believed in concentrated writing. If his allusions are sometimes esoteric, they are not vague. Witness, for example, the allusions offered to the unwitting reader of the word 'pomegranate' in *Bells and Pomegranates*: 'Giotto placed a pome-

---

1 In 'The Pertinaceous Victorian Poets,' *University of Toronto Quarterly* 21 (1952), 232–45

granate fruit in the hand of Dante, and Raffaello crowned his
Theology ... with blossoms of the same; as if the Bellari [Bellori] and
Vasari would be sure to come after, and explain that it was merely
"*simbolo delle buone opere* ..." ' This may expect a good deal; but it
also suggests that it is not over-ingenious to read inferences from, for
example, the components of the natural scene in *Two in the Campagna* or *By the Fireside*.

The tracing of certain images, and of their successive uses, in both
Browning's poetry and his letters, also helps to elaborate something
of the relationship between Browning the man and Browning the
poet. I do not mean the occasional connecting (which I offered almost
unwillingly) of this poem with that event. I mean the observation
of certain habits of mind, certain common reactions and concerns, a
certain irony and self-consciousness and reticence and assertiveness –
all of which operate in different ways in man and poet. Above all,
Browning is complex and self-aware, and his imagery is evidence of
this. If nothing else, I hope this book may discourage simplistic inter-
pretations of Browning's life or of his art.

With care, Browning's images can be made to elucidate each
other. This is not because they belong to a highly schematized system,
like Yeats'. Otherwise the system would hardly have escaped notice.
What Browning offers are glimpses of coherence, not a large synthesis;
his arcs are bits of a broken whole, not petals of a hundred-leaved
rose of God. Dante's rose is, of course, in heaven where the perfect
whole exists, but the point is that Browning chooses not to write about
this domain. It is the fugitive brief gleams, the crucial instants or
moments that possess him. And his poems themselves may be seen
as gleams, parts of a larger whole. In one sense, *The Ring and the
Book* is an intricately built unit; in another, it is deliberately frag-
mented. Browning cannot be read like Yeats or Blake or Dante. His
'R.B.' poem he never wrote.

He suggests, in the *Paracelsus* Preface, that the reader's 'cooperating fancy' must create a poem that is *Paracelsus*. Similarly, it
seems to me, the reader is called on to re-create the perceptions with
which Browning's poems began and to which they point, to use the
'many helps to the making out *the real painter's-picture as he had it
in his brain*' (Browning in *LRBEB*, I, 7; Jan. 13, 1845; italics mine).
It is the reader's job to make, if he cares to, the poem 'R.B.' There is
surely enough of the work "Shelley" to be known enduringly among

men, and, I believe, to be accepted of God, as human work may.' Thus Browning in his 'Essay on Shelley,' and thus he may have hoped men would read him. But this is hardly possible unless we try to apprehend the whole as well as the parts of his poetic structure.

If Browning makes his own poetic structure, it is not a new one or an old one, but an old one made new. He does not, like Yeats, fashion his own system, nor does he work traditionally within an accepted system. He re-forges traditional symbols for personal use, fearing both the solipsism of a private symbolism and the irrelevance of an unexamined conventional one. In this way, he is both dramatic and lyric, in Wasserman's sense of the words.[2] Browning would have sympathized with – and resisted – modern subjectivism and fragmentation. For him, the fragments still imply a whole – not a whole made up of the sum of gathered fragments, but a whole from which they were born and to which they will return, their beginning and end and reason. This is the pattern of his life and of his art.

2 'The lyric, in the sense in which I am here employing the term, limits itself to the constitution of self-sustaining reality; the dramatic advances beyond the entertained reality'; 'the mimetic theory was no longer tenable when man ceased to share the cosmic designs that made mimesis meaningful'; 'the poetry of the last century and a half has tended to be dramatic rather than lyric' (Earl R. Wasserman, *The Subtler Language: Critical Readings of Neoclassic and Romantic Poems* [Baltimore, 1959], 10, 11, 12).

SELECTED BIBLIOGRAPHY

POETRY

Manuscript
Pierpont Morgan Library, New York
- Manuscript of *One Word More* (entitled 'A Last Word')
- Manuscript of *Dramatis Personae*
- Manuscript of *Asolando*
Houghton Library, Harvard University
- Manuscript of *Love Among the Ruins* (entitled 'Sicilian Pastoral')
- Translations from the Greek Poets (Anacreontea)
Widener Collection, Harvard University
- Proof-sheets, *Bells and Pomegranates*, no. 3

Printed (in order of publication)
- *Men and Women* (London, 1855), 2 vols.
- *Dramatis Personae* (London, 1864)
- *Pacchiarotto and How He Worked in Distemper, with Other Poems* (London, 1876)
- *Asolando: Fancies and Facts* (London, 1890)
- *The Works of Robert Browning* (Centenary edition), ed. F.G. Kenyon (London, 1912), 10 vols.
- *New Poems by Robert Browning and Elizabeth Barrett Browning*, ed. Sir Frederic G. Kenyon (London, 1914)
- *Pauline by Robert Browning: The Text of 1833, Compared with That of 1867 and 1888*, ed. N. Hardy Wallis (London, 1931)
- *The Complete Works of Robert Browning, with Variant Readings and Annotations*, ed. Roma A. King, *et al.* (Athens, 1969–)

PROSE
'Introduction,' in *Thomas Jones, The Divine Order and Other Sermons and Addresses* (London, 1884), xi–xiii

'An Essay on Shelley,' in *The Complete Poetical Works of Browning* (Boston, 1895), 1008–14

REFERENCE

Broughton, L.N., C.S. Northup, and R. Pearsall, *Robert Browning: A Bibliography, 1830–1950* (Ithaca, 1953)

Broughton, L.N., and B.F. Stelter, *A Concordance to the Poems of Robert Browning* (New York, 1924)

The Browning Collections, to be sold May 1913 (London, Sotheby, Wilkinson, and Hodge Sale Catalogue, 1913)

DeVane, William Clyde, *A Browning Handbook* (New York, 1955; second edition)

Honan, Park, 'Robert Browning,' in *The Victorian Poets: A Guide to Research*, ed. F.E. Faverty (Cambridge, Mass., 1968; second edition), 81–120

Literary Anecdotes of the Nineteenth Century, ed. W.R. Nicoll and T.J. Wise (London, 1895), 'Materials for a Bibliography of the Writings of Robert Browning,' I, 359–627

Orr, Mrs Alexandra, *Handbook to the Works of Robert Browning* (London, 1923; sixth edition)

LETTERS

Collections (in order of publication)

– *The Letters of Elizabeth Barrett Browning*, ed. Frederic G. Kenyon (London, 1899), 2 vols. (*LEB*)

– *The Letters of Robert Browning and Elizabeth Barrett Barrett* (London, 1899), 2 vols.

– *Robert Browning and Alfred Domett*, ed. F.G. Kenyon (London, 1906) (*RBAD*)

– *Letters of Robert Browning*, ed. Thurman L. Hood (New Haven, 1933)

– *Robert Browning and Julia Wedgwood: A Broken Friendship as Revealed by Their Letters*, ed. Richard Curle (New York, 1937) (*RBJW*)

– *New Letters of Robert Browning*, ed. W.C. DeVane and K.L. Knicker-bocker (New Haven, 1950)

– *Dearest Isa: Browning's Letters to Isa Blagden*, ed. E.C. McAleer (Austin, 1950)

– *Letters of the Brownings to George Barrett*, ed. Paul Landis and Ronald E. Freeman (Urbana, 1958)

– *Browning to His American Friends: Letters between the Brownings, the* ..

Storys, and James Russell Lowell, 1841–1890, ed. Gertrude Reese Hudson (London, 1965). Supersedes the Browning letters in Henry James, *William Wetmore Story and His Friends*
– *Learned Lady: Letters from Robert Browning to Mrs. Thomas Fitzgerald, 1876–1889*, ed. E.C. McAleer (Cambridge, Mass., 1966)
– *The Letters of Robert Browning and Elizabeth Barrett Barrett, 1845–1846*, ed. Elvan Kintner (Cambridge, Mass., 1969), 2 vols. (*LRBEB*)

Other Published Letters

Letters of interest may also be found in:

– Allingham, Helen, and E.B. Williams, eds., *Letters to William Allingham* (London, 1911)
– Armytage, W.H.G., 'Robert Browning and Mrs Pattison: Some Unpublished Browning Letters,' *University of Toronto Quarterly* 21 (1952), 179–92
– *Athenaeum* (May 9, 1908), to A.E. Sloan, Feb. 6, 1871
– Bevington, Merle M., 'Three Letters of Robert Browning to the Editor of the *Pall Mall Gazette*,' *Modern Language Notes* 75 (1960), 304–9
– Blanc, Mme Marie T. de S. (pseud. Th. Bentzen), 'A French Friend of Browning – Joseph Milsand,' *Scribner's Magazine* 20 (1896), 108–20
– Carlyle A., ed., *Letters of Carlyle to Mill, Sterling and Browning* (London, 1923)
– Collingwood, W.G., *Life and Work of John Ruskin* (London, Methuen, 1893), 2 vols.
– Donner, H.W., ed., *The Browning Box or the Life and Works of Thomas Lovell Beddoes* (London, 1935), Section VII, 'The Correspondence of Robert Browning and Thomas Forbes Kelsall'
– Gray, John Miller, *Memoir and Remains* (Edinburgh, 1895), 2 vols.
– Greene, Herbert E., 'Browning's Knowledge of Music,' *Publications of the Modern Language Society* 62 (1947), 1095–9
– Harlan, A.B., and J.L., eds., *Letters of Owen Meredith (Robert, First Earl of Lytton) to Robert and Elizabeth Barrett Browning* (Waco, Texas, 1936)
– Kelley, Lachlan Phil, 'Robert Browning and George Smith: Selections from an Unpublished Correspondence,' *Quarterly Review* 299 (1961), 325–35
– Knight, William A., *Retrospects* (London, Smith, Elder, 1904), 69–101
– *A Letter from Robert Browning to John Ruskin*, Baylor Browning Interests 17 (Waco, Texas, 1958)

- Lehmann, R.C., *Memories of Half a Century: A Record of Friendships* (London, 1908)
- Millais, J.G., *Life and Letters of Sir John Everett Millais, by His Son* (New York, 1899), 2 vols.
- Palgrave, G.F., *Francis Turner Palgrave* (London, 1899)
- Phelps, William Lyon, 'Robert Browning on Spiritualism,' *Yale Review* 23 (1933), 125–38
- Ricks, Christopher, 'Two Letters by Browning,' *Times Literary Supplement* (June 3, 1965), 464
- Rossetti, W.M., *Rossetti Papers, 1862–1870* (London, 1903)
- Rossetti, W.M., *Ruskin: Rossetti: Preraphaelite Papers, 1854–1862* (London, 1899)
- Thackeray, Anne I., Lady Ritchie, *Records of Tennyson, Ruskin, and Browning* (London, 1892)
- Thomas, W., 'Lettres inédites de Robert Browning à Joseph Milsand,' *Revue Germanique* 14 (1923), 422–3

Unpublished Letters

Baylor University
- In W. Arthur Strain, 'Rare and Unpublished Letters of Robert Browning' (MA thesis, University of Colorado, 1925). All letters from this thesis are typewritten copies
- To Emily Marion Harris

British Museum
- Add. MS. 45563; to C.D. Browning, typewritten copy; to B. Paul Newman, copy by Mrs Griffin
- Ashley 5768, typewritten copies; most originals at the University of Texas

Columbia University
- To M.D. Conway

Houghton Library, Harvard University
- Holograph letters

Library of Congress
- Robert Browning Papers

University of Texas
- From the Robert Browning Papers

INDEX

THIS *book was designed by* ROBERT MACDONALD

under the direction of ALLAN FLEMING

and was printed by UNIVERSITY OF TORONTO PRESS.